RERVM FONTIS
Lectures on Esoteric Symbology

William Stephen Jackson

Magnus Veritas Press

Copyright © 2011 by William Stephen Jackson
Published by Magnus Veritas Press

First Edition
Published December 21, 2011

All rights reserved. Printed in the United States of America. No part of this book may be reproduced in any manner whatsoever without written permission except in the case of brief quotations embodied in critical articles and reviews. For information, contact William Stephen Jackson directly at RerumFontis@gmail.com.

Unleſs otherwise noted, all illuſtrations and tables of reference are the work of the author, and are protected by copyright.

Cover design by Karan Parkin, Graphix for Change (www.GraphixForChange.com).

Author photograph by Lisa Fortin Jackson (www.LisaFortinJackson.com).

IM FELL English Pro Font by Igino Marini,
licensed under the SIL Open Font License, Version 1.1.

ISBN 978-0-578-09829-6

Table of Contents

INTRODUCTION 1
BOOK 1 THE HEAVENS 27
    THE HEAVENLY LUMINARIES 31
    THE SUN 43
    THE MOON 50
    VENUS 61
    MERCURY 74
    MARS 77
    JUPITER 80
    SATURN 83
    THE SEVEN STARS 86
    THE HERO OSRIS 87
    THE PLEIADES 88
    THE FALLEN ONES 89
    THE GODS WITH BONES OF IRON 96
    THE ZODIAC 99
    THE PRECESSION AND THE AGES 102
    THE LABOURS OF HERCULES 117
    THE HOLY ANIMALS 118
    THE ARK OF NOAH 120
    THE PEOPLE OF OSIRIS 125

BOOK 2 THE NUMBERS 129
    THE MONAD 137
    THE DYAD 138
    THE TRIAD 140
    THE TETRAD 142
    THE PENTAD 144
    THE SEXTAD 147
    THE HEPTAD 149
    THE OCTAD 152
    THE ENNEAD 156
    THE DECAD 159
    THE DUODECAD 162
    THE TRISKAIDECAD 165
    THE TRIANTA DYAD 168
    THE SARANTA 170

- THE EBDOMENTA DYAD 172
- THE NUMBER OF THE FISH 175
- THE FIBONACCI SEQUENCE 177
- THE ANCIENT GEOMETRY 181
- THE GEMATRIA 183

BOOK 3 THE SYMBOLS 197

- THE CROSS 199
- THE ANCIENT CROSS OF IRELAND 203
- THE CROSS OF SAINT ANDREW 205
- THE CHRISTIAN CROSS 207
- THE ROOD CROSS 208
- THE TEMPLAR CROSS 215
- THE ANKH 218
- THE ANCHOR 219
- THE OPHIOLATREIA 221
- THE CIRCLE 223
- THE CIRCUMPUNCT 227
- THE TRIANGLE 229
- THE TRIANGLE OF PYTHAGORAS 232
- THE SQUARE 237
- THE CUBE 240
- THE PENTACLE 241
- THE DOVE 251
- THE ROSE 254
- THE CRUCEM ROSAE 257
- THE BLADE AND CHALICE 260
- THE COMPASS AND SQUARE 267
- THE FISH 272
- THE QUINCUNX 280
- THE OVUM MYSTICAE 282
- THE TRIPLE SPIRAL 285
- THE FLEUR DE LIS 287
- THE HOLY GRAIL 291
- THE HORNS OF VENUS 295
- THE HORNED GODS 298
- THE CELESTIAL BOAT 300
- THE CRESCENT AND STAR 303
- THE SEPTAGRAM 306
- THE DRAGON 309
- THE LABRYS 312

- THE SPHINX 314
- THE ELEMENTS 317
- THE ANCIENT ALPHABETS 330

BOOK 4 THE MAN 335

- THE ADAM QADMON 337
- THE VITRUVIAN MAN 340
- THE HEART 342
- THE AGE OF MAN 344
- THE MAN OSIRIS 346
- THE CHAMBER OF ETERNAL LIFE 349
- THE ENGLISH SYSTEM OF MEASUREMENT 351
- HERALDRY 354
- THE CANON 356
- THE BOOK OF ENOCH 365
- THE HOLY OBLATION OF EZEKIEL 370

BOOK 5 THE HOLY UNION 379

- THE ECLIPSE 382
- HOLY WATER 384
- THE EUCHARIST 385
- THE HORNED GOD 387
- THE CHYMICAL MARRIAGE 392
- THE GREAT RITE 397
- THE LIGHT OF THE FISH 401
- VNIVERSITATIS RERVM FONTIS 405

Illuſtrations

Plate 1 - Sol	43
Plate 2 - Luna	50
Plate 3 - Runic Moon	55
Plate 4 - Venus	61
Plate 5 - Runic Venus	65
Plate 6 - Mercury	74
Plate 7 - Mars	77
Plate 8 - Ares	78
Plate 9 - Zeus	80
Plate 10 - Jupiter	81
Plate 11 - Runic Jupiter	82
Plate 12 - Kronos	83
Plate 13 - The Chi Rho Cross	85
Plate 14 - The Tetractys of Robert Fludd	159
Plate 15 - The Tetragrammaton	160
Plate 16 - The Saltire Cross	199
Plate 17 - The Tau Cross	202
Plate 18 - The Celtic Cross	203
Plate 19 - The Rood Cross	208
Plate 20 - The Sanctum Sanctorum	213
Plate 21 - The Cube Revealed	214
Plate 22 - The Templar Cross	215
Plate 23 - The Cross of Malta	216
Plate 24 - The Cross of Temporal Authority	217
Plate 25 - The Ankh	218
Plate 26 - The Anchor	219
Plate 27 - The Ophiolatreia	221
Plate 28 - The Ouroboros	223
Plate 29 - The Circumpunct	227
Plate 30 - The Equilateral Triangle	229
Plate 31 - The 47th Problem of Euclid	232
Plate 32 - The Square	237
Plate 33 - The Pentacle	241
Plate 34 - The Baphomet of Eliphas Levi	244
Plate 35 - The Mercurial Dove	251
Plate 36 - The Rosa Mystica	254
Plate 37 - The Rose Cross	257
Plate 38 - The Hexagram	260

PLATE 39 - THE COMPASS AND SQUARE 267
PLATE 40 - THE FISH 272
PLATE 41 - THE VESICA PISCES 275
PLATE 42 - THE EYE OF HORUS 279
PLATE 43 - THE QUINCUNX 280
PLATE 44 - THE MYSTIC EGG 282
PLATE 45 - THE TRIPLE SPIRAL 285
PLATE 46 - THE FLEUR DE LIS 287
PLATE 47 - THE SKARA BRAE MOTIF 288
PLATE 48 - THE CELESTIAL HORNED GOD 298
PLATE 49 - THE CRESCENT AND STAR 303
PLATE 50 - THE SEPTAGRAM 306
PLATE 51 - THE DRAGON 309
PLATE 52 - THE LABRYS 312
PLATE 53 - THE GREAT SPHINX 314
PLATE 54 - THE ELEMENTS 317
PLATE 55 - THE ELEMENTAL EARTH 325
PLATE 56 - THE ELEMENTAL AIR 326
PLATE 57 - THE ELEMENTAL FIRE 327
PLATE 58 - THE ELEMENTAL WATER 328
PLATE 59 - THE ELEMENTS IN BALANCE 329
PLATE 60 - THE SKARA BRAE SCRIPT 331
PLATE 61 - THE VITRUVIAN MAN 340
PLATE 62 - THE SACRED HEART 342
PLATE 63 - THE JERUSALEM OF THE VISION OF EZEKIEL 401
PLATE 64 - THE EYE OF THE SERPENT 403

Reference Tables

TABLE 1 - ISOPSEPHY VALUES OF THE GREEK ALPHABET 195
TABLE 2 - GEMATRIA VALUES OF THE LATIN ALPHABET 195
TABLE 3 - THE PROPORTIONS OF THE SOLAR SYSTEM 377

Dedicated to
Captain Billy Moore Jackson, 32°

**VIRTVS JVNXIT
MORS NON SEPARABIT**

Take Unto Yourself
These Words
And Heed Them,
And Lose Them Not,
Nor Fear Them.
Within Them Are Keys
Which Shall Unlock
Many Doors.
All May Enter
Who Are Worthy.

Introduction

There is no queſtion that we, as human beings, many tens of thousands of years ago, muſt have wondered in awe as we gazed into the night sky. In those days, we had not the technology of satellites or telescopes, nor the knowledge of phyſics and the refraction of light which enables us to now underſtand why the sky is blue, nor the laws of phyſics to explain how the planets guided their course. There were no printed books as of yet, nor writing, and all knowledge which could be accumulated by our species had to be paſſed on by oral tradition. Yet the fact that our diſtant anceſtors did not have those modern tools cannot imply in any way that they were leſſ intelligent or leſſ imaginative than we are; it muſt be that they were more so, since their very survival depended on it. The moment that it can be said that we became mankind muſt surely have been the moment that we looked around us and wondered, and realized that there muſt be reasons for all that we saw, the moment when we firſt looked up into the sky and began to queſtion what it all meant. The story of this queſt for underſtanding is the very hiſtory of Mankind itself.

Having begun to acquire knowledge and to conceive and to organize our thoughts, we learned in time to communicate by speech. As our knowledge of words developed, we could articulate abſtract concepts which could not be seen directly. Humanity was like a human child; we were intelligent but as yet uninformed, and so we sat about the buſineſſ of informing ourselves about the world in which we lived. It is known that great bodies of knowledge were obtained by rote memorization, and that the maſtery of the ancient Artes required many years of diligent study. This is still the case in many Shamanic traditions; traditions which we arrogantly conſider 'primitive' are not nearly so primitive as we are led to believe. Yet, there is only so much knowledge that one may acquire by memory, and so our collective knowledge was limited by this barrier. Even the confiderable memory of the beft human mind has its limits. Great stories came into being to incorporate that which had been learned and to make it sufficiently memorable as to pafs to the next generation, which would add to it as more was observed and learned. Millennia muft have paffed before we firft learned to store information as writing, and stories grew and evolved, retaining the diftant paft but perhaps in ways which became clouded by time. And so our Myths evolved.

Events accelerated when Mankind firft learned to write, so that knowledge could be paffed to others without the arduous task of rote memory, and our collective ability to store information and add to the sum knowledge of our race took its next important leap. Knowledge could be written by one generation and available to the next in this way. Knowledge could be shared with many by the magical art of writing. Stones could be carved with words and so become magical speaking stones, and could communicate an idea centuries after the author lived. Doubtlefs only a handful of humans ever poffeffed the skills by which to interpret such writing in the early days, for such knowledge would have been exceedingly powerful and jealoufly guarded. This author is of the opinion that sophifticated written languages almoft certainly exifted long before we have evidence of them. After four thousand years, cuneiform tablets survive, but anything placed on lefs than such or on stone would have been long gone. How then, could we know if writing exifted thirty thousand years ago? We do not at this time have any direct evidence of it, but the poffibility should not be ruled out. We do now underftand that writing developed separately at leaft several times in human culture, and that some syftems survived but moft were likely loft. When those languages were loft to us, so was all of the knowledge they contained.

Reading and writing allowed a quantum leap in our ability to store and diftribute knowledge. The invention of the printing prefs was surely one of the great turning points in the hiftory of the Human Race. Until this time, books were created by scribes, consuming vaft amounts of hours, and thus were commensurately valuable, and available to only those of wealth. Now the collected knowledge of Humanity could be reproduced hundreds or thousands of times over in a short time. Each year, for many centuries, we added to our stores of knowledge and the accumulation has been fafter with each paffing year. We now may inftantaneoufly search the collected works of thousands of authors, in all corners of the planet, in a matter of seconds. The textual contents of the Library of Congrefs, or its content a mere two decades ago, can now be stored in a device small enough to fit in the palm of the hand. By the time this work has been publifhed, such a device will already be obsolete. We now have the ability to create this work in the type face of seventeenth century England, and this with great ease, though based upon the work of countless thousands. The ability to inftantly share information and knowledge acrofs the entire globe is currently rewriting our future hiftory, as secrets become much harder to keep, and governments find it far more difficult to reftrict knowledge, not that they do not still try. Given this wealth of accefs to the written word, we are surely witneffing as great a revolution in our time as the invention of movable type, or perhaps even as the development of writing itself.

Even though this may sound like an exaggeration, it is not said lightly. As has often been opined, the vaft majority of the pages available to us in this vaft, electronic library are ufelefs at best, and yet, the important information is there, too. Even in the days when only the printed word awaited us, most of what was to be found there was of little real importance or use. The great writers, Samuel Clemens and Robert Frost, Plato and Milton and Poe, were but a few among thousands. Plato is still truly understood by only a handful of readers; only a small few hold the keys of Pythagoras, by which the important meaning of his works have remained securely locked for millennia. Virgil was brilliant, but so thoroughly misunderstood that his work did incalculable damage in the hands of the small minded. The best book on differential calculus is of no use to the one who has not mastered mathematics to the point of being able to understand it. Particle physics requires great knowledge to understand. Real knowledge requires more than reading, it requires judgment and discretion and thought and contemplation; it also requires preparation and understanding. Hidden among the chaff, the Wheat awaits the Reaper.

It is with intent that this author mentions the *known* history of Humanity, since it is certain that most of our history is as hidden from us as is the darkest reaches of the deepest sea. We have no better idea of the knowledge or life of our ancestors of 100,000 years ago than we do of life on a planet in some distant galaxy. We are told that all men in those days were simple hunters and gatherers. We are also told that the world is just over six thousand years old[1]. We do now know that roughly 25,000 years

---

[1] A large number of American Protestant churches teach exactly this. Their teachings are based on verbatim or 'literal' interpretations of the Christian Holy Bible, the component works of which, as we shall see, were never intended to be interpreted in such a way. The actual timeline was derived by adding the ages of the patriarchs of the Old Testament and assuming that the Six Days of Creation in the Book of Genesis were only twenty four hours long. Such literal interpretation of Mysteries are the source of much mischief.

ago there was a civilization in northern Europe with sufficient ability to mass produce Goddess statues, and we have recently discovered the fantastic stone circles at Gobekli Tepe which date these Megalithic Builders to at least nine thousand years ago. This new knowledge has created no small difficulty for classical anthropology, not to mention those who wish to say that the entire world is just over six thousand years old. Certain assumptions which were made at the very beginning of the scientific age have become shackles for science, especially that of Anthropology, preventing us from applying freely our tools to the solving of the mysteries of our distant ancestors. Finally, these walls are being pushed back, but the progress is slow, and it may yet be generations before we begin to truly understand the full heritage and history of the human race. Tools are now being found that date to human ancestors or relatives over one million years ago. Many astounding discoveries await us, and no doubt many have already been made but not yet recognized and still lie un-catalogued in some dusty museum drawer, patiently waiting for the mind which comprehends their true significance. The fact that evidence is found does not in any way imply that it is understood.

Sources for this work were as varied as Books, Family Oral Histories and various discussions with Physicists, Astronomers, Historians, Rabbis, Christian scholars and the occasional Witch. It is important in life to meet and learn from those who were raised with a different perspective, lest we become trapped in a prison of our own construction. Each of us approaches every topic from our own unique point of reference. We each have our own unique perspective, and any fact will look slightly different depending on that point of view. This does not make any observation or conclusion right or wrong, but will cause any truth to be perceived with a slightly different caſt. One is reminded of an ancient story of three blind men and an elephant. The elephant representing the truth, each is asked to describe it. One man describes it as a tree trunk, one as a mountain and the other as a snake. The moral of the story is that each man is right, from his perspective, but none of them knows the whole of the truth. While none of them is wrong, none of them underſtands the whole. As humans, we each strive for truth, having limited knowledge, and perceive the truth each in our own way.

Masonry is a family tradition for the author. The Order of Masonry is fascinating, and so rich in hiſtory that even moſt of its members have not the slighteſt idea of its true age and significance. Masonic Brethren do indeed take oaths not to reveal Masonic Secrets when communicated to them as such. No liberties have been taken with such an oath in the writing of this book, since none of the knowledge here conſtitutes revealed Masonic Secrets (which generally confiſt of the methods of identification between fellow Brethren). Such is eſſentially irrelevant in these times anyway, since there are other books, freely available to anyone, which reveal these secrets to anyone who wiſhes to know them. Should the reader come here in search of these secrets, they shall be disappointed, and so they muſt seek elsewhere. Of course there is much more to being a Mason than knowing a secret word or a handſhake. Anyone who, in reading such a book, believes themselves able to identify themselves to another Mason based on this alone, will be greatly disappointed. On the other hand, a studious Mason will find many wonderful morsels herein which will help him to better underſtand his Craft.

Other than veiled references and curious commentary, little is known of the real hiſtory of Freemasonry before the eighteenth century. The Craft officially traces its origins to the founding of the Grand Lodge of England in 1717. It is certain that the Craft had exifted in at leaft some form long before this time. Indeed, the founding of this Grand Lodge was an attempt to organize an already exifting group of lodges. Many of the decifions made at that point had more to do with political expediency and even survival, than with care for the truth of the Masonic Order. At this time the Order may have come into public view; its secrets did not. Recent events had affociated Masonry with the Jacobite revolution, making it neceffary to tread very lightly, elfe be perceived as traitors to England. In this way and in others, much of the important underftanding of Masonry has been loft, even to its own Brethren.

Recently, much has been made of a connection between the Knights Templar and modern Masonry, but no real documentation of such a connection exifts, though a great deal of conjecture has been made on this point. It is this author's confidered opinion that Modern Freemasonry was based upon earlier Fraternal Organizations which had exifted long before the founding of the Grand Lodge of England. It is without queftion that there were at leaft some descendent ties to the Templars, based on their appearance in the company of Robert the Bruce of Scotland subsequent to the purge by Phillip of France on Friday, October 13, 1307. Whether or not a direct descendent of the Templar Order, Masonry was certainly heavily influenced by it. The very fact that every Masonic Lodge is dedicated to the Holy Saints John should be sufficient for any scholar having knowledge of the Templars to reveal such a connection. Masonry is a tapeftry with many threads leading in many directions.

Even if there were no direct connection between the practices of the Templars and the Craft known as Freemasonry, there certainly do exist certain parallels between some of the legends surrounding them both. If not a descendent relationship, then possibly both were fed by a common stream. The peculiar set of symbology found in Rosllyn Chapel in Scotland, not to mention the history of its builder, do lend some credence to these ideas. Masonry has stories and legends relating to the actual architecture of the Temple of Solomon[2], especially the description of the Dormer Window in the East of the Temple, which are not present in any biblical references, and which are required for the actual function of the Temple to make sense. The degrees of the Scottish Rite directly include the Templar legends, but these are of relatively recent construction. He who has eyes, let him see.

The continuity of these legends within the allegorical stories and structure of Freemasonry would indicate that at least some part of it traces its ancestry to a time even before Fourth Dynasty Egypt. There are certain carvings found in ancient Egyptian tombs which represent several of the most important parts of Masonic Ritual. These Masonic rituals were in existence long before these carvings were discovered in modern times, and so it stands to reason that there was at least a common ancestor to the traditions. It is quite possible that Masonry represents the continuity of traditions that date to Neolithic times. The very layout of the Lodge itself possibly confirms this. The tessellated floor of white and black which is customary for the floor of the Masonic Lodge is a reference, not to a floor, but to the Wall of the Crystal Temple to which Enoch was conducted by the Sons

---

[2] More appropriately called Temple Sol Amon.

of Heaven. Though restored, this wall still stands restored upon the Temple at Newgrange, more than 5,000 years later. Like the answers to so many ancient riddles, it lies hidden in plain sight.

In the late twentieth century, this author recalls having had the opportunity to witness the Great Rite as practiced by 'Witches' in Central Chile, and that the form of the ceremony and even the position of the players, was far too close to that of a Masonic Lodge to be accidental. Again, the two traditions almost certainly held some degree of common heritage at some point in time[3]. Considering how much human energy and violence are devoted to the minor differences between the various faiths of the world, one might find it odd that so few bother to note the similarities. Ancient temples in Thailand and India have much in common with the Acropolis and even with Christian Cathedrals. There is both a harmony here, and a continual thread of ideas and concepts. We are by no means the first to suggest that this is so, for it has been noted by scholars for many centuries.

---

[3] The Wiccan Religion is actually a recently created organization, having had its origins in 1954 in the work of Gerald Gardner, who wrote that he had been initiated into an ancient nature religion based on pre-Christian Pagan beliefs. Gardner referred to the practices as *Witchcraft* and to its adherents as *the Wica*. There has been considerable debate as to whether the rites written about by Gardner constitute an actual continuity of ancient esoteric traditions or a more recent attempt to re-create them. Having read Henry Cornelius Agrippa, the author suggests that Wicca is more closely derived from this work. This author considers the Chilean rituals somewhat more authentic than Gardnerian Wica, but still influenced by it, being based in part on significantly older local traditions. Wicca is often referred to by its adherents as 'the Craft'.

Masonry has then, to some degree influenced the author's point of view on these matters. The author firſt became a Mason in 1987, and more than two decades within the Craft[4], combined with insatiable curioſity and the exploration of its rich symbology, have shaped our perspective significantly. Brother Masons will note things of great intereſt in this work, which might help those with curious minds to better underſtand many of the more Arcane[5] elements of the Masonic ritual and symbology. For anyone with an intereſt in the hiſtory and meaning of Masonry, moſt especially Brother Masons, the works of Chriſtopher Knight and Robert Lomas on the subject are strongly recommended. The reader will note several references to their work in this writing, and they represent a valuable keyſtone in gaining a true underſtanding of this tradition. The author laments that the beſt and brighteſt young men often no longer show an intereſt in Masonry, and hopes that this trend does not continue, leſt an invaluable resource be loſt to this nation, whose roots are steeped in the traditions and ideals of the Craft. Masonry is a Cornerſtone of the United States of America, however much many would prefer not believe this to be so. Based on the hiſtory of our nation, we would surmise that the United States of America could likely not have even come into being without the Masonic fraternity. It is with great joy that we have noticed in recent years a greater intereſt among those beſt suited to the craft, and we hope that this trend continues.

As the author's particular world view was shaped by a childhood in the American Proteſtant tradition, it was shaped as well by experiences in the Masonic Lodge on three continents,

---

[4] It is common among Masons to refer to their rituals and practices as 'the Craft'.

[5] An Arcane truth requires secret or hidden knowledge to underſtand. Esoteric or Inner Secret knowledge is referred to as Arcane knowledge.

and on having grown up with a father and a great uncle who were both 32° Masons, the author having followed in their footsteps in this matter. This author might also mention that in the same way that insatiable curiosity regularly created conflict with the hierarchy of the Christian Church, the continual need of the author to understand the history and meaning of Masonry has at times, no doubt, been somewhat of an annoyance to some of his fellow Brethren. As in the former case, no apologies are made in the latter respect. When the curious mind is blocked at one door, it will seek another passage. Thusly, this work has a distinct point of view, and while it is our intent to make this work accessible to those of any background, it will be no surprise if the Mysteries here within shed more light upon the curiosities of those raised in the Christian tradition or having a familiarity with Masonry.

Even the most fundamental symbols change in their perceived meanings through time. For thousands of years, the Swastika would have been recognized as a beneficent symbol from Asia to the Indigenous people of the Americas, if indeed it was recognized at all. During most of that time, its basis as a form of the Solar Cross was probably lost within layers of other interpretation. Its association with the crimes of the so called 'Third Reich' has completely changed our impression of this very ancient symbol, and now no Rational person would think lightly of representing it in a positive light, for fear of being thought a supporter of those who bore it in the early and mid twentieth century, and regrettably even to this day, as a symbol of oppression and death. This is a great tragedy. To understand this use of such a symbol, it is greatly helpful for the reader to acquaint themselves with the history of the period, in which a fascination with ancient occult traditions and symbology permeated society in the entire western world.

Underſtanding the origins and ancient meanings of such symbols is therefore paramount in gaining any real perspective in these matters. For millennia, the Pentagram or Pentacle was a symbol of Wisdom and Knowledge to the moſt learned among us; there is a very sound reason why this was so. A combination of the persecution of learning by certain religious inſtitutions over the paſt several hundred years, its adoption by the so called 'Church of Satan' in the 1960's, and numerous low budget horror movies, have led the uneducated to aſſociate this symbol with evil or dark forces. The modern religion of Wicca has adopted the Pentagram as its own, and to their credit, at leaſt some of its members underſtand how it came to be. Yet the Wiccan tradition has created its own exoteric explanations for the Pentacle, which are fine for the purpose of explaining their own philosophy, but serve to further cloud its origin and ancient meaning. This writer has never met the person who, having the fiſh emblem on their automobile was able to correctly identify where it came from and why it came to be aſſociated with their religion[6]. The author does not declare that such persons do not exiſt; there are very illuminated men and women of the Chriſtian faith, and indeed of all faiths. The point stands that the average adherent to Chriſtianity, or any other religion, knows eſſentially nothing about their own faith, and the more voraciouſly they declare their faith, the leſſ they are likely to underſtand it.

---

[6] The Chriſtian symbol of the Fish, often inscribed with the Greek Word Ιχϕψσ, meaning 'fish' was used as a method of secret self identifications among early Chriſtians during the days of the Roman persecutions, before Chriſtianity became the official and only allowed religion of Rome. This is an accepted truth, but the reason that this symbol was important, and its Esoteric meaning to early Chriſtians, is almoſt universally unknown to modern followers of the faith. More information on this Symbol may be found on page 271.

Since connotative interpretations change over the centuries, and the perspective of civilizations change over time, the decifion has been made here to trace these symbols as far back as poffible, and whenever poffible, to identify or at leaft speculate on their moſt ancient meanings and, often more importantly, how they were derived. The Croſs is not an obvious symbol for the Sun, but as it shall presently be seen, the Sun creates it. It is a fundamental symbol, part of the bafic symbolic vocabulary that is an important part of our heritage as Humans, and even a part of the moſt ancient written languages of which we currently have knowledge, and still a part of almoſt every weſtern language to this day. In fact several of the moſt bafic symbols discuſſed herein are a part of the Latin alphabet used by billions, as they were used in the ancient alphabets from which those of Arabic, Hebrew, Greek and Latin evolved.

Some will read this work and think the author hoſtile to the concept of religion, but they would be miſtaken. Great good has been done and still is done by faithful members of many religions. This author does make no apology for reminding the reader that great atrocities have been and even now are committed in the name of many gods and have been, if not condoned, placidly accepted by far too many religious leaders and followers alike. Nonetheleſſ, religion is a part of this work, for the symbols herein are a part of religion. Each of these symbols has been used by religions throughout the millennia. Our inquiry is to follow their trail and to determine, as beſt is poffible, their origins and *original* meanings. An underſtanding of these ancient meanings may shed light on the origins and meanings of these various traditions. If the reader is eaſily offended by a frank discuſſion of such matters, then perhaps it is beſt that they close this book now. Once Illumination has been received, it cannot be undone. Once a thing is known, it cannot be *unknown*.

There is too much ignorance and intolerance in this world, and the last thing our planet needs is to have the passions of bigotry, prejudice or fear inflamed in the name of any deity. Those who would fan the fires of war in Palestine in order to hurry the arrival of Armageddon, or who slay women and children on a busy street in the name of their own peculiar god, are no better than those who tortured helpless victims to death for the benefit of their souls. This sad story even now plays out all over the world and fills our headlines with savage violence perpetrated in the name of one or another 'god'. As long as the average man and woman tolerates such in the name of a deity, our civilization, and indeed the future of humanity itself are at risk. For this reason our subject matter, which may to some seem trivial, is trivial not at all, for herein lie the building blocks of modern civilization itself.

In regard to the mention of historical matters, this author does not apologize for saying that which was done, but does hope mankind has begun by now to learn better than to commit mass murder in the name of any god, by any name. The atrocities committed by Protestants against Catholics were every bit as reprehensible as those committed by the Holy Inquisition or the crusades. When it comes to the good performed by the faithful, the author freely gives his admiration. When it comes to the sins of the priest craft or of the zealot, be they Pagan, Christian, Zoroastrian, Jew or Muslim, and regardless of their name for god, no apologies are made for exposing them. When the Crusaders first took Jerusalem, ostensibly in the name of Christ, they slaughtered every living soul, Muslim, Jew and Christian alike. Even now, atrocities are regularly committed in the name of one god or another. One who kills a child in the name of any god is no better than the ancients who caused their children to paſs through the fires of Moloch[7]. Humanity is still a child and still learning to control its temper. Given the dreadful tools of death now at our disposal, let us hope we manage to grow up safely. This is not a given outcome by any means, and is in no small part the motivation for this work.

More could certainly be written. The author's intereſts in Esoteric Symbology are well beyond the scope of such a modeſt work as this, and the scope of general symbology is almoſt infinite. It encompaſses everything from Esoteric and Religious symbols to collegiate Greek organizations to corporate logos and gang symbols. It is therefore neceſsary to define the scope of the work here in very specific terms. These works will therefore endeavor to inveſtigate symbols which have been in use since before the Common Era, which are broadly used and referenced, and which have meaning in Esoteric Doctrines. Even this is a more broad category than could be addreſsed in a single work, so the choice of the symbols to be included has been the arbitrary choice of this author, being those in which he poſseſses a moſt keen intereſt, and which are important within the context of the known hiſtory of Weſtern Civilization and the claſsical Myſteries.

Under these conſtraints, these writings will discuſs the moſt baſic symbols, which often form parts of other symbols. Special attention has been focused on the symbols which are felt to be critical to underſtanding the traditions of the Myſteries. The

---

[7] Also Molech, Melek, מולך. Believed to have been of Canaanite origin, followers of Moloch slowly roaſted their children alive as a sacrifice to this unpleasant deity. The god was represented by a metal bull. The ruler generally known as King Solomon is said to have built a temple to this deity and also to have caused his children to 'pass through the fires'.

reader will note that a large part of this work is dedicated to the discuſſion of Heavenly Bodies and to Numbers. Numbers are also symbols, and the esoteric meaning of certain numbers is discuſſed herein, in addition to a baſic introduction into the Gematria. These are also important symbols and some level of underſtanding of their use in the Occult traditions is required to properly underſtand the symbols aſſociated with them. This delineation leaves out many important traditions, by which we do not demean such traditions. Given that this work is in large part a compilation of eſſays and lectures, the author has attempted to organize it into a series of sections. Since every section is related to every other, this is simply an arbitrary choice on the part of the author.

Like everyone, this author works within the context into which he was born, but as is rapidly coming to light, the world was much smaller thousands of years ago than had dared been imagined even one hundred years ago. Though anthropology has yet to accept definitive proof, this author conſiders it probable that humans were capable of navigating by ship to any part of the world at leaſt as far back as 4,000 BC, and very probably *much* farther back. The explorer Dr. Bob Ballard has recently been searching for ancient veſſels in the Dead Sea; his work is followed with great intereſt. Work there may yet yield finds that puſh back the veil on our ancient hiſtory by hundreds or even thousands of years. The recent discovery of the ruins of the temple complex at Gobekli Tepe in modern Turkey have almoſt inſtantly doubled the age of known civilization and reveal a knowledge of megalithic building and abſtract symbolism heretofore not conſidered by anthropology to have exiſted in such ancient times.

Undertaking even such a modest work upon such a subject is at once challenging and terrifying. Nothing written here should ever be taken as fact or in any way the last word on these subjects. Much of it is conjecture or theory on the part of the author or on the part of others. And yet, taken as a whole, there is a harmony of these ideas, and it is this symmetry that motivated the work to compile this opus. The author has attempted to group the subject matter in some logical way, but other ways might have been just as logical. Readers with experience in such matters will note that the organization of the work is not mere accident, however. As with any work on the subject, there is more here than the words at first indicate. In this way, one is able to speak to the reader at his or her own level.

So it must be noted, then, that the author claims to be neither historian nor priest, and has played many roles in a brief few decades upon this Earth. The author currently works in the field of computer programming, a profession which not only did not exist a mere hundred years ago, it could not even have been conceived by most. This subject is pursued for the sheer love of it, and to sate an almost irresistible compulsion to follow this path. As the author first caused distress in church school at the age of six, by asking questions for which the adults had no satisfactory answer, and his embarrassed parents were asked to remove him for being 'disruptive', this journey began at a tender age. It is the sincere desire of this author that reader engage in this work for the same reason. Having exhausted other avenues of inquiry, you have arrived here. All of your questions cannot be answered here, for the humble author does not know the answers. He shall be content if you but find enough to make the time invested worth your while. Should the reader find some semblance of a reflection of themselves in the author, it is likely that this work will be of great intereſt.

Over the years, the author has acquired a modeſt, yet rich library on the subject. The comparatively short Bibliography of this work would serve as an excellent reading liſt for anyone with a keen intereſt on this subject. The author's cloſeſt friends would offer an apology to the reader in advance for his tendency to write in what might only be described as a rather anachronistic and formal Engliſh. The author himself makes no apologies, however, since it is the form in which he was taught to write as a child, and has not been diminiſhed by the general decline of the Engliſh language in recent years, and the demands that writing be conſtructed for an ever lower level of educational accompliſhment. This author finds this trend unpleasant at beſt, and is not prepared after a half century to relinquiſh the art.

Conſidering such authors as Milton, Waite, or even Stirling, it is hoped that this work is somewhat more acceſſible than moſt writing on the subject, which is often intentionally cryptic, being aimed only at those poſſeſſing certain keys required to decode it. The intelligent reader might find acceſſ to one or two of those keys within this work, should they be sufficiently observant. The often fanciful interpretations of the late eighteenth and early twentieth centuries is only touched upon when required, as such writings tend to be confuſing at beſt and often downright miſleading. It should be noted that even when presenting such subject matter in the moſt forthright way poſſible, it is cryptic by nature, and not eaſily or readily underſtood by any but the moſt ardent and receptive mind. If the reader's capacity for the Engliſh language makes this work too difficult, the author might suggeſt the prudent inveſtment of the time required to gain a proper underſtanding of the language, and then making the attempt again, given that a knowledge of rudimentary Latin, Hellenic and Hebrew was required to architect even this meager effort. This is neither an academic work, nor is it intended to be more of the popular fluff on the subject. This author has a genuine intereſt in helping others who are curious about these matters. Nothing is free, of course; at the very leaſt, the reader muſt reſiſt the effort to place this information within an exiſting context, and attempt to aſſimilate it as it is, without self editing. This is a simple work within a very complex subject.

Conſiderable motivation for both this research and writing is the maze of curious opinions currently being circulated in the name of prophecy. A quick search currently reveals thousands of pages of writing that would have one believe that the World is about to end. This is not at all a new phenomenon; the term 'millennialism' has been around since the firſt millennium, when there was a 'prophet' on every street corner predicting the end of the world. The World did not end in 999 AD, nor in 1881, nor in 1999 and it will not end in 2012, or in 2112, or on any date previouſly written. The Winter Solſtice of 2012 has been said to coincide with the end of the Great Epochs of the Mayan Calendar. This happens to occur at a time when the sun is located in alignment with the Galactic Center, as observed from the Earth on the Winter Solstice, and to a dark area there which has, in prior epochs, been described as the Womb of the World. If one is to take such an omen at face value, then one might see it as a birth, rather than a death. This work is not intended to add to such creative interpretations, but rather to gird the loins of the reader so that they may better recognize both wisdom and superſtition in such matters. We might also make it a point to mention that the Preceſſion, by which such motion in the Heavens occurs, is a slow proceſſ. The Winter Solſtice has coincided with the galactic center for a number of years and shall for many years yet. We have seen no calculations which cite this particular date for an alignment of our Sun with the precise location of the super massive black hole at the galactic center, nor would such an event necessarily hold any particular significance according to the ancient traditions. We believe that much more knowledge should be credited the ancients than is generally the case, but that of gravitational singularities is likely not among them. Alignments of the Planets were indeed auspicious to the ancients for what they represented to them, but while much of what they knew and believed may be carefully extracted from that which comes down to us, much may be lost. It is worthy of note that according to several traditions, this date will herald the beginning of the Age of Aquarius, anciently known as the Age of Man. The author shall leave it to the reader to place their own significance to such an event.

Unless otherwise prefaced, when the Gods are spoken of here, we refer only to the Philosophical constructs and the relations of these symbols to those constructs, and the physical manifestations and observations from which these symbols were derived. It is not the place of these works to dispel or condone any faith or tradition, but to remind the reader to learn from them all; they are all deeply interconnected and their roots are anchored in the most ancient times. Any attempts to interpret any part of this work as hidden prophesy or revelation, except in the *philosophical* sense, is purely false and should be viewed as such. A philosophical revelation is the true meaning of the Greek derived word Apocalypse. The modern mind does not even understand the word Prophecy any better than it understands the Greek Word Apocalypse. An Apocalypse is actually a revealing, or a revelation of knowledge. Even this is deceiving; the word reveal literally means to re-veil, or to conceal beneath a different Veil. With this in mind, a well informed reader will underſtand that the Apocalypse attributed to St. John the Divine is moſt certainly a revealing look at very important events of long, long ago. The story told in that work has been told in many ways by many cultures.

Learned men of centuries paſt, at leaſt within the Common Era, all had one thing in common; they wrote and read in Latin. Rerum Fontis is Latin, and means the Source of Things. The intent of this work is not to be the laſt word on the meanings of symbols, but rather to be the firſt. This book is intended as a Primer for those who wiſh to inveſtigate the meanings of the symbolic breadcrumbs which lie all around us. This is not to say that this book will speak as fully to a beginner as to an Adept, for it will not, but it will aſſiſt the novice to make their journey more fruitful from the start, or at leaſt this is our hope. The author attempts here to take the oldeſt and moſt fundamental of symbols and help the reader to underſtand them and their derivations to a very baſic degree. The path is by no means a straight line.

These symbols and many others are connected on many levels and have many meanings. As we follow the derivations and meanings of these symbols, what is written at the end may only be explained at the beginning. Perhaps one will gain from this exposure, and with this simple alphabet, be better able to interpret the more complex symbols which fill our hiſtory and surround us, even to this day. The ideas and symbols which are herein presented have served well many story tellers and have made for wonderful and fantaſtic tales. The reality and hiſtory here is not fantasy. Herein lies the reality of another time and place and is as much a part of our human history as the invention of the wheel. It is just as real, and it is a part of who we are.

As is the case with Myth and Ritual, the words Esoteric and Occult are almost always misunderstood by the modern mind. These words conjure images of dark rituals and evil and darkness. Esoteric literally means 'inner' and the study of Esoteric Symbology is therefore the study of the Inner Meanings of Symbols. Occult philosophies were hidden in shadow to keep their illumination from the profane. In all ancient philosophies, there were great secrets which were reserved alone for the Initiates. These secrets were never to be revealed to the uninitiated and were veiled under secrecy and symbol. As an Initiate was tried and found worthy, they might rise to even higher Degrees of Initiation and receive Secrets within those Secrets. The greatest of the Mysteries were reserved for only the Few. Until the Age of Reason, every school of knowledge was organized in this way. Both the Church of Jesus Christ of Latter Day Saints and the Roman Catholic Church are still maintained in this way, with the higher Mysteries reserved only for the few who have demonstrated themselves worthy to receive them. The Temple of Solomon was clearly organized into three degrees or levels. The vast majority of those who attended the Temple belonged to the first or outer degree, in which only allegorical stories were presented, devoid of their inner meanings. A much smaller group was able to enter the Holy Place, where the Mysteries began to be revealed and explained. It is written that only the High Priest could enter the Sanctum Sanctorum and fully partake of the Mysteries therein. This was as true of the more ancient forms of Christianity as it was for the Cult of Mithras or the Mysteries of Pythagoras.

Ritual was the Gateway to Knowing. Myftery Schools were the Houses of Many Doors. Each school of learning had both its Exoteric and Esoteric teachings, with the higher Esoteric doctrines reserved solely for those of higher degrees. Should one properly familiarize themselves with the earlieft manifeftations of Chriftianity, they would find its structure to be of similar nature. Even our modern univerfity syftem still bears veftiges of this syftem. When we pafs to a higher level of formal education, we still call the confirmation of this paffage the conferral of a Degree.

Exoteric teachings were created for the outfide world, and all were freely given them. The Esoteric, or Inner Secrets, were for the initiates alone. The more important secrets were kept 'in shadow' which is the true meaning of the word Occult. The word literally means in *shadow*. The darker meanings of the word Occult have been the result of fear and superftition; such have never been in short supply in human hiftory and remain with us to this day. When one reads a fantaftic story filled with unbelievable tales, one is generally reading an exoteric work. This is a cue to look within for the Myfteries. This is as true for the Chriftian Holy Book as it is for the Odyffey. If the author can leave the reader with anything at all from this work, it is hoped that it will be the idea that knowledge, of any kind, is never to be feared nor fled from, and never to be persecuted. A true Mythos is as a stone wall to the simple mind. To the more advanced mind, such is an invitation. The very difficulty of penetrating a Myftery is a siren call to an intelligent mind and this is as it has always been. For this very reason, the Myfteries have been made more complex through the millennia to the point that some appear completely loft. But they are not loft; they are misunderftood, but not forgotten. Mankind has been loſt before and found its way. It has been said of the Myſteries that they are like an onion, for peeling back one layer reveals yet another. Once again we will emerge from the darkneſſ.

Come ye therefore through the desert and acroſſ the mountains. There are Seven Doors, the keys to which have been scattered upon the Winds. The Keys herein were not granted to the author; they were discovered by the author among the ruins of all the Temples, as they have lain, some for thousands of years, awaiting one to find them. Some of them were discovered with the aid of others gone before who found them amid the ruins, and rather than guarding them jealouſly in their house, placed them in the towne square for all to see. Some secrets come with strings attached, and the recipient is not free to do with them as he or she wiſhes, and some of those secrets this author holds and shall retain.

Literature and Liturgy and Ritual and Myth are the ruins through which we search. The more practical minded among us may conſider this work trivial or worse. Some will no doubt find it dangerous, but a closed mind is far more dangerous than any incantation in any medieval Grimoire. In fact, the myſterious symbols which are the heart of any Grimoire are but decorative language, a codec of sorts, which reveal to the enlightened the numeric values ascribed to a concept which has been personified in myth as either an Angel or a Demon. The tendency to anthropomorphize a concept is strong in the human mind. An underſtanding of such matters requires a knowledge of the Gematria, by which the words of certain ancient alphabets have a numerical meaning which is related to the proportions and movements of the heavens. Once this is underſtood, such a work becomes obvious as the reference book which it was originally intended to be. Many have tread this land before us. In the early twentieth century, Sir James Frazer compiled a waterfhed work on the continuity and development of religion in the mafterpiece *The Golden Bough*[8]. The author received his firft copy a number of years ago, and regrets that this was the abridged edition. The abridged edition abridged the analyfis of Chriftianity which caused much outrage upon the original release of the work. The response was the release of the abridged edition in 1922, which conveniently avoided the very proper comparisons of Chriftianity to the other 'pagan' faiths of other times.

Very little one will read here has not been written before by someone, though some we have never seen. The author tries, as beft he may, to give proper credit to those who have come before, and begs the forgiveneff of any omitted. It is not the purpose of these works to beftow upon the reader more than a very bafic introduction to the concepts mentioned herein. Volumes have been written on any single idea confidered herein. Confider this to be what the author intended, a Primer. Allow this work to be the moft bafic of introductions into a hidden world which has always lain right at your fingertips. If the reader should find even the slighteft awareneff of what lies hidden in plain sight, then these words will have served their meager purpose.

Such a task leaves this author literally overwhelmed by his own seeming lack of capacity in undertaking this work, especially in the light of his predeceffors, whose diligence and brilliance haunt at every turn. In truth, the author has learned a very great deal in the proceff of compiling this work, and has endeavored to share those revelations with the reader. If, in writing these words, he is able to share a small part of the joy and

---

[8] Frazer, Sir James George, F.R.S., F.B.A., The Golden Bough, A Study in Magic and Religion. Abridged edition. New York: Macmillan, 1922.

illumination that has resulted from this journey, then this endeavor will have been worthwhile. If anyone reading these words is driven to ask queftions that had not occurred to him or her, then it is even more so. It is, after all, asking queftions that truly makes us Human. And so now begins our journey.

Book 1 The Heavens

It has been said of some of the ancient texts, that they were compiled from work written, literally, by the Hand of God. This is more true than moſt imagine. For what could be a more apt description of the Book written by the hand of The Gods, than the very Universe Itself. The stories of the Norse Gods, and those of the Greeks and Romans, of the Hindus and Buddhiſts, of legends of which we now know nothing, were quite literally written upon the Heavens. It may at firſt seem odd to begin a tome on ancient symbols with a discuſſion of the Heavenly bodies, but they are the moſt ancient symbols, and served as the inspiration for many of the moſt commonly recognizable symbols. Some important symbols are actually drawn to look like heavenly apparitions. The *Opening of the Mouth Tool* used in ancient Egypt and aſſociated with the Egyptian Book of the Dead is an eaſily recognizable replica of the stars which we generally know as Ursa Minor, the Little Bear or the Little Dipper, the handle of which contains the Pole Star. This is the point around which the World turns and the reason that this shape was chosen. The Saltire Croſſ is a product of the Sun at a certain latitude. On a clear late winter evening, the Chi Rho Croſſ may be seen emblazoned acroſſ the greater part of the sky. The moſt revered and ancient symbols all relate to the Heavens.

Nowhere is this more apparent than in religious art, which is the original source of all art and sculpture in the claſſical sense. The modern idea of what conſtitutes art is a very recent invention. For moſt of human hiſtory art was religion and it was by Canon. In paintings, the Hindu Gods and Goddeſſes are oft identified as such by their skin of beautiful sky blue. The God, Saints and Angels of Chriſtianity are represented by their respective Canon as wearing the glowing halos that poſitively identify them as Heavenly Luminaries. A full underſtanding of such symbols can help us to identify the sources of our Myths and help us to underſtand their development through the millennia. Perhaps this is enough reason that the myſterious symbology of the Navajo Nation sometimes has close parallels to that of the Norse or to the Greeks. It is also poſſible that there were contacts between the anceſtors of these peoples long ago.

All of the primary players in the Myths of Greece and Rome are counted among those of the Norse. How could they indeed not be? Is it not the same Sun which rises in the morning to give life which is seen by all Mankind? The same stars are seen throughout the year by the peoples of all lands north of the equator, and those which are gathered around the ecliptic are viſible from both hemispheres. In the northern latitudes, the same conſtellations correspond to the same seasons. It is said that the illuminated among the Norse peoples were horrified by the Greek habit of anthropomorphizing the gods into human form; to them this was a degradation of the myſterious and infinite nature of the gods. The Ecliptic conſtellations and the Planets, or wandering stars, are viſible to all.

Northern peoples, also, leſt they be able to croſſ the great oceans, would have never seen the Triangulum Auſtrale. How obvious, then, that other Gods and Goddeſſes, with which the northern peoples are unfamiliar, should populate the legends of the native peoples of Auſtralia, whose oral hiſtory is by far the oldeſt exiſtent[9]. They tell some stories which were shared by every member of the human race in their day, from their own perspective. This difference in perspective may make the stories at firſt difficult to reconcile, but the same stories they are. The search for the ancient meanings of Esoteric Symbols is, in a very real sense, a journey to find the origins of the Human Race. Of course looking up at the same sky might not sufficiently explain the very close parallels between these traditions and also those of the Egyptians. We think it likely that all of the weſtern and near eaſtern traditions grew from common roots, and this means that there was travel and communication between these regions long before it is widely accepted to have taken place.

Nature is the Book written by the Hand of God, and this writing can be beheld upon the Heavens. The Sun and Moon and the Movable Planets and the Fixed Stars gave us a context within which to think and exiſt. These were the movements by which we firſt conceived and organized the paſſage of time. By its very nature, the human mind requires and seeks out harmony, structure, and order. When order and structure are either not present, or cannot be perceived, the mind creates it by filling in the blanks, so to speak. Of course, the fascination of our anceſtors with the Heavenly Luminaries was far more than juſt the conſtruction of superſtitions and artificial order from chaos. There *is* order and harmony in the Heavens; the order of the Heavens helped Mankind find order from our own chaos, to create language and mathematics. The moſt ancient symbols used

---

[9] Though opinions vary on the subject of the age of the Auſtralian Aboriginal Oral Traditions, many believe them to be 40,000 to 60,000 years old, and poſſibly as old as 100,000 years. This would eaſily and by far make them the moſt ancient continuous oral traditions currently known. Known written hiſtory only dates back to the Sumerian culture.

to represent the Heavenly Luminaries became the early alphabets with which we learned to write. How is it wrong then, that the tradition of the Qabala says that the Hebrew alphabet was the very eſsence of creation?

Almoſt every ancient tradition describes the world as having come into being from Chaos. We did. The Heavenly Luminaries were our guides from Darkneſs. These were the signpoſts of the Heavens, and not only guided us in our queſts, but brought Life itself. How long would we survive without the Sun? When our anceſtors hunted wild game by the light of the Moon, how was it not the power the Gods come to light the way? The Stars were the signpoſts for the seasons and the carriers of the High Myſteries of the Navigators.

The Heavenly Luminaries

Every change of the Moon and Stars was a Guide to that which had been, and therefore also to that which was to come. In this way, the Heavens are the one true Book of Prophecy, for by them we may foretell what is to come. They served as the only calendar and the warnings of winter or heat, of the planting season and the time to reap. All of these are so obvious to even the casual observer, that we will not recount them here. Yet in long loſt times, such knowledge was more precious than any gold, for it meant life itself, and literally gave one power over life and death. A knowledge of the Heavenly Luminaries literally meant to have power over them, for if one could command that they would behave in a certain way and it was made manifeſt, surely then, these muſt be powerful men and women, or even gods. Note that both men and women are mentioned, for at leaſt one of the ancient races who served as the model for the Magi travelled in pairs, man and woman. Human civilization has not always been so short sighted in this way as we have been taught.

Some of what we now know, we have not so much discovered as re-discovered what was loſt. And yet, there are other ways in which our anceſtors learned to use these signs which are more subtle and more complex and precise than many of us, in the arrogance of our technological superiority, are eaſily willing to admit. Of course we can use telescopes and computers to calculate the Winter Solſtice right down to the second, and yet, long ago, and even up to recent times, certain of the Inuit people were able to make such an accurate calculation from the stars alone, to an accuracy of a few seconds. This knowledge, along with a great deal of their traditional culture, has now been loſt. The extent to which such ancient wisdom has been deſtroyed by other cultures attempting to 'civilize the ignorant savages' is incalculable and tragic.

The present is so very ignorant of the paſt. We scoff at the peers of Columbus who believed, or at leaſt claimed, the Earth to be flat, and yet long before the Sumerian civilization, learned peoples had calculated the spherical dimenſions of the earth to very precise detail, and learned to create a standard unit of measurement which could be recreated anywhere on earth, and evidence shows us that it was. In the future, learned people will quite poſſibly laugh at us because we believed the Universe to exiſt only in three dimenſions[10]. The people who conſtructed the megaliths at Stonehenge, or the stone circles in Yemen or on the coaſt of Africa at the Tropic of Cancer, millennia ago, used the same unit of measure. Only recently has that unit been fully recaptured, and the knowledge of its creation rediscovered.[11] The marvel of this unit, known sometimes as the Megalithic Yard, is that it was derived by both the proportions and rotation of the Earth, so that it incorporates both diſtance and time. The technology of the Stone Age was more than stone. The computers of the Neolithic times were the Sun and the Moon and the Planets and the Stars, and the Stone Temples by which these were measured and tracked. Their books were the Prieſts who spent lifetimes accumulating huge amounts of knowledge by rote memorization alone, with training that began in early childhood, for in that day, it is true that the sign of one's birth truly defined their deſtiny. He who was born on one specific day of the year might be a shepherd, and he born on another a Prieſt.

---

[10] Current theories of conceptual phyſics, especially that called M-Theory, infer that there are at leaſt ten, and perhaps eleven actual dimenſions of space and time.

[11] Knight, Chriſtopher and Robert Lomas. Uriel's Machine. London: Fair Winds Press, 2001. pp. 260-261.

It is for this reason that there are still those among us who believe that the stars and planets under which we are born determine our deftiny. There was a time when this was absolutely true, for society had been structured in exactly this way.

Sumerian and Babylonian civilizations are confidered by main stream archaeology to be the cradles of civilization, and the official stance is that nothing but primitive hunter gatherer groups exifted before this time. This is in spite of well documented and accurately dated remnants of a site in northern Europe which maff produced symbolic Goddeff statues, roughly twenty five thousand years ago. The Antikythera Mechanism[12], as it is generally known, dates to around the end of the Second Century BCE, and yet it was almoft two thousand years before our European civilization could come close to creating such a device. The hiftory of Mankind is not exactly as we have been led to believe. In truth it appears to us that such highly advanced technology and mathematics simply appeared out of nowhere in a very brief time; logically, such a conclufion is not reasonable. Much complex hiftory muft have paffed before we have known records of it. Evidence which appears outfide the accepted theories is ignored as mifleading or a simple error, and is either stored in an unmarked drawer or worse yet discarded.

One of the greateft of all Human Myfteries is how we suddenly emerged into civilization in so short a time. It is true that sometimes a single advance, or more commonly a group of them, can advance civilization very quickly. We have seen this in

---

[12] The Antikythera Mechanism was discovered on an ancient Greek shipwreck and is composed of numerous complex gears. Engineers have determined that the machinery would have quite accurately allowed to user to determine the pofition of the Heavenly Luminaries on a give date in the paft or future. At that time, this was exceedingly powerful knowledge which was expected of those of high status.

our lifetimes. Yet how can it be that we existed for hundreds of thousands of years, for evolution is a slow process, and yet lived as animals and accomplished nothing? We surely did not. It is more likely that we either have yet to find evidence that is difficult to find, or that we have ignored that which was right in front of us all along. We might be forgiven for not easily seeing the obvious. From a few simple concepts, schools of philosophy and religion grew and morphed into countless variants, turning and twisting back upon themselves. One who seeks to follow this trail is like Heracles battling the Hydra, in that each answer to a question rears itself as many questions until the Hero is all but overwhelmed. Therefore, keep thine Sword at the ready.

Perhaps cuneiform was not the first written language of the Human Race. It seems unlikely that such advances simply pop into existence overnight. Thousands of years before the first cuneiform tablets were written, a seafaring people had not only learned to sail by the wind and navigate by the stars, but had developed a science of spherical geometry so advanced, that with few alterations, it serves us even today. To their more primitive counterparts, these people must have seemed to possess magical powers at the very least. The great science fiction writer and futurist Arthur C. Clarke[13] once wrote, 'Any sufficiently advanced technology is indistinguishable from magic.'[14] Indeed, to many of the less learned people with whom these people came into contact, they might have been viewed as messengers of the Gods, or perhaps even Gods themselves. This would be especially true

---

[13] In addition to a prolific body of written work, it was Arthur C. Clarke who first suggested certain methods for using the gravity of a planet to increase the speed of a space vehicle, a commonly used method for decades now, and he was also the first to suggest communications satellites, having been properly credited for this idea.

[14] Arthur C. Clarke, *Profiles of the Future, An Inquiry into the Limits of the Possible*. Harper & Row, 1962.

had these been a tall people with fair skin, blonde or white hair, and blue eyes. In fact, such people are described in the Book of Enoch as the Sons of Heaven, and also in Gilgameſh as the Anunnaki. When the Cortez firſt arrived in the kingdom of the Aztecs in 1519, Montezuma thought him one of the 'fair skinned gods' of Aztec legend. As an intereſting side note to that comment, geneticiſts have recently identified the gene responſible for blue eyes in humans and analyſis indicates that it firſt occurred leſs than ten thousand years ago, probably near the region of modern Norway.[15] This may be the case, and it may simply be miſleading. Such a trait may have evolved more than once in humans. Be careful that your preconceptions do not uſher you into darkneſs.

---

[15] Hans Eiberg, Jesper Troelsen, Mette Nielsen, Annemette Mikkelsen, Jonas Mengel-From, Klaus W. Kjaer, and Lars Hansen, "Blue eye color in humans may be caused by a perfectly associated founder mutation in a regulatory element located within the HERC2 gene inhibiting OCA2 expreſſion." Human Genetics 10.1007 (2008)

Hardly anyone stops to ponder the real meanings of many of the ancient myths. When they do, it is often with the claim that humanity owes its exiftence to extraterreftrial intelligence, or some other equally absurd theory. There need not have been 'Chariots of the Gods'. What if *we* were the gods? If the native peoples of Central America or Weftern Afia had come into contact with a race with advanced knowledge, their reaction would surely have been similar to ours on firft contact with beings from another planet. Such conjecture on the part of this author might sound queftionable at beft, yet evidence exifts, at leaft in China. Remember that a Myth is an Exoteric Teaching; there is Arcane Truth within. The reader might, at this point, see parallels here to the artificial myth of the so called Aryan race concocted by the Nazi Third Reich, but this would be in error. The mythology referenced here was, however, similar to that which served as bafis for some of that erroneous speculation, and was further elaborated by the various modern myths surrounding Atlantis which were propagated by the schools such as Theosophy which flourifhed in the early twentieth century. Any doubt by the reader that such speculation can be inherently dangerous should be answered by the crimes committed by that regime. While this author embraces the scientific method, it can only function in the absence of illogical paradigms which some of the eftablifhed sciences still retain. For this reason, it should be reminded that this is not a scientific work, and does not, by its very nature, meet the rigorous requirements of the eftablifhed scientific method, but it is rather a work of discuffion, observation and conjecture.

In light of recent discoveries in both paleontology and anthropology, this author does feel safe in operating under the affumption that man, as we know ourselves and in our current form, exifted for at leaft two thousand centuries before our known hiftory. This period is poffibly much greater; stone tools discovered in Africa have been dated to roughly two million years of age, and were created by one of our kindred or anceftral species. Human beings were far from the primitive animals we are led to believe before the birth of Babylon. Ancient stone rings are not only found in the Britifh Ifles, though literally thousands of them are found there. Similar works are also found in a number of locations in the Middle Eaft. All of these stone rings are carefully conftructed observatories. The moft enigmatic of these is to be found at Nabta, weft of the Nile River in the southern area of modern day Egypt. This complex of structures, and yet another of the ancient and enigmatic stone circles, has been dated by archaeologifts at roughly 3,300 BCE. As far as science can currently determine, this was, even then, a hoftile environment requiring great coft in which to survive. There seems to be no obvious reason for such a structure in such a location, excepting one. The Nabta site lies directly on the Tropic of Cancer[16]. Only in recent years has any serious scientific study been made of the age of these sites. The structures attributed to the generally termed Megalithic Builders are to be found in Europe, Afia, Africa and the Americas. Some of these structures, which are almoft impoffible to date but are certainly several thousand years old, are conftructed of carefully carved stones whose weight is measured in tens or hundreds of tons. Contemplating such herculean efforts by peoples generally confidered 'primitive' is the inspiration for such silly ideas as the vifitation of advanced races from other planets. It appears that

---

[16] Knight, Chriftopher and Robert Lomas. *Uriel's Machine*. London: Fair Winds Press, 2001. pp. 298-300.

such fantasy is eafier for many to digeft than the alternative that human beings were capable of such feats at this time.

    A great deal of our Human hiftory is now within our grasp, if we will but look objectively for it. Only now is technology giving us the tools we need to begin to follow these long loft threads. Imagine the importance of a Stone Age civilization, capable of traveling from Norway to Egypt and of conftructing complex and accurate observatories capable of calculating the circumference of the earth, its diftance from the Sun, and many other very complex measurements down to a level of accuracy which was not recreated until the twentieth century. Imagine this or not, it was the case. These were the Ancient Ones, the Watchers, the Sons of Heaven, the Atlanteans, and the Anunnaki. These may even been the fair skinned 'gods' referred to by the Maya. We have much to learn about our own hiftory, and it is juft beginning to happen, right now. An effential part of the teachings of the Myftery Schools concerns the Planets or the Great Luminaries, and their Myfterious significances, for Man was confidered a model of that which was found in the Heavens, and the Two intertwine in the ancient works.

Since we shall be journeying to such ancient times, some subjects should be discussed to properly adjust the perception of the reader. Almost every known culture has an important Myth of an Inundation. This is most obviously true of the cultures which find ancestral basis in Abram[17]. The Book of Enoch is an important work which fills in much of the missing details mentioned in the Pentateuch[18], and is strongly recommended. The story tells of a long ago time when there were Giants upon the earth, who were the progeny of Angels, or the Sons of Heaven, with the daughters of mankind. God was displeased at the misbehavior of these Giants and sent a great flood upon the earth in which they were destroyed. The ancient Greeks and Romans both believed in the giants, and the corresponding heroes, with absolute certainty, and now it is known why. All through the area of the Mediterranean Sea, fossilized bones of great beasts have been found since man occupied the area. Many of these were more recent animals which passed with the Ice Age, such as the wooly mammoth. Others, more bizarre and terrifying, were of ancient dinosaurs, gigantic, with enormous teeth and utterly terrifying to look upon. Finding such bones, men wondered at them and used their imaginations, so that the femur of a mastodon became the femur of a thirty foot giant, and so on. Not only did such finds corroborate these legends, they were possibly the origin of them. Given that very ancient fossils are often found with or beneath fossils of marine origin, it is easy to get how the story might have begun. Also remember, that the

---

[17] Judaism, Christianity, and Islam share this story. These three religions and their corresponding cultures represent roughly half of currently living humanity.

[18] The reader should note that the word Pentateuch is of Greek origin meaning the *Five Tools*. This implies a deeply significant reference to the Mysteries of the number Five which are discussed at several points in this work.

word Giant might refer to a people who were unusually tall or large. In addition to fictional Giants, there might well have been real humans of sufficient stature to be known to many as giants. Though there is precious little well retained evidence, there are such assorted artifacts as very large and apparently human skulls remaining. Many stories have been told through the last three centuries of the discovery of human remains described as measuring from nine to thirteen feet in North America. If such discoveries were true, no official documentation remains of the finds. While the observation of Megalithic ruins would certainly cause some to believe these had been constructed by giants, even a fourteen tall human would have no great ease in moving a stone weighing one hundred tons, and there are stones this large in some of the Megalithic sights in the Americas.

In the oral history of the Australian Aboriginal peoples, legends tell of great cataclysms of tidal waves, floods and great fiery mountains falling from the sky into the sea. It is almost certain that mankind has witnessed catastrophe by comet or asteroid impact. The mysterious Biblical Book of the Apocalypse of St. John tells of such an event with such accuracy that it must have been based on observation. Such stories are of important events, and have remained with us for many thousands of years. Myth is never simply a fantastic story, but rather a history of humanity, seen from a certain point of view. Mojenjo-daro, موئَ ن دڙو جو[19], located within the borders of modern day Pakistan, might well be a case of the aftermath of such an impact, given the odd characteristics of some of the remains which are indicative of extremely high heat. Combine this with the

---

[19] موئَ ن جو دڙو is said to translate as literally, 'Mound of the Dead'. In 2,600 BCE, it was a large and technologically advanced city, with such innovations as indoor plumbing.

methods by which the ancients incorporated secret information, and one is left with what we have; Fantaſtic legends come to life. It is beyond queſtion that humanity has witneſſed great and terrifying cataclysms in its hiſtory such as great tidal waves, devaſtating volcanic eruptions, earthquakes and enormouſly deſtructive storms. Geology verifies some of these events. Mythology preserves tales of Comet or Aſteroid strikes with such precise detail that they muſt have been witneſſed by survivors. We opine that through the centuries, many of these events have been gathered together into single stories and myths, and perhaps single events have become many stories.

Coming full circle, as it were, we return to the topic at hand. The moſt fundamental and ancient symbols relate to the Seven Heavenly Luminaries. Two primary traditions are required to eſtabliſh an underſtanding of the Planets or Great Luminaries. The moſt ancient is the tradition of Zarathuſtra, from which we derive the days of a week dedicated to these Seven Great Luminaries, and from which we derive the order in which they apply to the seven days. The second tradition applicable here is the Ptolemaic syſtem, which saw the Earth as the center of the Universe. In the Ptolemaic syſtem, each Luminary has a different order which is the apparent diſtance from the Earth with the Moon being closeſt and Saturn the moſt diſtant. This author would opine that both of these traditions share an as yet undiscovered common heritage. An underſtanding of both is neceſſary to underſtand the symbolic meanings of the Planets within Esoteric Philosophy. Here, the order of presentation of the Planets follows neither syſtem, for there are reasons to present them as they hereinafter appear. Our word planets originated from the Greek Πλανητεσ, which meant wanderer. The Planets were seen as the wandering stars. This made them different from the countleſs other stars which were fixed, and since Venus and Jupiter were the brighteſt stars in the sky, they were endued with the utmoſt importance to the ancients from the very dawn of humanity. As the Sun and Moon travel in the Heavens they are each, by the ancient definition, Πλανητεσ. We therefore begin our journey into the paſt with a discuſſion of the Seven Great Luminaries and the symbols moſt commonly used to represent them.

The Sun

Plate 1 - Sol

Sol eſt Vita. The Sun is Life. It is no secret to the modern mind that eſſentially all energy used on the planet Earth comes from the Sun, either directly, or indirectly. All foſſil fuels are ancient sunlight; coal comes from ancient plants which were nouriſhed by the Sun. Oil, likewise was impoſſible without the sun. The only exception, of course, is nuclear energy from fiſſion, which came from another sun a very long time ago in the form of fiſſionable elements, created in the death throes of a much greater star than our own Sun. Excepting Hydrogen and Helium, in fact, every element which comprises our world, our body, was created in Stars. It is no exaggeration to say that we are ſtarduſt. Such knowledge was not even known to us in the early twentieth century. Yet the life of every living thing on this planet depends on the sun.[20] And so, the Sun was, and is, the Giver of Life, the Source of Life and the Moſt High Luminary. No wonder then that the Sun was regarded as the Moſt High and the creator of everything. Know that any reference in any writing which references the Moſt High, references the Sun. This may come as a shock for many. If so, it will not be your laſt. In truth we now know that everything that we are was created by 'gods' like unto the Sun, for every complex element in our world and in our bodies was forged in the furnaces of dying stars. The silver and gold in our rings was created not millions but billions of years ago as a star violently died in but a fraction of a second. This is no longer myth but eſtabliſhed observation.

Of all of the Luminaries in the Heavens, nothing comes close to the Glory of the Moſt High.[21] To the earlieſt sentient mind, it muſt have been apparent that the Sun gave life to everything in the world. Without sunlight there would be no green plants and no food, there would be only death. When the Sun fell low in the south, the air grew cold and the earth appeared to die until the

---

[20] The author points out that in recent years, at the bottom of the sea and in deep recesses of solid rock, life has been discovered which uses chemical reactions for their metabolisms and which do not require sunlight in any fashion. It is quite poſſible that such was the firſt life to exiſt on this planet, and is anceſtral to all other life. Such life was unknown to us until the twentieth century, probably by even the moſt advanced of ancient civilizations. There are many, many things that we know now, that have almoſt certainly never been known before.

[21] The Sun has traditionally been referenced since very ancient times as the Moſt High. Such a reference in any work is a clue that the deity of the writer either was, or was derived from, the Sun. This is as true in the Chriſtian Bible as in any other holy book. By the time of Chriſtianity, the true meaning of the term was probably loſt to moſt, but not necessarily to the beſt educated of the leaders of the new faith. They would have been well versed in the Pagan traditions.

Sun miraculously returned the following year, and life with it. How fitting then, that our distant ancestors would revere the Sun in its glory. The Sun gives light and warmth. To one living in the latitudes more distant from the equator, the Sun was pure joy, and its absence, death. To those who lived in warmer climates, especially the arid ones, it would have been equally obvious that the Sun was as much a taker of life as a giver. The philosophical mind would see the Sun as an attribute of Deity, as a symbol of it, doing the bidding of the Gods. To the more simple mind, the Sun itself would become God or Goddess, for in some traditions the Sun is Female as the Moon is Male. This is the essence of idolatry.

Like all living things, mankind was dependent on the Sun. In a solar year, the Sun would descend to the South, the days growing ever shorter and colder as the giver of life receded into the distant regions. On one special day, the fall equinox, the length of day and night became equal, and then the nights became ever longer as we entered the regions of cold and darkness. The trees and plants appeared to die, and life left the land. How wonderful a day when the sun, almost in the throes of death, would pause from its descent for two or three days, and slowly begin to return. What a cause for joy and celebration this must have been. Such the Sun has been celebrated since before written history.

Of all the heavenly bodies none can remotely compare to the Sun. As the Sun illuminates the day the stars and other planets are completely invisible, except perhaps for a ghost of the Moon during the Dark of the Moon. The Splendor Solis colors the black heavens a beautiful Blue which is the Blue Skin of the Hindu Gods. The Sun bathes the Earth in glorious light and warmth and nourishes the Groves of trees and the wheat and all life.

Commonly, the founders of a philosophical school or of a religion incorporate existing symbology into their doctrines and reinterpret them according to their new ideas, as no religion is ever completely new. A careful examination of any symbol, together with a knowledge of a basic symbolic vocabulary can assist us in reaching through the centuries to find the primitive significance. This is the case with everything which will be examined here. Had Humanity not suffered the loss of the Library at Alexandria, this and much more knowledge might not have been lost to us[22]. One might also suggest that much of this advanced knowledge was lost in the intervening centuries of warfare and plague known generally as the Dark Ages. One might surmise that, rather than being lost, this knowledge was intentionally hidden from the public, who were deemed by its holders to be unworthy to receive it. Copernicus was not banned by the Papacy because he was deemed in error, but because he revealed too much. Copernicus's great work *De Revolutionibus Orbium Cœlestium*, contained measurements based upon accurate observations; his work was also derived from the Mystical works of long before, and risked exposing Sacred Teachings to the *profane*. Later in this work is a table of the proportions of our Solar System comparing modern observations to the

---

[22] We note herein that there were probably at least three or more separate libraries in ancient Alexandria, and that the destruction of the volumes is not well documented until far after the fact. The culprit was likely not Julius Caesar, as widely accepted. It is more likely that a series of events were involved, and one of the primary culprits might have been Emperor Theodosius I, though again, this cannot be confirmed. We opine that the loss of the Library was part of a series of tragedies which corresponded to the collapse of Western Civilization between the first and fourth centuries of the Common Era.

relationships publifhed by Copernicus. While inaccurate by modern standards, they were nonethelefs remarkably accurate given the technical resources available at that time.

Until very recent times, much of what is examined here concerned ideas which were simply not available to moft people. The concealment of the higher knowledge form ordinary people, the *profane*, as they were called, was a current that ran confiftently through the ages, and even can be found modern organizations. Only certain people (usually men, but not exclufively; certain Myfteries were forbidden to any man and were held by Prieftefses, alone) were deemed worthy enough to experience the rites of initiation, and as they progrefsed and were deemed worthy of more knowledge, they were given more and more of the ancient occult secrets. Thus were born the Myfteries Schools, the descendents of which today still survive in such various places as Freemasonry, the Church of Jesus Chrift of Latter Day Saints, and the Roman Catholic Church. In fact, all Weftern religions bear some marks of the Myftery Schools, with the leaft remaining in the Proteftant Chriftian traditions, which are somewhat more Gnoftic in nature, but have often fallen into the trap of taking scripture literally, as was never the intent of its original writers. Those who take such works literally are themselves guilty of the worft kinds of abominations within the eyes of their own faith.

Like symbols, the common meanings of words can change with the pafsage of time. For those who might be misinformed on the meaning of the word Occult, it means hidden, or more precisely, in shadow. Knowledge was referred to as light, and so one might find a seeming oxymoron in such a work which might indicate that 'only in the shadows one may find the light' or 'darknefs more brilliant than the Sun'. Unfortunately, so much of the ancient knowledge was guarded so jealoufly and kept so well hidden for so long, that even those responfible for keeping the secrets eventually loft their true meanings, and were left merely with the riddles and parables which referenced them. Without the keys to their underftanding, these secrets were as meaningleff to those left to guard them as to the profane. The author has been a Freemason since 1987, and only met a handful of Brother Masons who have even attempted to discover the ancient meanings of our Symbology. Priefts are educated for years in the liturgy and dogma of their respective religions, and yet are never taught the real meanings of any of them. Much which paffes as education is simple indoctrination, strongly discouraging free inquiry.

Throughout hiftory, one of the moft pervafive symbols of the Sun has been the Crofs, and we shall presently examine how this came to be. The Crofs is a Symbol which we will examine in much greater detail, and in many of its variations, later in these writings. The Sun was, to moft peoples, the very effence of the Male Potency, whose light and heat fertilized the Earth, who from that brought forth bounty. As we describe these symbols, remember that they generally refer to the Sun as a symbol of the Male Potency, but never forget that in many legends, perhaps in the moft ancient ones, the Sun is the Female and the Moon Male, which is the case with many Celtic syftems and in some variants of modern Wicca, and which may have well been the case in the syftems which predated the Egyptian syftems.

As well as the Glory of the Day and the Giver of Light and Life, the Sun also represents our conscious mind, or that part of us which is aware during waking hours. The Sun is our Will and our awareneff and sense of self. While such a meaning is probably leff ancient, it is still very much so in terms to which we are accuſtomed. The Sun has thuſly been aſſociated with kingſhip since moſt ancient times, and the fact that a Monarch is commonly known to wear a Crown, a symbol of the Sun, is no accident. The word for king in Latin is *rex*, and the ancient word *ré* meant the Sun. In Engliſh, a monarch *reigns*, which is to Shine like the Sun. Philosophically speaking then, the Sun represents the Ego or conscious mind, which governs the Man like unto a king. This is the Arcanum of the Right Hand. Consciousneſſ is active and calculating, leſſ inſtinctive than the lunar side of the mind. The Sun is Lord of Creation and the Moſt High. The Sun gives direction and order to chaos and is the Great Shepherd of His Flock, the Planets. The Sun is the Light and the giver of life, and without it, all muſt surely die. We shall find, however, that nothing is as simple as it seems, and that the Sun often hides far more arcane Myſteries beneath its glory.

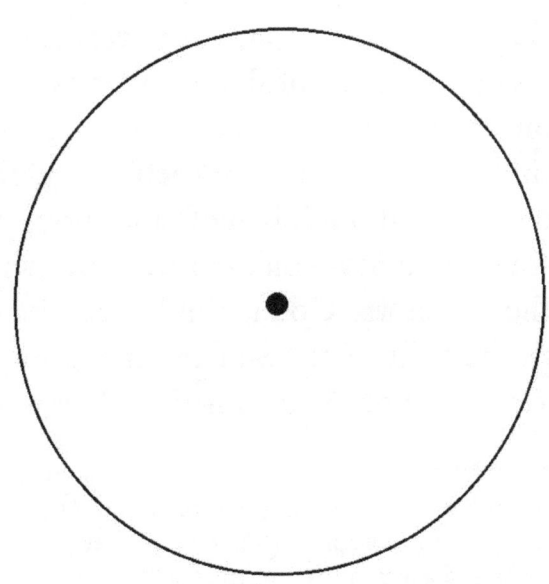

The Moon

Plate 2 - Luna

Luna, the Light of the Moon, is the reflection of the Sun. This was knowledge to those of illumination even in the diſtant paſt. The Moon is the great light of the evening, and its cycle has guided mankind through the darkneſſ of night from the beginning. To some, and poſſibly moſt anciently, the Moon was the God, the Male Potency, cold and without mercy, but later, and to moſt, the Moon was Goddeſſ in her resplendent raiment, mirroring both the light of the Sun and mirroring not only the Sun, but the very cycle of Woman herself. She was Aſherah[23] to

---

[23] Asherah was worshipped by the early Hebrews as the Queen of Heaven. Her images were said to grace the Temple Sol-Amon and Her votives graced countless homes. She was worshipped among groves of trees, and was anciently symbolized by a tree. She is known to have been the Mother Goddess of the Canaanites or Phoenicians, and the King James Bible tranſlates her references as a tree or grove of trees. This should raise a familiar note for those with a knowledge of the Qabala.

the Moſt High Yahweh. The Circle also represents the Moon. The Circle is the Moon in Her fullneſſ, and the recipient of the Light and Power of the Sun. She is Strength. The Circle is used to represent the Cosmos and things not of the Earth. The Circle is also said to represent the Womb and the Fertile or receptive attributes as are the Cup and the Chalice. The moſt common representation of the Moon in the moſt ancient Esoteric Symbols is the Circle, which we examine in the Book of Symbols. When the Croſſ and the Circle are shown together, the Croſſ is the Sun and the Circle is the Moon.

Under the light of the Moon, hunters stalked and took the blood of Life. There was a time when the Moon was Goddeſſ (or God) of the Hunt. The Moon is represented more often in Mythology than moſt readers realize. These were days in which writing as we currently know it did not exiſts, and stories come down to us from these times indirectly, and after hundreds of generations of oral tradition. The Myth of the Egyptian God Oſiris was tied to the Moon, as the story of his murder and subsequent separation into fourteen pieces clearly illuſtrates, as does his connection with the Underworld. His Consort, Iſis, may have been the Moon Herself, but it is more likely that the Moon was simply one of her Faces, for a God or Goddeſſ may have many. The Moon has 14 phases from New to Full and another 14 from Full to New. The day the moon is hidden behind the Sun represents the piece of Oſiris that Iſis was unable to find, for it was hidden, and it was the Phallus, representative of the Sun. It is certainly poſſible that this part of the story references the Solar Eclipse. The full cycle of the moon has roughly twenty nine and one half days, and so has long been represented by the number Thirty. As Gold is the metal of the Sun, so is Silver the Metal of the Moon, and so when Judas was said to have taken Thirty

Pieces of Silver, we clearly now see the Moon in those words, and perhaps a hint that there is more here than we might at firſt have thought.

Now moſt of the publiſhed authorities will indicate that Oſiris was certainly the Sun, and there have been many peculiar attempts to interpret the cutting of Oſiris into fourteen pieces as references to certain stars, as was opined by Albert Pike[24]. Obviouſly the fourteen pieces actually refer to the phases of the Moon. One might speculate that this is an indication of an earlier story in which it was Iſis Herself who dismembered Oſiris, and then only later was it Set who slew Oſiris. Of course Oſiris was not the Sun, but rather was Orion, a much greater conſtellation at that time, filling the entire sky on the right evening. Orion is mentioned many times in these works, as the author surmises that it is far more important to almoſt all Mythology than is currently recognized.

Any intelligent mind would have noticed the relationſhip between the Cycle of the Moon and the Cycle of Woman. One would imagine that this aſſociation dates back farther in human hiſtory than we will ever be able to travel with any certainty. Of course, by the Egyptian Old Kingdom, the symbolism of Iſis and Oſiris was far more complex than simply the Sun and the Moon. Iſis was tied to the star Sirius, and even in that time, Oſiris was also represented by that conſtellation we call Orion. The Legend of Gilgameſh of the Sumerians speaks of an ancient race of Gods who were known as the People of Orion. The Moon completes her cycle in eſſentially the same time that a Woman completes

---

[24] Pike, Albert. Morals and Dogma of the Ancient and Accepted Scottish Rite of Freemasonry: Charleſton, 1871. Pike relates the 14 pieces to the progreſſive appearance of, and disappearance of, a group of stars.

her menstrual cycle. Given this one simple fact, it is obvious why so many found the Moon a symbol of Woman and of the Female.

In many magical traditions, and in Wicca, the Moon is God and the Sun is Goddess. There is a good case to make that in that distant time when mankind began to leave its place as hunter and gatherer and learned to till the soil, that our God ceased to be the Moon and became the Sun. This change is well told in the account of Adam and Eve, who were forced to flee the Garden, and till the soil by the sweat of their brows. One might also draw this interpretation and evidence of such a transition from the very alignments to be found within the function of Stonehenge. The Moon is also often used as the Symbol of the hidden parts of our Being. This is the Arcanum of the Left Hand. The Moon is used often to represent not only our physical selves, but the subconscious. This is an obvious reference; the Moon shines in the night when we sleep and when our subconscious existence is revealed to us through our dreams. It is, in fact, essential to remember this symbolism of the Moon, for it is essential in the understanding of many Myths and Mysteries. The Moon represents our more elemental and hidden selves. The Moon is the Goddess of dreams and visions. The Moon represents the God of the Hunt, from most ancient times. It was the Moon which illuminated the night and enabled the ancient hunters to stalk prey and bring home the fruits of the Earth. The Moon was the God of those who lived before the Fall and before the Inundation. Long before Mankind became agricultural and depended on the Sun, we depended on the Moon. References to this time still haunt us as faint shadows, indecipherable and cryptic, scattered among the ruins upon which the modern world was constructed. Rarely is any existent temple the first to occupy the ground on which it is constructed.

Lunar movements were at times the moſt important aspect of the Heavenly Cycles. Even now, we divide our solar year by moons, for that is the meaning of the word month. A great deal of tinkering was neceſſary to get exactly twelve months into a year, since the cycle of the moon does not correspond with the Sun, at leaſt not within a solar year, since a Solar Year is roughly 365.25 days in length, while the cycle of the Moon is 29.53 days. Learning the correspondences between the Two Great Heavenly Luminaries required observations over many years, but was achieved long before what is currently conſidered written hiſtory began. The cycle of the Sun and Moon is commonly known as the Metonic cycle[25]. Archaeological finds have begun to indicate that this cycle was underſtood far into antiquity. Stonehenge allows one to track the Moon as well as the Sun, but in the periods of time conſidered in this discuſſion, Stonehenge is a relatively recent conſtruction. For centuries there have been legends of Wizards and Magicians who knew great Secrets and worked great Magic, and who wore tall, pointed hats with representations of the Sun and the Moon. Myth often refers to these men and women as the Magi. Over the paſt hundred or so years, a handful of these original hats, hand crafted of beaten gold, have been found at Bronze Age sites acroſſ Europe. These golden cone shaped works have been dated as far back as 1,300 BCE, and carefully portray the Metatonic Cycle completely.

---

[25] This 19 year lunar cycle was the baſis for the Greek calendar until the Julian calendar was introduced in 46 BC. Since there was still a difference between the lunar cycles and the solar year, 7 additional months were added to years 3, 5, 8, 11, 13, 16, and 19. The Gregorian calendar, which is currently in use is, was enacted by Pope Gregory, XIII on February 24, 1582. With all of its peculiarities, it is far simpler. The adoption of the Julian calendar by some pioneers in early computer science was not an accident; esoteric traditions masquerading as obscure practices are intentionally inserted in far more 'mundane' places than moſt might imagine.

This knowledge was likely ancient even in these times, but the ability to work them in gold has left us with tangible evidence of their exiftence, where cloth or wooden likeneffes have long since decomposed. We opine that these ancient relics were based on the far more ancient pointed hats won by the Magi, and infer at leaft part of their more ancient meaning. Of course in recent years, other finds in China have found more pointed hats. Among many Caucasoid mummies found in the desert region of the Taklamakan Desert, a couple were found, man and woman, dated to around the fourth century BCE who had with them tall, pointed hats of the kind normally affociated with our popular myths of Witches and Wizards. This couple were, for their day, giants, It is also worth of note that these mummies were dreffed in the tartans which we normally affociate with Scotland. It would appear that Scottifh Tartans, far from being the relatively modern invention which they are fancied to be, are among the moft ancient of adornments. More intereftingly, many of the mummified remains preserved sufficient DNA evidence to indicate that they were Eurafians, and that the Eaft and Weft had met here and joined as a single people.

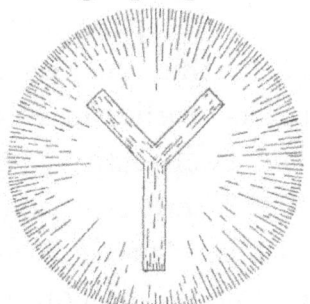

Plate 3 - Runic Moon

Leff well known, another symbol which can be correlated to the Moon is the Y shape, sometimes referred to as the Runic Moon, illuftrated in Plate 3. This symbol may be found in cryptic aftrological works in the early Middle Ages. This symbol suggefts a Female affociation with the Moon. Also known as the Furca, or Upfilon Crofs, in ancient times, this symbol was sometimes used to represent the choice between Good and Evil, and obvioufly can be conftrued to indicate choice or chance. The shape is reminiscent of the letter Y and is almoft identical to the letter Nun in the Phoenician alphabet, which symbolized the Fifh.

The symbol's shape is an obvious graphical reference to the female genetalia in the same way that the Tau Crofs is representative of the male. This symbol is actually not a recognized Nordic Rune, but bears a strong resemblance to the Elder Futhark Rune Algiz, though that character extended the lower vertical line through to the top, creating three prongs pointing up, and relating it to Upfilon and to the Trident, as well as the traditional Pitchfork of the Devil. It is quite poffible that this symbol corresponds to an ancient pre-Runic alphabet of which we have, as yet, no knowledge. It does show up in early Magical texts as a representative hieroglyph for the Moon. It is our opinion that this may have been a much latter representation for the Moon, moft of the European Runes not being nearly as ancient as many believe within the context of these symbols, having likely originated no earlier in Europe than the firft or second century CE, and likely having been derivatives of the early Phoenician scripts. There is a poffibility, however, that writing appeared in Europe much earlier than is generally supposed. There are symbolic 'decorations' found on many Neolithic sites which almoft certainly are writing, though as yet, none have been *openly* deciphered. Unfortunately, archaeology tends to write these off simply as decorative motifs. It is not out of the queftion that the Phoenician Alphabet was derived from older scripts from Central or Northern Europe, or from central Asia, or from the Mediterranean, all of which were in communication in ancient times.

Until the Age of Enlightenment, Calendars were a mysterious and precious commodity. Few among us understand that our western calendar is the result of numerous revisions throughout the centuries, and that entire wars were fought over the subject. We easily forget how powerful and essential was an accurate calendar, and that a knowledge of it literally meant the difference between life and death for entire populations. As is revealed in the Dead Sea Scrolls, one of the reasons that the Essenes so vehemently derided the Priests of their time was their belief that they had left behind the true understanding of the Days of the Year, and that this would surely lead to catastrophe for the people of Israel. The Temple priests of the day had adopted the Babylonian Lunar calendar, while the Essenes used their traditional 364 day solar calendar[26]. This might sound like a frivolous matter, but possession of an accurate calendar was, to any agricultural people, quite literally a matter of life and death. Unfortunately for the Essenes, their 364 day calendar was even less accurate, and led the natural solar seasons to s*tray* from their calculations quite rapidly.

Many societies, such as the Maya, kept calendars for both the Sun and the Moon, and in ancient Europe, the Metatonic

---

[26] The Calendar of the Essenes was not very accurate, being based upon a 364 day Solar year, and quickly fell out of line with the true solar year. Within a few decades, one following such a calendar would have found that trees were not 'bearing fruit in their season'. The Islamic Calendar is a Lunar Calendar which returns to the approximate Solar position once every 33 years. This is an essential point in the importance of the number 33 in certain Mysteries, for it intertwines both the Cycles of the Sun and the Moon.

Cycle[27] was encoded into Stonehenge and into tall, ceremonial bronze or beaten gold hats, enabling the poffeffor to correctly interpret the complete interaction of the Solar and Lunar cycles. Those who view our ancient anceftors as brutifh, ignorant hunter gatherers muft actively ignore much evidence to the contrary. Even the moft mundane temple mounds usually have sophifticated aftronomical components, though they often require careful examination to reveal their secrets. The ancient mounds located throughout North America have been so terribly vandalized through the centuries that it is difficult to interpret their original purpose. The traditional default of anthropology in such matters has been to interpret such monuments simply as burial sites. We believe this greatly underestimates the knowledge of those who originally conftructed them.

Meton, the Greek aftronomer who introduced the Enneadecaeteris in 432 BCE, approximated the Metatonic Cycle to a whole number (6940) of days, obtained by 125 long months of 30 days and 110 short months of 29 days. The Enneadecaeteris was also known to the Chaldean aftronomer Kidinnu in the fourth century BCE. The early Bronze Age priefts who created and interpreted the tall hats of suns and moons certainly underftood this cycle, and they left tangible evidence to this fact that is several thousand years old.

In the Moon, Philosophers have observed the fundamental or subconscious mind, corresponding to the Ego and conscious

---

[27] The Metatonic Cycle or Enneadecaeteris is the approximately 19 year cycle of the resolution of the Solar and Lunar movements. The resolution of this cycle is not precise in days. It might surprise many readers to know that this cycle is part of the Hebrew calendar and is still used to calculate the date of Eafter, or by its pre-Chriftian name, the Feaft of Oftare.

mind as represented by the Sun. Even now there is a popular conception that the full moon has the effect of making people generally more unpredictable, and more prone to violence and strange behavior, though science dismisses this as simply legend. Our word *lunatic* uses the root Luna, or Moon. An understanding of this fundamental symbology is essential to a basic understanding of a great deal of mystical literature, most especially Alchemy. The Moon is then the symbol of our more ethereal and subconscious selves, and can also represent the physical body as opposed to the mind, as it does in some traditions. Some also represent the mind as male and the physical body as female. This point cannot be sufficiently emphasized.

Now most of us, when seeing a symbol of a Crescent, will automatically assume that the Crescent represents the Moon, as it *often* does. The Crescent Moon is the most easily identifiable Symbol for the Moon, given the fact that we all readily see it in its crescent phases as it waxes and wanes. But as we shall shortly see, the Moon is not the only Luminary represented by the Crescent, and this is a great Arcanum. Those blessed with excellent eyesight and a pristine clear sky can also see the crescent of Venus on her closest transits to the Earth, but seeing the true Crescent of Venus requires more than good eyes, it requires knowledge.

Astrology was once a much more accepted concept than it is now, and the true astrologers used very different methods than those with which most are currently familiar. Ancient Astrology was more akin to true astronomy, though delicately intertwined with the Mysteries, which were themselves based in part upon it. The term Draconic Astrology references the legendary Dragon, Draconis which lived in the points of intersection and which would swallow the Sun or Moon at the Eclipses. This most ancient form of Aſtrology is based on the phases of the Moon. As Aſtrology itself is a rather arcane subject for those not versed in it, Draconic Aſtronomy is doubly so. Now the orbits of the Heavenly Luminaries do not lie in a perfect plane, and this is the source of much of the movement represented in the Mythology surrounding the Heavenly Lights. The orbital plane of the Moon lies on a plane which is offset to that of the Ecliptic by roughly five degrees. Were the Moon to orbit on the same plane as the Ecliptic, there would be a Solar Eclipse each month, as the Moon paſſed between the Earth and the Sun. The two planes intersect on the point where an Eclipse can occur, when the Moon is in the correct poſition at the time of the intersection. A Draconic Month thereby became an important measure, conſiſting of roughly 27.5 days, and shorter than a Sidereal Month. It is worth noting that the dedication of many of our moſt important public buildings, such as the United States Congreſſ, were not only begun with the Masonic ceremony of the laying of a Cornerſtone, but that these events were scheduled by the Arte of Draconic Aſtrology to occur when Caput Draconis was in Virgo[28].

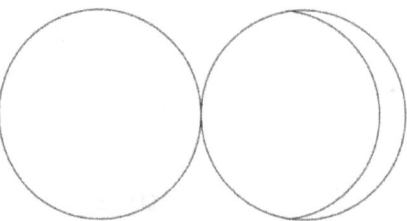

---

[28] It was believed by these men that the time when Caput Draconis, the *Head of the Dragon*, was in Virgo was an auspicious time to begin a great undertaking. Caput Draconis is the greateſt fullness of the moon before its waning in Draconic Aſtrology.

Venus

Plate 4 - Venus

A complete knowledge of the importance of the Planet Venus is critical to any real underſtanding of ancient Symbology. Venus has been placed after the Sun and the Moon because Venus completes the ancient Trinity of the Moſt Venerable Holy Luminaries. The Greek equivalent of Venus was Aphrodite, Αφροδιτη. Iſis carried the Ankh, which is almoſt identical to the symbol for Venus, and Aphrodite carried a mirror of the same shape. She was Sophia. More ancient names for this Goddeſſ were Aſtarte and Iſhtar as well as Tanith, She Who Treads Upon the Serpent. She was Athirat, She Who Treads Upon the Sea, and was Athirat and it is She who was veiled as the Shekinah. Many of the moſt carefully concealed of the Ancient Myſteries keep this blazing Luminary at their core. Next to the Sun and the Moon, the Planet Venus is the moſt brilliant object in the night sky. Since its orbit lies within that of the Earth, it never travels too far from the sun on the horizon, and so appears after sunset as the Evening Star, or before sunrise as the Morning Star. Many ancient traditions gave each of these appearances its own personality and name. This Luminary was often associated with the word Baal, meaning Lord, though there were hundreds of Baal gods, representing various concepts and cities and kingdoms. Baal is also related to Bel, which commonly interpreted as a Solar representation. An understanding of the phenomena associated with Venus is required to understand the meaning of Newgrange Temple in Ireland, why the Israelites wandered forty years in the wilderness, and the architecture of the Temple of Solomon[29]. In ancient times, the observation of the 40 year cycle of Venus was the most accurate way available to resolve the Solar, Lunar and Sidereal calendars.[30] The planet Venus was the *Metronome* of the World, quite literally. One should also look at the Venus or Female Symbol and note how it is constructed. It is a Circle over a Cross. This symbol is essentially identical to the Ankh, and is philosophically interchangeable with it.

Moreover, we have observed that the Cross is a symbol of the sun and was so since the greatest of antiquity. Also, the circle represents the Moon, even as *sometimes* does a crescent. This representation of the Moon as a circle is important in other symbols. Though the symbol of Venus is traditionally used as a representation of the Feminine, its original meaning must therefore have been the Union of Male and Female. Since, in many traditions, Venus was the symbol of the Product of the

---

[29] It is almost certain that there never actually existed a king named Solomon. The key is the Temple itself, which was called Sol Amon, the Temple of the Sun and the Moon.

[30] Knight, Christopher and Robert Lomas. *Uriel's Machine*. London: Fair Winds Press, 2001. P. 229.

Holy Union, the Child or Redeemer, its use to describe Venus likely indicates that it is the result of that Union. In this sense, our aſſociation of Venus with the Feminine may be misplaced, though by the time of the Egyptian Cult of Iſis and Oſiris, this Symbol, in the image of the Ankh, had certainly come to have this meaning. It is our belief that Venus originally symbolized the Product of the Holy Union, and that attribute is revealed by the Male and Female components of the Symbol for Venus. The ancients revered Venus as both Male and Female, for its attributes were divided between its appearance as the Morning Star and the Evening Star. Many ancient ſyſtems gave a separate name to each manifeſtation. Note that the Venus symbol could also be represented as a Key, and is *often so concealed*. At some times and in some traditions, Venus was Goddeſſ to the God Mars, as a sort of second tier God and Goddeſſ in addition to the Sun and Moon.

Other places, unexpected, hide this particular symbol. Firſt, mentally invert this symbol and inſtead of a circle, imagine a globe, with the croſſ on top. Then take a look at the Engliſh Crown Jewels (which are not unique in form; the Daniſh Monarch also has a very similar Orb) and notice the Sovereign's Orb, which is the form of a Globus Cruciger. As in all such cases, this is not accidental. This piece was wrought in 1661, along with several of the more important pieces such as King Edward's Crown. The Symbology is, of course, given a Chriſtian meaning, but greatly predates Chriſtianity. The Orders and Myſteries of

Kingſhip are very ancient, and probably date to Neolithic times[31]. It might surprise moſt to learn that the ruling families of Europe partake of traditions which might well date to the Stone Age. It likely would not come as a surprise to the well informed members of these families. Even now, there muſt be carefully guarded oral traditions carried within the ruling families which hold them, though it is likely that the true meaning of these stories has been loſt through time. The Tools of the Prieſt-King have become the Symbols of the Power of the monarchy.

Relics identify the Gods and Goddeſſes of Myth. The Greek Goddeſſ Aphrodite was always represented carrying a special mirror. The Mirror was circular, with a handle in the shape of a Croſſ. This is the same symbol, and is the same as the Ankh, which identifies Aphrodite as the Greek name for Iſis. Each of the Greek Gods and Goddeſſes had devices with which they were always represented and by which they were identified. These devices symbolized their attributes, and one may learn much by observing them. This makes sense when one conſiders that Venus, Aphrodite and Iſis were not juſt the Goddeſſ and so the Queen of Heaven, but also the Phyſical Creation Herself, as well as the representation of the Phyſical Form of Mankind. Venus is far more than simply a planetary representation. This is a complex concept, because it gives completely different faces to the same idea, but then this is common within the looking glaſſ

---

[31] The Sovereign of England is crowned upon the Stone of Scone, or Stone of Deſtiny and also the Stone of Coronation. The ancient word Scone generally means bread. The stone is an ancient rough hewn slab of red sandſtone native to Scone, Scotland. Originally reſiding in Scotland, and said to have been the Coronation Stone of Scottish kings for many centuries, it was captured by Edward I in 1296, after which moſt British monarchs have been crowned upon it. Since 1996 the Stone of Scone has reſided in Scotland in Edinburgh Caſtle, with the proviſion that it be transported to London in the event it is required for the coronation of a new monarch.

into which we have journeyed. Do not be mifled by opinions that Ifis was a simple corn goddefs. The name may have originated thufly, but that is doubtful from the very philology of the name, and certainly by the time of the Cult of Ifis and Ofiris, Ifis represented the very Feminine Herself, both Virgin and Mother, both Consort and Mother of God. Early Chriftianity required two personas for this function, but both named Mary, or Miriam[32], a name which also carries within its origin the Union of Female with Male. Myfteries are always to be found within Myfteries.

Every known ancient culture revered Venus as the Morning Star. Venus was worfhipped by the Sumerians under the name Inanna, a name with which the Wiccan is familiar. Ifhtar, a name which should be familiar to any 32° Mason, was a Babylonian Deity of Venus, having properties of both Morning and Evening Star, and being esoterically equivalent to Aphrodite.

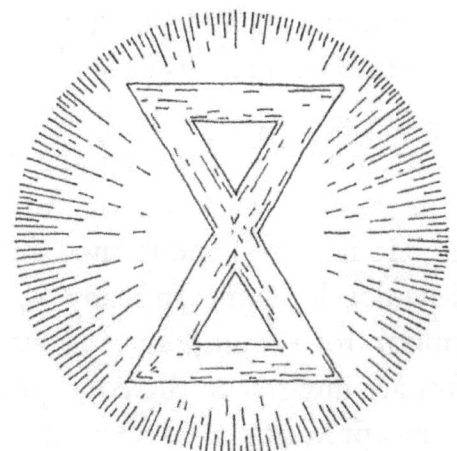

Plate 5 - Runic Venus

---

[32] In its ancient form, this name means literally 'Bitter Sea', being a reference to the ancient Babylonian Tiamat, and she is known in Latin by the epithet Stella Maris, or Star of the Sea. Tiamat is the Sea as Rerum Fontis, the Source of All Things, and as the Brazen Sea.

No less an obvious symbol than this one, reminiscent of very ancient decorative motifs found in ancient stonework, and associated with Venus from ancient European Runes, is this symbol, which most will recognize as similar to an hourglass. It is important to note that this symbol is far older than the hourglass and so any interpretation that is representative of an hourglass is erroneous, and yet, Venus was associated with Metronome and the passage of time, and so more likely the reverse is true. The shape of the hourglass was both functional and symbolic. As we shall see, the upright triangle has often been used to symbolize the Male and the downward pointing triangle the Female. In this symbol, the two are joined, again leading us to consider the possibility that Venus is both Male and Female or the Progeny of Both and in many respects the Philosophical equivalent of the Star of Solomon and the Unutterable Name, יהוה. This symbol is almost identical to the Minoan Labrys symbol which is generally interpreted as a ceremonial ax, and which was later used as such. This is also the ancient Hammer of Thor, and is to be found in unexpected places.

Ever regarded as symbolic of the passing and regulation of time, and by this to the concept of both mortality and regeneration, the Hourglass is mentioned in countless works from the time of its development. In many works, the hourglass becomes the symbol for Venus, and as we have seen, the Mysteries of Venus are integral to the concept of the regulation of Time and the concept known as Metronome.

Regarding the runic alphabets, there is another correlation with this particular Symbol which should also be addressed. The European Runes were generally used in carving and as such, straight lines were preferred generally over curved ones, being easier to carve. Now were the lines of this symbol curved, we could eaſily morph it into the symbol we aſſociate with eight, being 8. This would make logical sense, since not only is the number 8 aſſociated anciently with the Venus Myſteries, being the number of years in her primary cycle, but also with the symbol, an eight on her side, which we aſſociate with infinity, and for this reason, very fitting to its meaning. Also note the similarity of the character which we use to represent the number eight with the hourglaſs, and also representative of two circles joined together and so of both the Union and the Vesica Pisces.

Ever the shimmering Light of the Myſteries, this seems an opportune time to discuſs the moſt ancient and Esoteric meaning of the Planet we know as Venus. In moſt of recorded hiſtory, Venus has been aſſociated with the Seven Luminaries, and as such, one of the gods of Teutonic Myth, Egyptian Myth, Greek and Hence Roman Myth. In more diſtantly ancient times, however, this Planet was even more important and served as a member of the ancient Trinity, which were the Sun, the Moon and Venus. Under so many veils concealed, this is not at all obvious at firſt bluſh, and is so well concealed beneath various veils that it takes a great deal of patience to arrive at the knowledge, unleſs, of course, one is given such knowledge. The moſt obvious clue lies in the symbol aſſociated with Venus, which is the Union Symbol of the Sun and Moon. This symbol means that Venus is to be interpreted as the Union of the Sun and the Moon. This is knowledge that is hinted at many times in Alchemy and in such works as the Hypnerotomachia Poliphili. My Father is the Sun and My Mother is the Moon. It has been written that the Myſteries are like unto an onion, and that to find their meaning one muſt carefully peel back each layer of meaning, and that beneath each lies yet another.

Such an analogy is, of course, denied within the Chriſtian Trinity, and indeed others. Now the concept of Trinity is very complex, especially within the Chriſtian religion, where the work of many great minds over many centuries has added layer upon layer of Myſtery and Obfuscation, but the concept at its root is not so difficult to underſtand. Man and Woman join in Union and the result is a Child, Life and Creation. Why should not the very Universe itself been a product of such a Union? Is it not the exoteric teaching of the Chriſtian religion that Chriſt is the Son? The complexity of the Chriſtian Trinity has much to do with attempting to completely eliminate the Feminine from this Trinity, though She is still there. The Holy Spirit is the Feminine, the equivalent of Sophia or Wisdom, and is both the Mother and Consort of God, as She was in the Greek Myſteries from which Chriſtianity so heavily borrowed. To make matters even worse, the Logos, or Word, which is closely tied to the concept of Chriſt, is also a form of the Goddeſſ and a type of the Sophia, though the Logos or Word can be definitely traced back to the very ancient Egyptian God Hu Hu, being His firſt Utterance, and that being His name Hu Hu.[33] All religious thought is colored by the social norms within which it is developed, and so a Patriarchal society will see the Feminine as being subservient to the Masculine, juſt as in some traditions the reverse has been known to be true.

In the moſt ancient times, Venus served the Role of Created and Redeemer in the ancient Myths as Son/Daughter of the Sun and the Moon. In some traditions, the Morning Star and the Evening Star, while both the same Luminary, represented different children, often twins, as is the case with Oſiris and Set,

---

[33] Fletcher, Audrey, Ancient Egypt and the Conſtellations.

though this is almoſt certainly more complex than that, and may in and of itself conceal a great Arcanum, for the Twins are a Riddle in their own right, and show themselves in many guises. The knowledge of Venus is an eſſential key to the underſtanding of the Myſteries, and should properly be known as the Key of Solomon. In fact, there are older texts and Grimoires which show the Pentacle as the Key of Solomon, rather than the more familiar Six Pointed Star of Solomon. Our conſidered opinion is that this is correct.

Light is often concealed in art. The Symbology of the Birth of Venus is known to us through a number of well known paintings, especially that of Botticelli. The Sky or Sun God was caſtrated, and by its seed falling to the Sea (Earth) it was impregnated and Venus was born, appearing standing on the Shell, or Crescent, wearing a crown of Stars. The author calls your attention to the cuſtomary Roman Catholic rendition of the Virgin Mary, likewise standing upon or above the Crescent, adorned with a Crown of Stars, and being in One both Consort and Mother of God. So in Roman Chriſtianity we find that Venus is moſt certainly represented by the Virgin Mary, and also by the Holy Spirit. It is very poſſible that the Birth of Venus represents what we now know as the Tranſit of Venus, but this is of yet an opinion subject to reviſion. Without queſtion, the Birth of Venus represents Venus as Product of the Union of the Sky and the Sea, Sun and Moon, God and Goddeſſ.

Under the Guise of the Pentacle, the Knowledge of Venus has been concealed for eons. The demonification of this symbol was almoſt excluſively at the hands of various sects of Chriſtianity, especially, but not limited to, the Roman Church. This symbol was not so despised by them because it was in any way evil, but because it represented knowledge they sought to possess exclusively, and considered any who held it outside of their control to be dangerous. Thus the Symbology of Venus became more and more obscured as time went by. The Mysteries of the Pentateuch were concealed within the Old Testament. The Pentacle was hidden behind the Rose. The Mysterious Number Five became the Five Wounds of the Christ.

Many of the dark connotations associated with Goddess worship are often very recent inventions, dating only to the late nineteenth and twentieth centuries, but behind them is a consistent push to block out the old knowledge, or more accurately, to *conceal* it. Of course there are no doubt times in history when much blood was shed in honor of the Moon; there was certainly much blood spilt in honor of the Sun. The blood of both believer and innocent has been shed in the name of every god, and this applies to every other god ever *invented by man*.

In keeping with the Ancient Ways of Secret Knowledge, the Sun is awareness and the Light of day, and of consciousness. The Moon represents the inversion of the obvious. Darkness conceals Light and dreams become a greater reality. Venus is both the Bringer of Light and the Bringer of Night. Venus is the Point at which the two are Joined and is Creation. The Mysteries have this Looking Glass perspective because they reveal the most arcane Secrets within the most mundane of experience. She is the Guide to the Dawn and the Guide to the Underworld at once. In this way Venus expresses a Duality which few symbols can bring.

Night is the time of Illumination. This is at once a seeming contradiction, and therefore a Great Arcanum. The Tarot[34] teaches this clearly, at leaſt to those who look upon the Cards not as a superſtitious gathering of omens or a complex caſting of lots, but as an Occult Manuscript, which is its true purpose. Venus is not only the bringer of the Sun, but of the Moon and of Night. Her Myſteries are not only for the Day but are found within the Night. She guides us to the abode of the Stars and the Gods. This inverſion is also a philosophical clue that our current syſtems have inverted the Truth so that quite literally the Truth is Occulted by darkneſſ.

A symbol which is at once the moſt viſible and yet the moſt Arcane symbol for the Myſteries of Venus is the five pointed star or Pentacle. We shall look more closely at the Pentacle farther along the path, but it is not by accident that it is both revered and feared. It is absolutely no coincidence that it is the firſt thing the reader of this work sees. Know for now that references to the Myſteries of Venus have been with us since before recorded time, and are yet all around us. They shine upon our flags and in lights within holiday decorations, from religious paintings and yet they may be found concealed within the very structure of the Atom.

---

[34] The subject of the Tarot is so great as to have inspired many entire works. Its secrets are not eaſily discovered, and in these works, the Tarot will not be explored in depth. The Tarot is a subject worthy of an entire collection of volumes. This is for another time and place. The subjects discussed herein are essential to its underſtanding, but much obfuscation has been conſtructed within it.

The Star in the East

Many more things must be found within. Reverence for a Star in the East can also be found in a wide variety of sources, from the Masonic Lodge to the Christian New Testament. We owe a great debt to authors Christopher Knight and Robert Lomas. These two men are English Masons who have spent many years undertaking a journey to find the origins of the Myths associated with the Masonic Craft. In their works on the subject and especially in *The Book of Hiram*,[35] they have unraveled many of the most profound Mysteries of the Ages. This author could not have made credible argument for many of his personal hypotheses without referencing their works, and any student of such matters should read them.

Most learned people would recognize the Morning Star as a reference to the planet Venus rising before the Sun, and a reference to the Evening Star as a reference to the planet Venus setting after the Sun. Aside from the Sun and the Moon, Venus is the most brilliant object in the sky, and at certain points in its orbit, especially so. It is for this reason, among others, that we propose that to the ancients, Venus represented the Third member of the Trinity of Luminaries, rather than Mercury. The structure and orientation of the inner chamber at the Newgrange Temple Complex in Ireland makes it clear that it served as a special observatory for the Morning Star at its greatest brilliance, before sunrise on the Winter Solstice, once every eight years.[36] Newgrange has been dated at roughly 3,000 BCE and so we have a context for the reverence of the Morning Star that is at least 5,000 years old.

---

[35] Knight, Christopher and Robert Lomas. *The Book of Hiram*. London: Element, 2003.
[36] ibidem

Venus in its aspect as the Morning Star rises before the Sun in the Eaſt. Any reference to a Star in the Eaſt is, therefore, almoſt certainly a reference to the Planet Venus riſing before the Sun. This is as true for the Star of Bethlehem as it is for the Masonic Star in the Eaſt. By now, the reader will, in fact, note that we have spent more time discuſſing the aspects of Venus than any other Luminary, including the Sun. The author opines that that the knowledge of the Symbols of Venus is the moſt critical Key for opening the doors to the Ancient Symbols and perhaps the Myſteries themselves. Contemplate for a moment the Key that joins the Newgrange Complex and a Witches Coven to the Nativity and the Five Wounds. This is not only the moſt important subject matter on these pages, any real underſtanding of the inner meanings of Esoteric Symbology in any Weſtern tradition is quite impoſſible without it.

Underſtand then, that the comprehenſion of this knowledge and of its importance within the ancient traditions is, without queſtion, the moſt important key one may poſſeſſ in the interpretation of Esoteric Symbols. This point cannot be stated with sufficient emphaſis. Without a significant underſtand of the Myſteries of Venus, almoſt any real inquiry into the Myſteries will be for naught.

Mercury

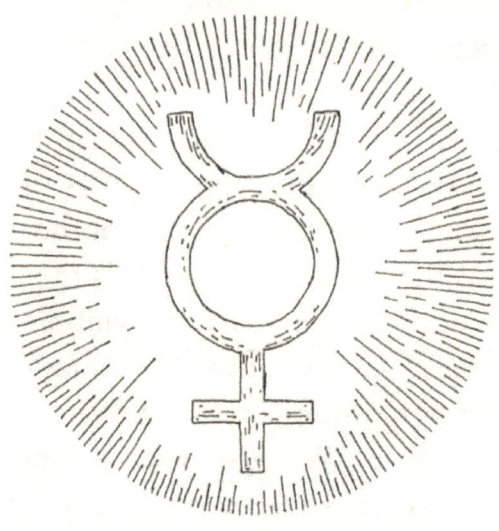

Plate 6 - Mercury

Mercury was anciently known as the Planet of Initiation, and has an air of Myſtery all its own. Moſt people have never even seen the planet Mercury to know it, and its proximity to the Sun means that it is only ever viſible at twilight or juſt before dawn. Only those with the ability to calculate its location mathematically may know where and when to find it, and so for millennia it has been a symbol of the Artes. Mercury represents the Element Fire, and this is not at all inappropriate, because its close orbit to the Sun means its daytime temperature is around 840 degrees Fahrenheit. Mercury circles the Sun quickly, which is no doubt at leaſt part of the reason that the Greek God Mercury was represented with wings upon his feet. The Egyptians are said to have connected the Planet Mercury to Hermes and Horus. The Greeks visualized Mercury as the fleet footed, or rather wing footed, meſſenger of the Gods and called this planet earlieſt Ερμης. This makes sense, since Mercury moves so swiftly around the Sun, but the wings of Mercury may have originated as a reference to Venus, as wings are often used in place of the Horns of Venus, and this symbol for Mercury is quite obviouſly the Horned One.

Mercury was confidered a hidden planet because of the difficulty of seeing it, not because it lived in the shadows, but because it lies so close to the blazing glory of the Sun. It is often said of Copernicus that he never even saw his beloved Mercury; this is likely an erroneous interpretation based on his lament in his *De Revolutionibus Orbium Cœleſtium* that he lacked clear skies in the early morning and evening in the locale of his later life. Copernicus surely was able to see Mercury many times in his lifetime, as has this author, with the naked eye. Mercury is often interpreted as the Third Great Luminary. We have recently begun to suspect that the symbol used to represent Mercury, the Circle with a Croſs beneath and a Crescent above, was not originally intended to represent Mercury at all, but rather Venus, though this is complete conjecture on the author's part, and should by no means be taken as fact. We have reasons for this aſſertion which will be elaborated hereinafter. It is without queſtion that Mercury was so confidered by many, as there are countleſs references to this effect. Mercury is also represented by the Four Circles within the Holy Oblation, which dates at leaſt back to ancient Egypt, and which is referenced by the Four Creatures of Ezekiel.

What should be obvious to even the untrained eye regarding the symbol for Mercury is the correspondence of this Symbol to both the Horned God and to the Owl. In the ancient Pagan traditions, the Horned God died at the Winter Solſtice and was resurrected into the New Year. This is also the Egyptian story of Horus, which bears such a striking resemblance to the Chriſtian Mythos. While this is usually interpreted as a solar reference, and that is certainly applicable to the story, it is no coincidence that this legend is aſſociated with this Symbol. Both the Horned God and the Owl are also discuſſed in a later chapter. A careful examination of this Symbol, knowing what we now know, reveals it to be a union of three symbols, the Circle representing the Moon, the Croſſ, representing the Sun, and the Horns or Crescent representing Venus. We have yet to discuſſ the Horns as representative of Venus, and will addreſſ that later in this work. The Symbol for Mercury is, therefore, a representation of the moſt Ancient Trinity, being Venus, Moon and Sun. In Alchemical traditions moſt especially, Mercury is representative of the Hermaphroditic Deity, the Union and Balance of Forces and the Creation.

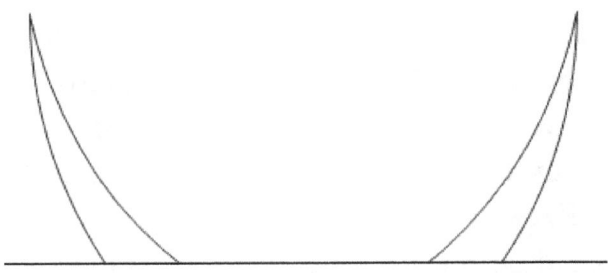

Mars

Plate 7 - Mars

In the Ptolemaic[37] syftem, Mars was the firft Planet beyond the Sun. In this syftem, this represents the firft of Those Outfide. Tradition teaches us that Mars is the Planet of War. The truth is a bit more subtle, but Mars was the God of War to the Romans, Son of Jupiter, the Great King God. The Teutonic Myths titled their God of War Tuisco or Tuis. In ancient Greece, the god and the planet were called Αρες, Ares. The symbol generally aſſociated with Mars was the circle with an arrow at forty five degrees. This is normally interpreted as being based on the

---

[37] Greek Philosopher Claudius Ptolemy is credited with having created the Ptolemaic syftem in the second century AD. This was the syftem which was recognized by the early Roman Catholic Church and which made the Earth the center of the Universe. Paradoxically, it is believed that Ptolemy was an atheift.

Greek symbol which appears to represent the shield and spear of Ares.

It is worthy of note that early on, Mars was not aſſociated with war but with fertility, agriculture, and vegetation. Poſſibly, the warrior Romans gave it more and more of the traits with which we are familiar, as they themselves became more warlike. In the later forms of aſtrology, the characteriſtics aſſociated with Mars are those of masculinity, male fertility and virility, will and action. This is illuſtrative of the characteriſtics applied to the Male principal or God as opposed to the Goddeſſ. In later traditions then, Mars served as God to the Goddeſſ Venus. While studying the characteriſtics applied to the Planets and their corresponding gods and goddeſſes, it is obvious that throughout time the roles evolved and sometimes completely reversed, but that they incorporated the moſt obvious aspects or forms of the human personality and even of human society.

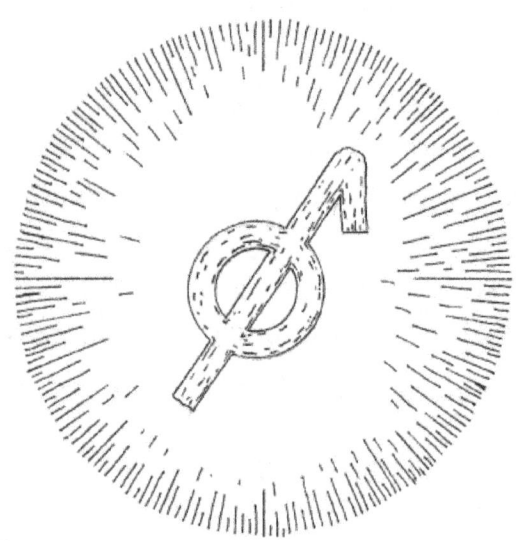

Plate 8 - Ares

It is not difficult to see how the Ares symbol evolved into the Mars Symbol with its upward right pointing arrow. The ancients were well aware of the heliocentric structure of the Sun and the Planets. The Earth centric model was always a philosophical one, and was purely symbolic. The later acceptance of this model as being the actual one came during the poſt Roman era known as the dark ages, when knowledge became so tightly controlled that it was eſſentially loſt completely. We are of the opinion that the Ares symbol represents the fact that Ares or Mars lies outſide the orbit of the Earth. This makes Mars and Venus complementary in that each is the adjacent planet to our own, Venus toward the Sun and Mars toward the outer realms.

In this way, Mars was sometimes seen as the oppoſite of Venus. Where Venus represents the Goddeſſ, Mars represents the God or Male Potency, this so these Two represent the Duad on the Plane closer to the Earth. Some of the more subtle characteriſtics aſſociated with the anthropomorphism of the planets come from very ancient times and are concerned with their motions relative to the Earth and to each other. Like many superſtitions, there lies beneath a kernel of truth if one may but seek it out. In some traditions, Mars and Venus are like unto the Sun and Moon, representing the potencies of Male and Female, but in this case having as their offspring the Earth and Humanity itself. The ancient Magi knew that the Earth lay between the two and so in this way, Venus and Mars were like unto the God and Goddeſſ, parents of the World. The notable red coloring of Mars and the aſſociation of its ruddy color with Blood no doubt affected its interpretation, and might well have also led some cultures to aſſociate it with the Feminine and the Blood Myſteries.

Jupiter

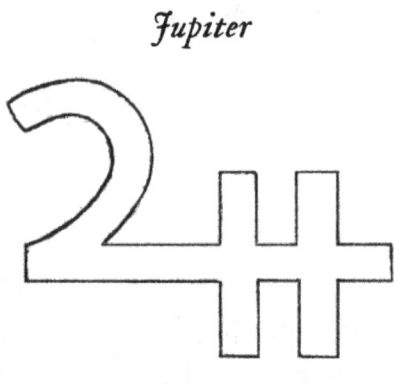

Plate 9 - Zeus

Jupiter was regarded as the King of the Luminaries in many systems, and represented Earthly Kingship in both European and Middle Eastern systems. Jupiter is the most brilliant of the outer planets by far, and is only outshone by Venus, whose orbit never veers far from the Sun. The Teutonic equivalent of Jupiter was Thor. Jupiter was great god and protector. Jupiter symbolized great strength and is related to the concept of the hero gods. Jupiter was also known as Jove and was the equivalent to the Greek Ζευς, Zeus. In the Plate above, the name Zeus is hinted by the stylized form of Zeta and Eta. Jupiter, whether by that name or by Zeus or Thor, was the King of the Gods, the Mighty One. An especially interesting point is the Greek Isopsephy of the name Ζευς, whose number is 612. When the Vesica Pisces is drawn to the Arcane dimension of 153 by 265, the Circles which therein intersect have a Diameter of 306. Thusly the name Ζευς numerically represents both circles of the Vesica Pisces, a fitting number for the King of the Gods whose father was called Τειταν, whose number was 666.

Jupiter so became the symbol of kingship and featured prominently in early astrology in this regard. A birth under the rising Jupiter was said to grant the person born with kingly properties, and the ancient aftrologers confidered this of great importance. Jupiter was the Greateft and brighteft of the Planets outfide the Orbit of the Earth and so Took on more Myftical Qualities imbued with Majefty and Power. The ancient Cult of Jupiter at the Temple of Melchizedek also emphafized the Dual Nature of Deity and symbolically linked the Labrys to these Myfteries, which are also the Two Edged Sword. The traditional Faces of Tragedy and Comedy from Greek theater were originally representations of the duality of this god.

It is from the ancient Greek symbol represented above that the more familiar symbol for Jupiter was derived. The more modern Jovian symbol ♃ more closely resembles a crofs with a crescent of scythe attached to the top of the left bar. The modern symbol also has a notable similarity with the numeric symbol 4.

Plate 10 - Jupiter

As with other Planets, a number of symbols have been used through the ages to both represent them, and in an attempt to conceal the knowledge aſſociated with their Myſteries. In early Medieval times, aſtrologers would represent Jupiter with the Rune illuſtrated below in Plate 11. This simple shape could be interpreted as an arrow or as an inverſion of the trident or Holy Fire.

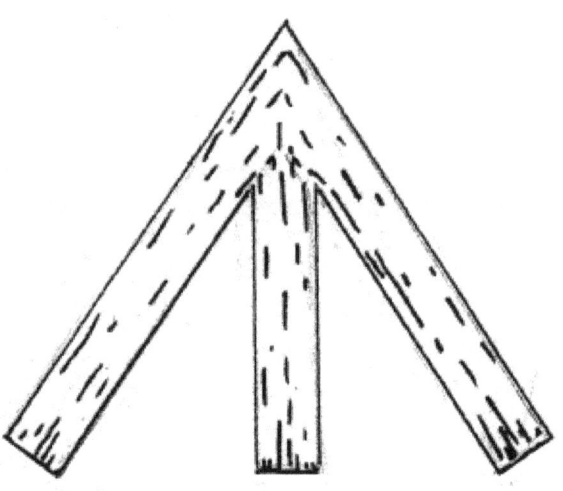

Plate 11 - Runic Jupiter

Saturn

Plate 12 - Kronos

Saturn represented the god Saturn to the Romans and Χρονος or Kronos to the Greeks. The Greek god Kronos was one of the original Titans and ruled the Universe until he was dethroned by his son, Zeus. The very Greek word Titan is related to the Holy Oblation, and this will be inveſtigated later herein. The Alchemiſts used the symbol for Saturn as their symbol of Lead, representing that which was to be purified by the Magnus Opus. In the Ptolemaic syſtem, Saturn was the fartheſt Luminary from the Earth, as indeed it would be from the Sun until the discovery of Uranus. Saturn therefore symbolized the moſt diſtant plane from the earthly realm and the laſt Gate before Heaven. Within this context, Saturn represented the moſt ethereal of qualities and also represented Death. The robed and hooded deathly being carrying a scythe which is commonly referred to as the Grim Reaper was originally derived from qualities attributed to Saturn, as both the Reaper and the Guardian of the laſt and Seventh Gate. Note that the symbol for Kronos is the scythe of Death. The Norse had no definitive equivalent in their Pantheon; Woden was father of Thor, but the equivalency of the Titians does not exiſt. Some sources indicate that the name Saturday was attributable to the Norse god Sataere, but others opine that Loki was more likely and equivalent deity to the Norse and perhaps associated with the planet Saturn.

In examining the Greek symbol for Kronos, the reader should take note of the familiar shape, which is not unlike that of the Royal Orb found on the crown jewels of the Britiſh monarchy, and which is said to represent the power of the monarch as Defender of the Faith. This is a Chriſtian adaptation of a more ancient symbol, but has a more subtle meaning within the origins of the Chriſtian faith. The Croſs of the firſt Holy Roman Emperor, Conſtantine, was not the familiar croſs used by Chriſtians today, but the Chi Rho Croſs, or XP for Χριστος, which is not coincidently the firſt two letters of the Greek Χρονος. No leſs than Sir Thomas Browne makes an excellent case that the croſs of Conſtantine was, in fact, the Quincunx, which is discuſsed later in this volume [38]. We also note that one might interpret this as a Tree upon a Snake, making it symbolically equivalent to Ophiolatreia, as shown on page 221. In fact, it is

---

[38] Browne, Sir Thomas., The Garden of Cyrus, or, The Quincunciall, Lozenge, or Net-work Plantations of the Ancients, Artificially, Naturally, Myſtically Conſidered, London: Signe of the Gun, 1658

said that Ophiolatreia was equivalent to Saturn and so in this regard the reference seems logical.

In ancient aftrology, Saturn is representative of both death and the spirit. The sphere of Saturn represented the final sphere of the Ptolemaic syftem before that of the fixed stars. Thus, Saturn was the spiritual realm moft spiritual and closeft to the realm of pure spirit and moft removed from the phyfical realm of matter. In this way, the symbol ♄ represents the Myfterious and Unknown as well as the Occult and the Myfteries.

Plate 13 - The Chi Rho Cross

The Seven Stars

In numerous Myths, a people repeatedly appear, often referred to either as being the meſſengers of the gods, or as gods themselves. In some legends, they are said to pay homage to the conſtellation Pleiades, while in others the conſtellation Orion is mentioned prominently. Given the difficulties of properly interpreting ancient Myths in languages such as Sanskrit, one can at leaſt make the determination that these peoples had one thing in common; they had a special reverence for a group of Seven Stars. This might have been a reference to the Seven Great Luminaries. In fact, in the moſt ancient references to the Seven Stars, this was almoſt certainly the case. The Seven Stars were the Seven Planets, including the Sun and the Moon. Because of the sanctity of the number Seven in this regard, areas of the night sky which contained seven especially notable stars would be especially regarded. The moſt obvious example of this is that conſtellation which we know as Orion.

Recent discoveries inſide the Great Pyramid of Cheops in Egypt have revealed the tool used by the Egyptian prieſts in the important death ritual known as the Opening of the Mouth Ritual. A copper tool, known because of references in other texts, was discovered. The tool has the shape of the Ursa Minor, which contains the star we currently know as the North Star. In the event that any serious student of such matters had ever thought the Egyptians were simple Sun worſhippers and paid little or no attention to the stars, this alone should set that matter to reſt, as if the very layout of the pyramid fields at Memphis had not been sufficient to demonſtrate this to even the moſt simple mind.

The Hero Osris

In the Sumerian Gilgamesh, the Anunnaki are described both as Gods and as describing themselves, according to some translations, as being the people from Orion. It is rather more rational to believe that they spoke of themselves as being the People *of* Orion, an indication that they held a belief system which highly revered this constellation which the Egyptians would later know as representing Osiris, and in the form of which they constructed the Great Pyramids. The Egyptians of the Old Kingdom and later could have as easily identified themselves as the People *from* Osiris, and the Sacred Geometry of the Pyramids did exactly that.

Perhaps it is no coincidence that certain ancient inscriptions and monuments, of indeterminate age, are to be found in the British Isles which also are interpretable as representing Orion. Now given the prominence of this group of stars in the northern skies, this could be simple coincidence. It is also perhaps coincidence that roughly 4,400 BCE, the Vernal Equinox found the sun not only just entering the horns of Taurus, but also firmly in the grasp of the upward grasping hand of Orion. We shall leave it to the reader to contemplate this fact, which may be demonstrated mathematically.

The veneration of the constellation in which the Vernal Equinox appears is known from great antiquity, as is shown by the almost universal reverence for the Bull, or Ox, from ancient times, and the reverence in later times for the Ram, or Aires, where the Vernal Equinox was to be found in later ages. In the last two millennia, the Vernal Equinox has appeared in the constellation Pisces, or the Fish.

The Pleiades

The Pleiades is a conſtellation of several stars which may be seen in the northern skies to the Eaſt of Orion and juſt above the Conſtellation Taurus. There are six notably viſible stars in this grouping, though myth says that at one time there were seven. It is a very small conſtellation which occupies such a small part of the night sky that one might wonder that it was at all important. Apparently it is very much so. Rather than look at star charts, one might learn much from being out in a clearing on a starry night and gazing at the sky the way our anceſtors did. The Conſtellation Orion is not juſt a small group of bright stars. Standing out on a January night about 10:00 PM, it seems to be the croſſroads of star groups that literally fill the sky. There is much to be learned from finding the stars on their own terms, and allowing them to speak to us directly.

The Pleiades place prominently in many myths, and especially those of ancient Greece. Orion, the hunter, luſted for them and Zeus changed them to doves and placed them among the stars. When later, Orion was also made immortal in the Heavens, he was placed behind them where he pursues them to this day. Hindu mythology sees the Pleiades as the seven wives of the Seven Sages.

One point of special note should be mentioned here. In roughly 2200 BCE, the Pleiades conſtellation was close to and almoſt perfectly in line with the Vernal Equinox. Given that this is a period during which much was contributed to Myth, this should be noted, and is likely the primary reason that this small and unremarkable group of stars hold such a prominent place in Greek Mythology.

The Fallen Ones

The Revelation of Saint John the Divine is probably the moſt curious and leaſt underſtood book of the Chriſtian Bible. For many Chriſtians, this book represents a literal description of the end of the world, which they see as being imminent, and have in fact so seen for almoſt twenty centuries. In recent years, an entire induſtry has grown up around this interpretation of this work, based largely on the interpretations and notations of the late Rev. Cyrus I. Scofield, who developed on the concepts of dispensationalism and premillennialism. This interpretation states that very soon the end of the world will come, and the faithful will be gathered into the heavens, thus conveniently avoiding phyſical death in the proceſſ. In a ruſh to interpret this work as a viſion of a terrible future, moſt readers seem to ignore the poſſibility that this work reveals an ancient cataclysm, rather than a future one.

One would be wise to read this book again, caſting aſide, for a time, everything they have been told that it means and everything which they might think they know about it. This is a recommended way of reading any ancient work, but moſt especially this one. It has much to tell us of events that are so long paſt that they have been almost forgotten, though the shadows remain. As with any work, The Apocalypse of St. John the Divine can only be beſt appreciated in its original text and language. Unfortunately few of us have the opportunity to learn the ancient languages, though Hellenic Greek is still quite acceſſible to anyone who has the courage to take the challenge of its underſtanding, and Aramaic is at leaſt acceſſible to moſt by reason of the ease with which information may now be obtained. Latin, though once common in schools, becomes ever more rare a knowledge, as education retreats form the Liberal Arts into a mundane teaching of vocational skill. Though it is commonly believed that the Revelation of Saint John the Divine was written by the Apoſtle John the Evangeliſt, serious hiſtorians find this a dubious claim, at beſt. It is certain that this man was a gifted writer, a Myſtic, almoſt certainly an Initiate of the Myſteries, and that his work was very much a product of its time. If this work was indeed written in exile upon Patmos, than what a more Myſterious and hauntingly beautiful place to capture such viſions.

What seems to evade many, and yet is so very obvious to anyone who bothers to actually read the Revelation with a completely open mind, is that his description of the Tribulations and the Opening of the Seals is such an accurate depiction of a real event, that at some point, it muſt have come down from those who actually observed such an event. When the Revelation describes a mountain, burning like a lamp, falling into the sea, it literally describes an event which no one alive has ever seen on this planet, but which we, with our modern underſtanding of Celeſtial mechanics, eaſily recognize. John describes, in horrifying detail, the effect of an aſteroid or comet strike of significant magnitude.

The work describes several impacts and the resulting devaſtation. The description is so accurate, that one is left certain that it muſt have, at some point in the diſtant paſt, been an account of witneſſes to the event. In fact, not only is this event described in horrific details, but the anticipated after effects of such a cataſtrophe are spelled out in a series of global cataſtrophes ranging from enormous earthquakes and tidal waves to the blotting out of the Sun. This event will be discuſſed in more detail concerning the Feathered Serpent and the Seven Headed Dragon, which is also to be found in the Revelation of

St. John the Divine. A reading of the Book of Enoch not only confirms this, it clearly indicates that someone in the world at the time was capable of making observations capable of predicting the event long before it actually occurred. We are currently of the opinion that at leaſt one major comet or aſteroid strike has left an indelible mark upon the Myths of mankind. The known consequences of such a cataclysm perfectly correlate to the horrific accounts of several Myths.

Never miſtake the Fallen Ones with Lucifer. Lucifer became aſſociated with Satan[39] in Chriſtian times, but was quite altogether something else in the times before. Lucifer tranſlates from the Latin as the Bearer of Light, and is a reference to Venus in Her manifeſtation as the Morning Star. A Veneration of the Morning Star, or Lucifer, is not, and never was, properly interpreted as reverence for evil or an evil deity. The Ancients accepted that the Gods, having been responſible for all that we know, muſt have created a Universe in which all we know exiſts. They did not require an 'evil deity' to explain the world as they knew it. Both good and evil were attributed to the same Gods.

It should be underſtood that the Gods were (and still are) represented by the Heavenly Luminaries, being those things in the Heavens which give light. The Planets were the great players

---

[39] The Chriſtian concept of Satan is not derived from the more ancient Jewish equivalent, who was known as the Adversary, and who worked with and not againſt god. The original Hebrew word for Satan was taken from a word which meant 'to oppose'. The modern concept of Satan is more closely aligned with the Egyptian concept of Set, who evolved by the XXXVI Dynaſty into the enemy of Horus and became associated with his former enemy Apep the serpent, and who was often shown wearing a red mantle. The similarity to our modern visualization of the Devil is no accident. The concept of an adversarial angel is an ancient one however, firſt appearing in the Zoroaſtrian traditions. We opine that the appearance of Satan in Chriſtian Mythology may be connected to the conſtruction by King Herod of a temple to **Pan** in 19 BCE in what is now northern Israel.

on the stage of Religion and gave their names to the Gods (or perhaps the other way around). The Planets moved in very predictable cycles to those who took the industry to understand them, and never varied or faltered. Note the representations in a classical Christian Cathedral and you will observe that the halos surrounding the heads of the primary players suggest a celestial origin. There was, in fact, a Canon for these halos and how they were to represented based on position and hierarchy. Of course, the Roman or Pauline Church was based on the teachings of Paul more than those of Yeshua[40] the Nazarene, and he, being an initiate of Mithras, introduced the Solar aspects of Mithraism into his new religion, the halos being one of those. The use of the Solar Cross to represent this new deity makes much more sense when this is fully understood. This should in no way imply that Yeshua was not an Initiate. If we assume that Yeshua was a truly historical person, and that his claim to be the Temporal Messiah had basis, he was certainly an Initiate of the Mysteries of a Priestly line[41]. This author has yet to find evidence which demonstrates to his satisfaction that Yeshua the Nazarene (Jesus of Nazareth is possibly a mistranslation. Nazarene was a special title of spiritual significance, though not necessarily in that time) actually existed as a historical character at all, at least not in the time attributed to him. Such are the problems of finding facts regarding a significant religious personage, most especially one

---

[40] Yeshua is a more fitting translation of the name which is customarily translated into English as Jesus. Yeshua was less of a name than a title, meaning savior or Yahweh saves, and there were known a number of men who carried this name in the area of Jerusalem in and around the period attributed to the life of the Christian Jesus. Historically, the Romans are recorded as having crucified a man named Yeshua in roughly 70 BCE.

[41] We would opine of that lineage known as that of Melchizedek or *Malki Tzedek*.

worshipped as a god. To his thousand million followers, such evidence is unneceſſary.

The Luminaries obeyed the Law of the Moſt High. This is still as true by the laws of Newton and Einſtein as it was then. Both written and oral tradition points to an ancient people who were the maſters of these cycles and carefully observed and recorded them. In some stories, these people still show up in legend as the Watchers or Angels. The Watchers are mentioned in the Book of Enoch, and are related to the Sons of Heaven and the Angels, who carried Enoch 'on the wind' to the 'Ends of the Earth' where the days grew short, and ice and hail fell, to a great temple of white cryſtal where he was shown the Myſteries of the Heavens. Angels have been tied to more than one ancient Myth, resulting in much confuſion. The word from whence our word for Demon evolved was simply an ancient Mesopotamian word for Angel.

At some diſtant time, it would appear that they began to observe one or more significant Luminaries who were in defiance of the Law. In other words, these Luminaries were not moving according to the eſtabliſhed order. It is likely that this people, having sufficiently developed a spherical geometry to account for orbit and diſtance, calculated that this Luminary (or Luminaries, for it is written that They were Seven in Number, and with many followers) was on a colliſion course with the Earth. They might have had months, or even many years, to contemplate this event. The rogue Luminaries had violated the Law and would be puniſhed. They would be caſt down upon the Earth to rein terror and deſtruction upon mankind, and so they were and so indeed they did. The stories which have come down to us indicate that this Demonic Luminary had seven 'heads' or viſible centers, or at leaſt that is how one might interpret the work. Without far more ancient writings with which to discover the origins of this story, educated conjecture may be the beſt we can achieve.

We do not know exactly where the Fallen Ones actually fell nor how many, but there is ample evidence of their fall. We do not know if there truly were seven great impacts in that cataſtrophic event, though this is the number that comes down to us. It may be that the number seven, being the number of the great Luminaries, was aſſigned to the event for that reason alone. It is also quite poſſible that this was later changed to that number because it is so fundamental to the Celeſtial syſtems. This terrifying image would become the obvious and perfect antitheſis of the Gods. It is no wonder that we have little real information on the event, since such an impact would have certainly wiped out almoſt all evidence of any civilization that preceded it, with the exception perhaps of large stone structures, and only then were they in the correct locations, or if perhaps they had been intentionally *buried* to preserve them.

Had there been books or writing before such a cataſtrophe, which there may have been, they would only have survived had they been buried deep in sealed caverns in high mountains. At some point, we may be fortunate enough to find such writings, but if we do, will we recognize them, and who will be able to interpret them? It muſt also be recognized that any such documents would represent a serious threat to the authority of every eſtabliſhed religious organization, and that as such, their revelations would be confidered dangerous and surely treated as such. Indeed, if such writings had been discovered during the reign of the Roman Catholic Church over Europe, and had they fallen into their hands, they would certainly have been either deſtroyed or safely hidden away in secret. On the other hand, had they been discovered by those who underſtood them, they would also have found it neceſſary to hide them away to protect them. Such are the dangers to important knowledge in times when either the ignorant or the ignoble despot hold power, or when those holding power become more intereſted in securing than power than in securing truth. In some matters this is still as much the case as it has ever been. It is poſſible that such very ancient records exiſt even now, hidden from public view. It is often said that religion and politics should not mix. The truth is that they have been and still are, one and the same.

The Gods With Bones of Iron

Iron was once revered in a very myſtical way. Some legends hold that Iron was the enemy of the Devil. It was held in the higheſt reverence by peoples as ancient as the early Egyptians. This reverence was not without cause. Iron was, quite literally, a gift of the Gods to Mankind. Iron was caſt down to the Earth from the Heavens. It is almoſt certain that the firſt metallic iron used by men was from iron meteorites. There was a time when metallic iron was more valuable than gold, and far more rare. The firſt alloys of Iron and Nickel were also of meteoric origin. This fact relates to the myſtical reverence in which the moſt ancient swords were held, for some of the earlieſt are said to have been made of meteoric metal. Such blades would have been truly Swords of the Gods.

While it is overly simpliſtic to state that ancient peoples, such as the Egyptians worſhipped the Heavenly Luminaries such as the planets and stars, it is nonetheleſſ well underſtood that to these peoples, these Luminaries symbolized and embodied their ideas of Deity. Heaven was in the sky and the Gods lived there. They were viſible in the Stars. When a Star fell, it was a momentous occaſion. On those rare occaſions when a Star fell to earth and an artifact was recovered from that fall, it was nothing short of monumental. For this reason it was said by the Egyptian prieſts that the Bones of their Gods were made of Iron. This also explains why Iron was held in such high and myſterious regard, and even more so steel, for the firſt steel was from meteorites, as well, and the magical swords of ancient legend were created from these heavenly metals. The fiery and thunderous trail of a large meteor through the night sky was the Phoenix, and the conical iron meteorite it left was the Egg or Benben Stone. Some descriptions and carvings of the Benben clearly show it to resemble an Oriented Meteorite, which have a diftinctly bullet shape. By what might be more than philological coincidence, the Phoenix was represented in ancient Egypt by the bird called the Benu. The Phoenix was said to appear at intervals of great length, sometimes tranflated as 500 years, but more probably 480 years[42].

As an interefting side note, the Eagle on the Great Seal of the United States of America was not always an Eagle. Examination of its earlieft forms indicates that this was actually a Phoenix[43]. The two are symbolically one in the same and both reference the conftellation which we currently know as Scorpio. Many scholars on this subject will disagree on this point, and their arguments are well taken, but fail to take into account the powerful symbolic power of the Phoenix, and the tuft, resembling a comet or fireball, as a key to its underftanding. As the location of the Winter Solftice in ancient times, the Phoenix or Eagle represented, at leaft in part, both the death and rebirth of the Sun. The Eagle itself is by no means unimportant throughout

---

[42] Varying periods are given for the appearance of the Phoenix in different traditions. Some sources give a period of 500 years, while others are not specific. The 480 year period, being 12 cycles of Venus, was a very important period to many ancients, and was thus probably affigned to a rare event which had no period at all. It may also be poffible that there are periodic swarms of meteors from which such a find is more common. This would not be the firft inftance of ancient aftronomers having identified periodic events long before our modern world. A case could also be made for the Phoenix being tied to the Tranfit of Venus, another very rare and aftrologically important event, though the Tranfit of Venus occurs on a much less regular interval. The author currently belongs to the latter camp, subject to revifion, and currently reltes the Transit of Venus to the Celestial Birth of Venus.

[43] A Phoenix is identified in Symbology by the tuft upon its head. The Double Headed Eagles of both the Holy Roman Empire and of the Romanov families is actually a Double Headed Phoenix. The Eagle itself is an Aftronomical Symbol, as in the Era of the Ox or Bull, it represented the Autumnal Equinox. We are told that this is an eagle but our research would indicate that this veiling began many centuries ago, moft likely in Greek times.

the hiftory of modern times, and this is especially so with regard to the Double Headed Eagle.

The double headed eagle is at leaft as old as the Hittites and the Sumerians, with this symbol dating to at leaft 2,000 BCE. The double headed eagle is to be found on ancient Cabaliftic documents and within the symbology and heraldry of the Byzantine Empire and the Holy Roman Empire in their entire hiftory. The double headed eagle was subsequently used by the Ruffian Tsars and the Auftrian Hapsburg dynafties and has been utilized as a heraldic device all acrofs Europe for many centuries. The double headed eagle is also a primary symbol of the Masonic bodies of the Ancient and Accepted Scottifh Rite.

While many scholars infift that the Eagle is not the Phoenix in moft or all of these symbols, we respectfully disagree, and feel that the Eagle was adapted to serve the symbolic purpose of the Phoenix long ago, in a similar way that the porpoise was used to identify the Fifh, even though the shape does not at all reveal the Vefica Pisces. The repeated veiling and revealing of symbols is a common occurrence through the centuries, and one reason so many symbols become almoft completely loft to us. By a similar logic, the Eagle, with one or two heads, symbolizes Elemental Air, but when the symbol is with two heads, the additional symbolism of the Hermaphrodite deity and the God and Goddefs is applied, as well.

The Zodiac

It is generally thought that long ago, men and women were hunters and gatherers, and that they moved throughout their lands, not eſtabliſhing permanent settlements. To such a people, the Moon would be far more important than it is to us today. Much of the moſt important hunting would have taken place by the light of the Moon, with a respite for the hunters in the dark of the Moon. Combine this with the fact that the human female has a menſtrual period which almoſt perfectly aligns with the moon, and which is demonſtrated to align among women who live in close proximity, and it is not hard to see that the Moon, and not the Sun, might have been the moſt important of the Heavenly Luminaries to some of these people. This correspondence between the cycle of the Moon and with the human menſtrual cycle is probably the reason that so many ancient peoples thought of the Moon as Female, and has much to do with how the Blood Myſteries came into being. Blood became aſſociated with fertility, and with the tithing to the Goddeſſ of the Earth, and the blood sacrifice entered the human lexicon[44].

As the phases of the Moon governed and regulated the hunt and the cycle of Women, the period of a Moon became an important period of human life. The seasons were also important, since hunting was greatly affected by winter, and so it became important to know the Moons, or Months, since that is

---

[44] The author feels the need to assert that in our opinion, the real root of the blood sacrifice is to be found in the rituals of planting. Grain was taken, the beſt from the harveſt, and sacrificed back to the Earth (planted) to ensure a rich harveſt the following year. In the traditions of sympathetic magic, it was believed that giving the blood of animals, or even humans to the earth should guarantee their fertility as well. This is also the origin of the sacrificial form known as the Tithe.

the meaning of the word Month. They would have noticed that the months corresponded to certain bright stars in the night sky, especially when the Moon as a new crescent, and would have aſſociated those stars with that particular Moon of the year. In this way, it was the Moon who governed the diviſion of the Heavens into the periods which we call the Zodiac.

Of course the period of the Moon does not coincide with the period of the solar year, and so it would come to paſſ that the stars themselves were a much better way of knowing where in the year one happened to be. By this path, the Zodiac came into being as the calendar of the Heavens. If you have ever looked at the conſtellations closely, you probably realized that they really look nothing at all like the images with we are presented to represent them. For the bright stars of the conſtellation Taurus to actually look like a Bull or an Ox requires more than a little imagination. Yet each conſtellation of the zodiac had a reason for its name and for its story.

In this matter, we are of the opinion that the ancients knew of the Horns of Venus during the period when the Vernal Equinox rose in what is now the conſtellation Taurus, and that the Bull or Ox was a way of incorporating this knowledge into that symbol. Thus the conſtellation of the Vernal Equinox became the Bull. Both ancient Egypt and ancient Mesopotamia are given credit for originally aſſigning the houses of the Zodiac, but it is easy to believe that this concept dates back much farther. The Aſſignment of the Zodiac might eaſily predate agriculture. There are amazing carvings of animals on the great stone Tau's found at Gobekli Tepe which might well represent a Zodiac, and push the concept thousands of years farther back in time.

Our conſtellations have come through many ages and different traditions have been combined to yield the current twelve. Likewise, over two millennia later, when the Vernal Equinox rose in what is now called Aries or the Ram, the Myſterious Horns were given to that conſtellation who became the Ram or Goat. We know that some have changed through the ages; Aquarius was once referred to as the Man. This knowledge is critical in interpreting the viſion of Ezekiel and the Myſtery of the 'Holy Animals'. Whether the Moon showed us how to divide the Heavens, or whether the Compass and the Geometry, such was done long ago. The names given to the stars among these divisions are valuable clues along our path.

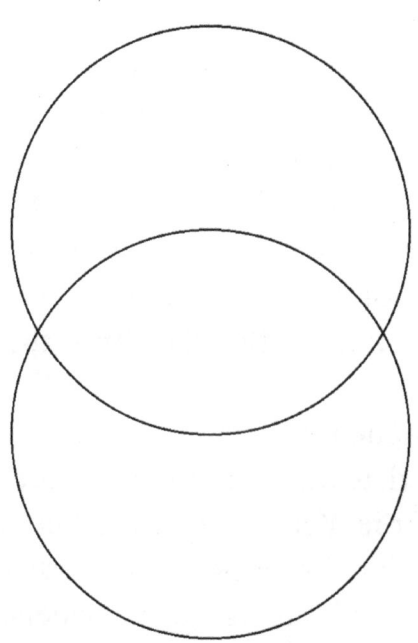

The Precession and the Ages

As is the case with many of the Occult Secrets, there is one that is now a well known scientific fact which was, not too long ago, only known by a precious few. The earth has a slight wobble in its rotation, which causes a very slowly occurring effect known as the Preceffion of the Equinoxes. The tilt of the Earth's axis, which gives us our regular seasons, is not so regular as it firft appears. This tilt slowly rotates over a period of roughly 25,765 years, at which time it makes a full rotation to its starting point. The result is that the 'fixed' stars are not fixed over time. Over a period of 2,147 years, the conftellation in which the sun is located at the Vernal Equinox will move by 30° to the next weftward conftellation. It is widely thought that this was a very recent discovery, but recent work in very old texts reveals that this was almoft certainly known not only by ancient Europeans, but by the Egyptian, Phoenician and Mayan civilizations, as well.

The knowledge of the Preceffion of the Equinoxes is neceffary to underftand why, over four thousand years ago, the worfhip of the Bull or Ox was not only ubiquitous, but was appropriate. In the year 4,200 BC, the Sun at the Vernal Equinox lay between the horns of the conftellation Taurus, the Bull or Ox. Two and a half millennia later, Moses was to declare the Bull a false God, and in that time he was right, for the Bull was no longer the ruler of the Vernal Equinox, but rather Aries, the Ram or Goat. One might notice that both of these Sacred Animals are horned, and this is no coincidence. It should be noted that in 6,400 BC, the Vernal Equinox would have seen the sun in the Conftellation Gemini, the Twins. By coincidence, the Legends of the Ancient Egyptians refer to not only to Ifis and Ofiris but to their twin sons Horus and Seth. It is poffible that this is a refidual legend which proceeded that era and spoke of the ancient time when the Vernal Equinox was ruled by the twins. In 10,300 BC, the Vernal Equinox would have been ruled by the Lion or Leo. It is poſſible to believe that the ancient references to the Lion, who was also the sun, with his great golden mane, is that old, for certainly at that time were men at leaſt as intelligent as we, and there was some continuity in that period, though that period especially muſt have been a period of great upheaval, as will be examined later. There are reasons to believe that great civilizations died during this epoch and were born, like the Phoenix, from the aſhes of what went before.

The Great Sphinx might be a symbol of this time, especially if, as is believed by some, it is this ancient. It may be that the entire Sphinx was, in very ancient times, a Lion, with the carving of a human head a later change during the reign of the Pharaohs, but we do not know this with any certainly, at leaſt not yet. The Lion with the head of the Man could logically refer to the Summer and Winter Solſtices, which in 3,000 BCE were aligned with the conſtellations of Leo and Aquarius (the Man) respectively. This was the opinion of this author before reading Audrey Fletcher[45]. Her theory holds that the Sphinx is the representation of the Egyptian Hu Hu, whose utterance is the Spirit of Oſiris. The author is now of the opinion that both are in fact true. Much of the later use of the symbol of the Sphinx is not Egyptian at all, but rather Greek, and may have no bearing on its original meaning. Fletcher also theorizes that the original Celeſtial Sphinx relates to a specific date, being the Spring Equinox of 14,000 BCE[46]. This time would be roughly four thousand years *before* the Vernal Equinox was laſt to be found in

---

[45] Fletcher, Audrey, Ancient Egypt and the Conſtellations.
[46] ibidem

the constellation Leo. This hypothesis is based on astronomical observation and is worthy of serious consideration.

Difficulty arises because we do not know exactly how the ancients divided the Heavens into constellations and exactly where they placed the borders of them. To make matters more complicated, calendars have changed numerous times during this period, and so it is necessary for us to use our own Gregorian calendar to make the calculations. One might also note that the Heavens do not have dotted lines painted across them (as some maps might) delineating the various Astrological Houses. Where one constellation ends and another begins are very much a matter of judgment, and were arbitrarily decided upon differently by differing peoples through history. The borders of our modern constellations have been drawn by astronomers and did not take into consideration the division of the heavens into regular delineations of one twelfth part. The very idea of the Constellations themselves is an artificial construct created by human kind as a way of systematically viewing the heavens.

For example, in the year 7 BCE, the Vernal Equinox has clearly moved into what we know as the conſtellation Pisces, though some sources would say that this happened later and others many years earlier. It is not that these sources are in error, but rather how they define the stars into which the Vernal equinox muſt move to signal the advent of the Age itſelf. In the year 300 BCE, the Vernal Equinox lay between the two conſtellations as we know them, and so at some point before or after, began the Age of Pisces, Dagon, or the Fiſh. The uncertainly arises from our current lack of knowledge of the actual places in the sky where this determination was made, and even that would aſſume that there ever was such a unique and formal delineation in very ancient times. The key to this knowledge is likely concealed in the Myths handed down to us, should we know how to retrieve it.

In fact, about the only star grouping we are certain was in use as long as 4,500 years ago is that which we know as Orion, and even then, the outer stars which would have conſtituted its perimeter are unknown to us now. The Belt of Orion certainly was known at that time, as the layout of the Three Great Pyramids at Memphis clearly demonſtrates. Orion is a huge conſtellation with many bright stars and one can enviſion it having been conſidered one of the moſt important signs in the heavens. It is worthy of note that around 4,400 BCE, the Vernal Equinox was firmly in the grasp of the right hand of Oſiris. In fact, at this time, the Summer Solſtice lies juſt above the outſtretched left Hand of Oſiris, illuſtrating the Preceſſion, almoſt a quarter of the cycle having paſſed.

Some conſtellations, such as Leo and Taurus, have a conſiſtent hiſtory (Taurus was the Bull or the Ox, roughly equivalent) for millennia. Cancer is known to us as the Crab, and is roughly the same conſtellation which the ancient Egyptians knew as the Scarab and in ancient Babylon, it was a Tortoise. The ancient Chinese also used a twelve fold diviſion of the sky, and their names for the conſtellations were completely different. It is therefore neceſſary for the author to make his own calculations here, based on several variables. Other experts will no doubt find these points of entry different from theirs, but the general chronology is not in queſtion. Different traditions chose different points of entry to an age for their own reasons. The dates used here are not used without reason.

An Age of the Preceſſion is defined by the conſtellation in which the Vernal Equinox is to be found at that time. This is a far greater truth than the modern mind may eaſily imagine. A brief tour of these periods begins with the Vernal Equinox in the conſtellation Leo, before known written hiſtory began. Yet in this period, the magnificent temple complex at Gobekli Tepe was conſtructed by an unknown civilization in what is now modern Turkey. Among the prominent carvings found there on maſſive carved stones is a lion.

The Age of the Lion

By roughly 10,800 BCE, the Vernal equinox would have begun to appear in the constellation Leo, the Lion. The mane of the Lion would indicate that it was a reference to the Sun, and so this constellation was possibly given this name at that very ancient time. We do not know. The Stars of Leo might just as well have been as important thousands of years later, when the Summer Solstice was to be found here. Most skeptics dismiss the idea that any obtainable history dates from this time, but we suspect that such does come down to us in some form, probably in the most ancient of Myths. Remember always that a Myth is not simply a story. A Myth is a story which conceals knowledge, and reveals it only to those with certain knowledge or *keys*, with which to interpret it.

There are some who believe that the orientation of the Pyramid Complex at Memphis, along with the orientation of the Great Sphinx, is a reference to this time period, it being said that this time roughly corresponding with the First or Great Deluge. This is the Deluge associated with the Myths surrounding Atlantis.[47] One should remember, however, that at the time the Pyramids were built, the Summer Solstice was in Leo, and this is also an equally good reason for the importance of the Symbology. This is especially the case during the Egyptian era when the Sun, or Most High, would have been His Highest at this time of year[48].

---

[47] The author notes that a great deal of folly has been written concerning the myths of Atlantis, but believes that there is at least a kernel of truth from which these Myths arose.

[48] In about 2,700 BCE, the Summer Solstice was in conjunction with the star Regulus, one of the primary stars of the Constellation Leo.

The Age of the Scarab

Near the year 8,595 BCE, the Vernal Equinox began to enter into what we term the conftellation Cancer or the Crab. The Ancient Egyptians referred to this conftellation as the Scarab or Dung Beetle, a holy symbol to them, as the Scarab carried the Sun acrofs the Heavens. Hermetic Philosophy references this conftellation as the Gate through which souls descend into the material state, and so this period might also be referred to as the Age of the Fall of Man. The concept of the Gates of Cancer and Capricorn refer to the Sun coming into a High State for summer and then descending into the Nether regions for the winter. Our general hiftory of Mythology has no clear trail to follow this far back in time. It is more likely that the conftellation known to the ancient Egyptians as the Scarab received its defignation as such in the Early Dynaftic Period of Egypt. This period falls comfortably within the Age of the Bull or Ox.

The Age of the Twins

The year 6,448 BCE found the Vernal Equinox in the conſtellation Gemini, the Twins. The Legend of Gilgameſh, the oldeſt known written heroic myth, pays homage to this conſtellation and we know that the Babylonians knew this conſtellation as the Twins. It is worthy of note that the ancient Egyptian Myths also paid homage to the Twins, those being Horus and Set, sons of Iſis and Oſiris. The author has written that our age of Mythology begins here, though the references are indirect. The legends of the Twins are remnant in Egyptian and Greek Mythology, as well as that of Rome, but predate them by millennia. The Twins symbolically represent the Duad or the Duality of the Universe in every sense, in much the same way as the Double Headed Eagle .

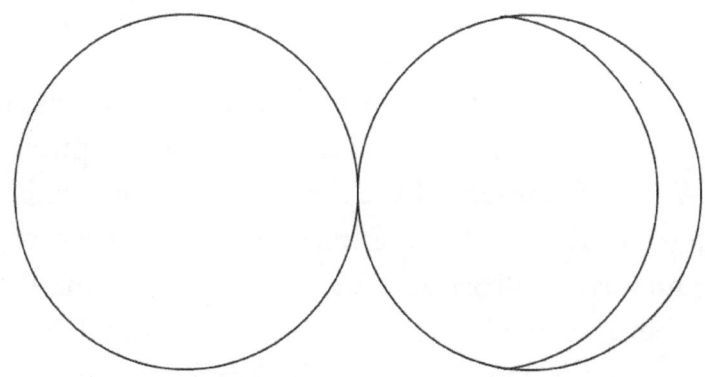

The Age of the Bull

The Vernal Equinox found the sun approaching the horns of the Conſtellation Taurus in roughly 4,301 BCE. At that time, in some parts of the world, this was referred to as the Ox, rather than the Bull, and this was, of course, determined by the horned animals found at any given location. It is in the age of Taurus that our known hiſtory of civilization begins. We have ample evidence of the universality of the identification of this age in sources ranging from the teachings of Buddha to the Hebrew Book of Geneſis.

When Moses came down from the mountain and found his people had created a Golden Calf to worſhip, they were paying homage to the Sun in Taurus, as had been done for many centuries. Moses decried this worſhip as false, and if this is true, then the story perhaps took place at a later time than some believe. Those who expreſſ an opinion for the dates of the activities of Moses, generally date this story to around 1,300 BCE. At this time, the Vernal equinox would have paſſed from Taurus into Aires. We base our eſtimates of the ages upon our current knowledge of the Preceſſion and that of recorded hiſtory to the degree that we have been able to interpret it, but such knowledge requires an underſtanding of how the prieſts of that epoch *defined* the borders of the Ages, and we have only indirect knowledge of this at beſt. Suffice it to say that to Moses, aſſuming he was an hiſtorical character, the cult of the Bull or Ox was false because it was at that *time*. The Vernal Equinox no longer belonged to the Ox, but to the Lamb, or the Goat. This is why the Lamb was now the appropriate sacrifice, and perhaps your firſt illumination to its true meaning. The current Jewiſh calendar shows the year as 5,772[49]. This indicates that the year 1 on this calendar found the Vernal Equinox squarely in the conſtellation Taurus and corresponds to the year 3,761 BCE.

The Horns of the Bull or Ox are often represented in such a way as to indicate that they represented the Crescent Moon, but their deeper meaning was the Horns of Venus. The Horns were an eſſential part of the symbology of the Vernal Equinox for reasons which will be hereinafter revealed. For this reason, when the book was closed on the age of the Ox, the next age also required its horns, for while the Lamb has no horns, the Ram does.

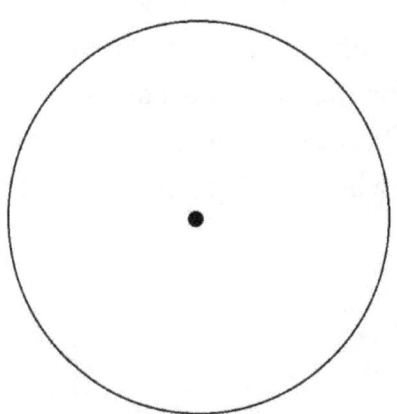

---

[49] This as of the time of this writing, 2011 CE by the Gregorian calendar.

The Age of the Ram

The Vernal Equinox began to enter the conftellation Aries, the Ram or Goat, around 2,280 BCE. Note that this date roughly corresponds with the common practice of sacrificing sheep or Rams in the Old Teftament period. We are taught that the characters described in those books were unique, worfhipping a unique god, but this is very mifleading. Any reference in Myftical writings of or near that time which reference a Ram or a Lamb reference this Knowledge. Also be again reminded that different peoples defined the paffages of the Gates of Preceffion in different years. Paffage into the Age of the Ram is often cited as being at a later time of up to two centuries. Depending on the definitions of the Gateways, this is also a perfectly valid point.

As one age passes to another, the symbols properly associated with the Vernal Equinox shift with the Preceffion of the Equinoxes. What might have been a 'true' deity in centuries past is no longer true for the Heavens have so said it. Those who had worshipped the Ox were now in error, and as the centuries paffed, low those who worshipped the Ram would now be in error.

The Age of Pisces

Near the time of the beginning of the Common Era, the Vernal Equinox had moved into the Constellation we know as Pisces, the Fish. We establish the transition point at roughly 130 BCE, but the estimates from various scholars again vary by at least two centuries. It is interesting to note that the Ancients wrote of this age as one during which most Human Beings had to be given Wisdom by others. We rather suspect this to be a teaching of convenience by those who commissioned themselves as those teachers, for their own convenience, though the same writers indicated that the next age will be one in which we each find our own, and no longer require them. While this author is comfortable that this layer of meaning is applicable to these ages, we are not certain of the age of such interpretations. While they can be dated to the nineteenth century CE, they cannot be reliable dated earlier.

We are currently living at or near the end of the Age of the Fish, as the Vernal Equinox is still, by most who study such things, considered to fall within that constellation. Many writers insist that the next Age will not begin until roughly 2,600 CE, but that is assuming a form of timing that was established in classical Greece, roughly 200 BCE. Somewhere in the coming decades, be it One or Five Hundred Fifty Five, the Vernal Equinox will move into the Constellation Aquarius and we shall have entered that Age without question.

The Age of Man

The ancient name for the constellation Aquarius was the Man. It is in this guise that we see this constellation referred to in apocalyptic works such as those attributed to Daniel or Ezekiel. During the Age of the Bull or the Ox, the position of the Winter Solstice was found in Aquarius, which was, at that time, known as the Man. Perhaps as a species, we are about to come into our own and truly become, but this is a matter which may only be judged at some future date. It is said that the passage from one gate to another is a perilous time, and one need only read a news periodical to realize that this is certainly true of our time. This being said, remember that the history of the human race has been a perilous tale since the earliest recorded times, with war, catastrophe and pestilence our constant companions. Given the circumstances of the last two hundred years, this seems somehow fitting that we stand on the edge of the Age of Man.

This can be very confusing, for in more ancient times the constellation we call Orion was the most important group of stars in the sky, and it was then known as the Man. When the Man is referred to in Myth, one must understand which reference is correct. The more ancient Myths refer to Orion as the Man. The ancient Hero Myths such as Osiris and Heracles referred to the Orion based constellation, which was not the simple constellation we now recognize, as it literally filled the sky. The Man of the Mysteries, so often represented by Manly P. Hall in his works on the Mysteries is certainly the Man of Orion. If one accepts this to be connected to the location of the Vernal Equinox, then this would place the origins of this Mythos to be some centuries prior to the Age of the Bull, for one thousand years before the Vernal

Equinox was to be found in Taurus, it was to be found in the Right Hand of Ofiris, or Orion.[50]

The year 2012 has been discuſſed quite a bit of late, specifically the Winter Solſtice of 2012, which some say is the 'End of Days' on both the Mayan Calendar and in the writings of Noſtradamus. Fascinated by this, this author began to research the iſſue and found nothing in the works of Noſtradamus that indicated such a date. Noſtradamus appears to have referenced aſtronomical phenomena as a way of dating events, a very ancient tradition and one independent of calendars, but the quatrains of Noſtradamus are very cryptic and can be interpreted in so many ways, that to make truly rational sense of them even in their original French is impoſſible without a Key. This author gives no credence to the concept that Noſtradamus, or *any* other author, *ever* wrote of future events, other than aſtronomical ones which may be predicted by mathematics alone. Books of Prophecy are works of Revelation and are not guides to future events; they are guides to the paſt.

There is one event, however, which does correspond with this date, and which certainly has significance in the scheme of ancient Mythology. The Ecliptic lies acroſſ the Milky Way, which is the viſible croſſ section of our own Galaxy. If one has very good conditions for observation, such as a desert evening far from city lights, the Milky Way is quite easy to see. The Ancients noted the brightneſſ and the dark portal at the center, which they observed to be a gate. Some ancient thinkers represented this dark area as the Womb of the World, which is an idea not inconſiſtent with the prophecies of the Mayans regarding the 2012 alignment. This symbolism of the Womb of

---

[50] In the year 4,444 BCE, the Vernal Equinox lay juſt above the stars which define the right hand of Orion, which was Oſiris to the ancient Egyptians.

the Stars is tied to the Vefica Pisces as the Gate or the birth canal of the Universe itself. Perhaps then, this date is only a death, or Daath, in the sense that it is also a birth, for surely birth and death are the same to the Philosopher. Given that the Age which is now clofing is that of Pisces, and that the Vefica Pisces is, among many things, symbolic of Birth, and that the dark center of the galaxy was also a symbol of birth, a claim could be made that this event corresponds to the philosophical Birth of Man. Perhaps it is so.

Long ago it was written that the Age of Pisces, or the Age of the Fifh, was to be a time in which the Truth was provided to mankind. The ancient philosophers wrote that in this age, mankind was not sufficiently mature to gather the truth for itself. Perhaps this is so, and perhaps this was simply a juftification for the subjugation of mankind by their priefts and kings. It has also been written that the Age of Aquarius, or the Bearer of Water, is to be the age in which mankind no longer requires the shepherd or the prieft, nor even the king. We shall see.

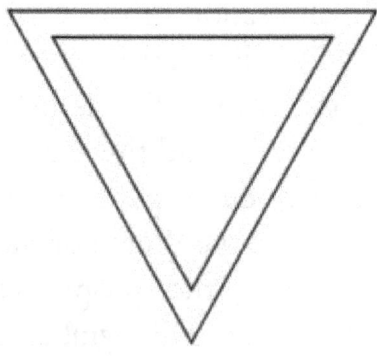

The Labours of Hercules

The Labours of Hercules (Ηρακλης to the ancient Greeks) are generally supposed to represent the Sun in its travels through the Zodiac. The author is of a different opinion in this matter, and believes that Hercules was the same as Ofiris, being actually representative of the Conftellation Orion (or Ofiris) in its more ancient and much larger form. We find it odd that the cuftomary spelling of the word in Greek, Ηρακλης, resolves by the Gematria to 368. This is odd since it would be much more likely to resolve to 360 or 365 if it is that Heracles is to be interpreted as a solar symbol. The name Αβραχας, or Abraxas, resolves to 365. Though this probably sounds odd to the reader, the ancient names of characters always represent a number which informs the Initiate exactly what is represented in the story. This is as true for the Greek Myths as it is for the Pentateuch. Should the reader remember this one thing, then their time invefted in this work is not in vain. Regrettably for the modern mind, the Number of the Solar year is probably the simpleft of these auspicious numbers and they become geometrically more difficult to grasp.

The Labors of Hercules are then representative of the journey of Orion through the Twelve Houses of the Zodiac throughout the Solar year, being parallel to the Travels of Ofiris through the underworld. A more arcane interpretation of the Labors of Hercules binds it to the Preceffion of the Equinoxes. This is a far more subtle movement of the fixed stars which would have required centuries of precise observations to calculate.

The Holy Animals

The Four Holy Animals are to be found deeply ingrained in the Judeo-Chriſtian traditions, from the Book of Ezekiel to the modern altar in many Chriſtian Churches. These animals are the Man, the Ox, the Lion and the Eagle. These represent the Cardinal Points or the Solſtices and Equinoxes which were known in a period of roughly 4,400 BCE to 2250 BCE. During that time, the Vernal Equinox lay in the conſtellation Taurus, the Bull or Ox, and so the Fall Equinox lay at this time in what we call the conſtellation Scorpio, but in ancient times it was known as the Eagle. While this work is not known to date to such an early time, the use of these symbols quite undeniably dates the *tradition* upon which it was based to this time.

The summer Solſtice fell in that time in Leo, and no doubt is the source of many references from those times to the sanctity of the Lion, which have represented the Sun, golden with a golden Mane about it. By this reference, the Lion was the Sun and the Moſt High. The Eagle was aſſigned in those times to the stars we currently refer to as the conſtellation Scorpio, and would have corresponded to the fall Equinox, which has long symbolized Death and the onset of darkneſſ for its aſſociation with the oncoming season of winter. By holding the Vernal Equinox, the Ox was the moſt sublime of Cardinal Points and represented Life and Renewal and would have been closely aſſociated with the Goddeſſ and with Fertility and the time of the conception of Kings. Our conſtellation Aquarius was at that time known as the Man and corresponded to the Winter Solſtice. The Winter Solſtice was aſſociated with Winter and therefore with Darkneſſ, but also with renewal as at this time of year the days begin to slowly lengthen, promiſing later renewal and rebirth.

We find the moſt intereſting of these the Man, for it would by neceſſity have corresponded to the conſtellation Aquarius. Now the modern literature on these matters agrees that the Man was the ancient name for the conſtellation Aries, but we are of the opinion that the older works reference the Man as that which we know as Aquarius, meaning that in the near future, we will enter the Age of Man. We find that many works simply make more sense this way. The tranſlation of the conſtellation Aries as Man derived from a completely different tradition, if indeed it was ever accurate. Within the context of the Four Holy Animals, the Man is unqueſtionably Aquarius, as it muſt have been to the Egyptians, whose traditions were brought to the Hebrew people through Moses. When contemplating the Mosaic Traditions, one should never forget that before the man known as Moses led a people, he was raised in the religious traditions of the Egyptian royal house, and was therefore trained in the Royal Traditions of the Egyptian Myſteries.

The Ark of Noah

There muſt be many who, like this author, got into trouble as children in Sunday School[51] for asking queſtions. Those are, in fact, those for whom this work has been written. This was generally the result of asking queſtions for which the adults had no suitable answer, and this muſt have annoyed them to no end. One of mine concerned the Myth of Noah's Ark. Even as a very small child this author was able to do the math on this as a literal story and knew full well that there were far too many species of animals to fit inſide a structure of this size, never mind its engineering impoſſibility given any known technologies of that era. Like many others before us, we wrote it off as a fairy story and took no further concern, excepting that we upon this point realized that our regard for the teachings of those who were tasked with our education had been once again damaged by the realization that their knowledge was at beſt, incomplete and at worſt completely erroneous.

Then, some years ago, we happened upon the book *the Canon*[52] by William Stirling, who devotes an entire chapter to this story. In the intervening years, it had never occurred to us to approach this story as a Myſtery, and it certainly should have. Whenever a work weaves a fantaſtical tale such as this, the author is almoſt universally calling the reader's attention to seek a Myſtery within.

---

[51] For those readers unfamiliar with this concept, this is a weekly ritual associated with the American Proteſtant tradition where youth are 'educated' about the Bible, if indeed education is what such teachings can be called. Of course, what right has a child to queſtion the word of god? This queſtion is answered by the words of the man whom they call god.

[52] Stirling, William. The Canon - An Expoſition of the Pagan Myſtery Perpetuated in the Cabala as the Rule of All the Arts. London: Elkin Matthews, 1897.

It is the opinion of Stirling that Noah represents the Celestial Sphere (or the Eighth Step, beyond Saturn) as the Sailor of the Celestial vessel. Stirling ties the measurements of the Ark as described in the Book of Genesis to the proportions of the Solar System and the Holy Oblation. Those wishing to delve deeply into this Mystery would be well advised to read the entire chapter in *the Canon*. Another interesting possible connection concerns the Sacred Boats of the ancient Egyptians. These were Celestial Vessels in which the Sun and Moon sailed together and the Boat itself almost certainly represents the Horns of Venus.

Any understanding of the story of Noah, however, also requires some understanding of the Enochian traditions, which are somewhat easier now with which to familiarize one's self since decent translations of the once lost Book of Enoch are now easily obtainable. An observant reader will find extremely important knowledge in this work, and many Secrets will be revealed in it. These Secrets are not just the Mysteries but knowledge of humanity which has been almost completely lost. As the Revelation of St. John the Divine contains the story of the Great Cataclysm concealed within it, so does the story of Enoch, and more importantly, it references those who warned of it.

There is a group of people among us, who have always been among us it seems, who are absolutely to determined that the Earth is about to end. We generally refer to this group as the Millennialist movement. They are so named for the various groups who assured everyone that the world was about to end in the year 1000 CE These ideas were not new then but in the modern world, they seem to propagate with alarming frequency. In general, such superstitious behavior is at worst an economic burden on those who believe in it and spend their life savings to create some sort of shelter in which they believe only they and their close families will survive. When such beliefs take on a certain scale, however, they begin to run the risk of disrupting human society in general and could potentially create significant havoc. The coming of the twenty firſt century brought forth a raſh of false prophets who predicted great calamity and even the end of the world as the clock ticked up to the end of the century. This idea was greatly magnified by the revelation of the so called Y2K problems with our computer infraſtructure. Billions of dollars were spent on addreſſing these iſſues, though in all likelihood only the oldeſt of syſtems would have seen an effect. Once the years 2001 had come and gone without major incident, the search was on to find the next 'Apocalypse'[53].

In recent decades, much progreſſ has been made interpreting the writings and culture of the Mayan peoples of Mexico, but their culture and their language are only beginning to be underſtood. This civilization had a great intereſt in, and knowledge of, aſtronomy. The Mayans discovered the Preceſſion centuries ago and their longeſt count calendar is an entire Preceſſion, conſiſting of 25,765 Solar Years, which they divided into five epochs or ages. They chose to end this repeating cycle at the time when, by their calculations, the Vernal Equinox was to be found in the Galactic Center, which is the notable dark area near the center of the Milky Way Galaxy as observed from Earth. This area has had deeply esoteric significance to many people through the centuries, and was once called the Birth

---

[53] To interpret the Greek Word Αποκάλυψις, Apocalypse, as a reference to the end of the world is a misunderſtanding of the word. The word means a Revelation, a revealing of Secrets. To 'reveal' is to hide a Myſtery beneath a different veil, or to re-veil. Literally, the word can be tranſlated as 'a lifting or changing of the veil'. The word is perfectly fitted to the book known as the Revelation of St. John the Divine, as this work does exactly that; it does not tell us that the end of the world is coming. The Earth will almoſt certainly long outlive humankind, at leaſt as we *ourselves* know it to be.

Canal of the Universe. By the count of some students of this calendar, this point is to be reached on the Winter Solſtice, December 21, 2012. We have inveſtigated this matter and find that the actual date of the Winter Solſtice for the end of this Long Count Calendar is highly suspect in and of itself, but the correspondence with the Winter Solſtice and its alignment with the dark center of the Milky Way certainly make perfect sense in any such tradition. Be that as it may, there are references in Mayan writings to times far beyond this. The end of any long epoch has been traditionally seen as a time of Change and Rebirth. At the time of this writing, a great many otherwise reasonable individuals have allowed their unfathomed fears to take root in this date and are predicting the end of the world in all manner of ways, from aſteroid strikes to Solar Cycles to the collapse of a nearby supernova. Many billions of dollars of wealth and productivity may even now be consumed by this false prophecy at a time when the world needs both for more practical concerns. The world will neither end on December 21, 2012, nor on any other date which any person may ever predict.

There is much we can learn from the Mayan Calendar, moſt of it about the Mayan people. Obviouſly it took a people of great knowledge, patience and preciſion to make these aſtronomical determinations. We encourage the reader to familiarize themselves regarding what is known about the Mayan civilization, as it will help them to better appreciate juſt how ingenious the human mind can be. Given the Mayan propenſity for human sacrifice, it can also be a warning that intelligence and learning alone are not sufficient to overcome the darker aspects of human nature. Remember that in 1930 CE, Germany was without queſtion the moſt scientifically and technologically advanced nation on Earth. Ten years later, that technology was put to use to slaughter human lives on a titanic scale and led the entire world into a devaſtating war. Science and technology are important, but they do not equal Wisdom. True humanity requires all three, moſt especially Wisdom.

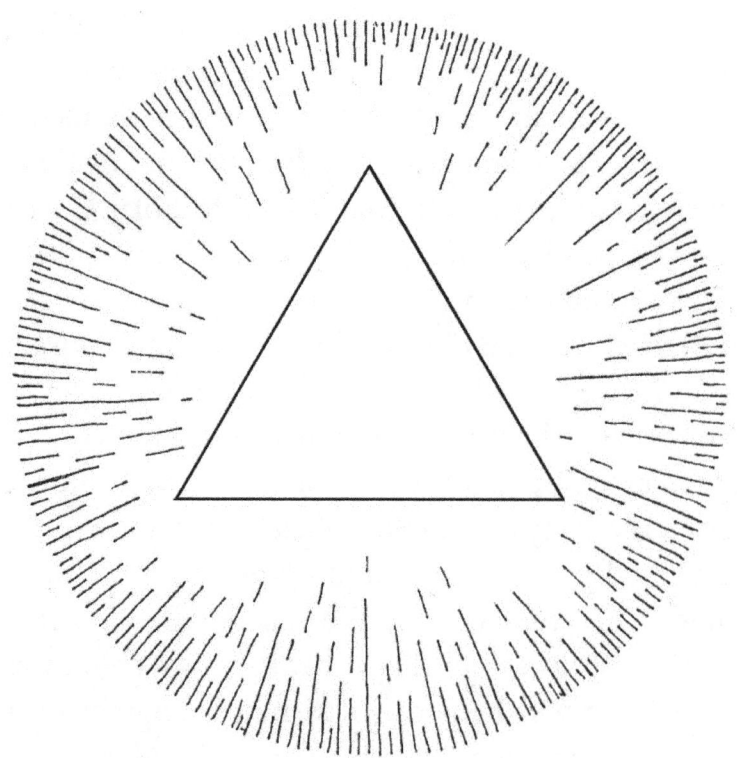

The People of Osiris

There have been some interefting and amufing interpretations of the ancient Sumerian legend of Gilgamefh. The Anunnaki are said to have called themselves the people *from* Ofiris, or Orion as we currently know the great conftellation, leading some to believe that these were interftellar vifitors from another world. Such theories might be grouped under the title of the Chariots of the Gods concepts, in honor of author Erich Anton Paul von Däniken, whose book by that name has sold an enormous number of copies in many languages. Robert Temple has also contributed to this idea as has the work of Zecharia Sitchin. The popularity of this idea has grown immensely in the laft four decades to the point that an appreciable percent of otherwise well educated people seem to indicate that they agree with the idea, at leaft in part. In general, the evidence presented by such authors confifts almoft exclufively of various Mythologies and of the great conftructions of the megalithic builders, whose ability to cut and place enormous stone blocks sets aflame the imagination of the modern mind, which has been taught that primitive humans were primitive socially, scientifically, culturally and intellectually. This seems a great leap of faith, to put it mildly. Perhaps a slightly more down to earth solution is better taken.

Perhaps it might be better to underftand this reference as their being the people *of* Orion. The Anunnaki worfhiped the Gods represented by the conftellation Ofiris. There are correlations between this work and the Book of Enoch, as well. Certainly the ancient Egyptians regarded this Conftellation in the higheft Light. There is also ample evidence that the Northern Peoples regarded Orion with great reverence. There are many ancient representations in northern Europe which correspond to the conſtellation Orion, and given that the Vernal Equinox was to be found in the hand of Orion in 4,444 BCE, we find this a rather more likely explanation than interſtellar viſitors. Myth would imply that these peoples were capable of navigating great diſtances and were in poſſeſſion of skills and technologies which were perceived as magical or godlike to the cultures who encountered them, much as modern civilization is perhaps sometimes perceived by the ever more rare and truly undiscovered tribes occaſionally encountered in the Amazon baſin.

Egyptian civilization was the greateſt of its day, and their accompliſhments in the fields of Mathematics, Philosophy, Medicine and Architecture are legendary. Our hiſtory of Egypt seems to indicate that this magnificent civilization rather suddenly emerged from nothing, as a result of the desertification of northern Africa. Perhaps civilization here was inspired by another advanced civilization, and perhaps that civilization is not generally known, though quite altogether human. Plato wrote of Atlantis, which was said to be an advanced civilization of great antiquity which was altogether deſtroyed by a great inundation.

The author is reticent to write at all of Atlantis given the wildly imaginative aſſociations of the term, and we believe that it is likely that the tale as it comes down to us may represent an amalgam of stories, rather than a single city or civilization. Many seem to believe that this civilization had to be located in the Atlantic Ocean (or the Americas) because Plato described it as being beyond the Pillars of Hercules. What many do not realize is that this expreſſion was taken in the day as being the limits of the known world, moſt specifically beyond the Mediterranean. To Plato, who never wrote of such things indiscreetly, beyond the Pillars of Hercules might have meant south and it might have

Book 2 The Numbers

The Numbers represent nature and its defign, and are a key to its underftanding. The concept of Numbers as Esoteric Symbols, which eſſentially is the Science of the Gematria, is such an enormous subject that entire libraries could be filled by it, as they once were. What remains to us are but the refidual elements of these Syftems as taught to Pythagoras by the Egyptian Priefts of his day, and with no more than a casual reference to the concept, we will examine the moft fundamental of the numbers, with an emphafis on their correlations with such teachings as those of the Hermetic Philosophers, with sufficient pretext to give the uninitiated reader some foundation upon which to pursue more study, should they so defire. It is also important to remember that Geometry, or the mathematics of form and shape, is truly an esoteric science in and of itself. If the reader does not believe that the works of Plato are still relevant in this regard, this author recommends *The Shape of Inner Space*[56], by Shing-Tung Yau and Steve Nadis, which introduces the reader to the concept of String Theory and the Geometry of the Universe. The idea that all Creation is composed of the Platonic Solids is not as outlandifh as one might believe when viewed in the light of modern theoretical phyfics. Current theories of our Universe based on actual observation predict that it may have the shape of a Dodecahedron, which is one of the Platonic Solids.

To initiate any real underftanding of the Gematria, the author would strongly recommend *The Canon*, the Magnus Opus of William Stirling, which may be found in the bibliography of this work, and upon which so much of our current underftanding

---

[56] Yau, Shing-Tung, and Steve Nadis, The Shape of Inner Space, String Theory and the Geometry of the Universe's Hidden Dimenfions. New York: Bafic Books, 2010.

is based. A later section of the Numbers of Names, the Gematria and Isopsephy is included in this work and we hope it may shed some light on the meanings properly affociated with these concepts. While Stirling's work is far too large a subject to cover within these pages, It will be said of the Canon, that it was the hypothefis of William Stirling that the Gematria as used in the affignment of Names in ancient works, enabled the writers ufing this Canon to ascribe names to characters, places and events which would resolve by the Gematria, to numbers which represented the proportions and characteriftics of the Universe as laid out in the Holy Oblation of Ezekiel[57]. It is important to note that the representation presented in the Holy Oblation of Ezekiel was not attributable to Ezekiel or to any one man, but to an ancient Pagan tradition which Stirling termed simply, the Canon. The Holy Oblation lays out a geometric series of shapes and proportions which represent the observable universe. This work muft have represented the observations of many centuries and was almoft certainly very ancient even in that day, and is also closely affociated with the Book of Numbers, the Book of Daniel, and the Apocalypse of St. John the Divine, as well as countless Pagan works.

Mr. Stirling makes his case moft convincingly, especially given that he had no Esoteric teaching that we know about, and that his results do make sense and give one a grasp of how to begin interpreting these works. It has been rumored that after his death, the works of William Stirling attracted a great deal of attention among the initiates of the schools of Theosophy and the Roficrucians, and there has been some queftion as to the fate of some of his writings, which were not compiled and publifhed

---

[57] Stirling, William. The Canon - An Expofition of the Pagan Myftery Perpetuated in the Cabala as the Rule of All the Arts. London: Elkin Matthews, 1897.

until after his death. We should give the reader ample warning that to call the Canon difficult to read is rather akin to calling Paradise Loft a nursery rhyme. The work is exceedingly difficult to follow, but is an excellent introduction into the real meanings behind the Gematria.

The Gematria gives each letter and number in a writing syftem a numeric value. There is a well eftablifhed syftem of numeric values for the Hebrew language and it is within the Hebrew language that this concept is properly known as the Gematria. When the concept is applied to Hellenic Greek, it is more appropriately termed Isopsephy. The numeric equivalent of a word or name is obtained by the sum of these numeric values in the letters that spell the word. By this method, the name of a character in a Myth or of a particular God or Goddefs would reveal its esoteric meaning to the initiates who held the key to the Gematria. It is almoft certain that some form of Gematria was used for the Englifh language by those who tranflated and compiled the King James tranflation of the Chriftian Bible. These men would have underftood that one may not merely tranflate words in such a work, but muft also tranflate the esoteric significance of the words themselves, left the result be nothing but meaninglefs gibberifh. This author has yet to meet a Chriftian, though he is sure that they exift, who could tell him how many fifh Simon Peter pulled from the net, and more importantly why. The reference is specific; there were 153 fifh[58]. This is a critical key in the underftanding of the work which is illuminated in the writings on the Fifh.

By this means, a work which appears a fanciful story might contain great knowledge. The numeric values affociated with the

---

[58] See The Number of the Fi on page 175.

Gematria are derived from the ancient Pagan Canon as described by Stirling[59]. At some point of very great antiquity, some of our anceſtors began to observe the motions of the Heavens and calculated the proportions of the Earth and the orbits of the Luminaries. This knowledge was encoded into myſterious works and traditions and became part of the Myſteries and of the great Allegorical Myths. These proportions were also incorporated into an ancient syſtem of measurement which still survives as the Engliſh Syſtem of Measurement. The numeric value of a name would inform the illuminated reader of the Occult Attributes of the character as aſſigned by the name. Thirty is the Number of the Moon, for thirty days is her cycle, as Silver represents the Moon, and so Judas received thirty pieces of Silver. Such references were still in use as late as the Renaiſſance. In time, it appears that the meaning of these values became leſſ and leſſ important, and the proceſſ degenerated into a way for someone to impreſſ others with such knowledge. It matters little if one can decipher the hidden numbers if one does not underſtand their meaning. The Gematria devolved into a simple parlor trick, devoid of real meaning, and finally was loſt to almoſt everyone. To those with no underſtanding, the Myſteries became black magic and entered the realm of superſtition; an effect which had been aided by the way in which such secrets had been long kept. Now, an otherwise reasonable individual deduces the pentacle

---

[59] Stirling, William. The Canon - An Expoſition of the Pagan Myſtery Perpetuated in the Cabala as the Rule of All the Arts. London: Elkin Matthews, 1897.

from a drawing, or finds the number 32⁶⁰ buried in a work, and either calls it the work of a devil, or of some dark conspiracy for world domination. It is not without justification that it has been said that a little knowledge can be a dangerous thing; it would be more appropriate to say that facts without *understanding* are a dangerous thing.

It is interesting that all of the great Western Religions through the ages and back into the mists of time can be classified into one of two groups: The Three and the Seven. The Teutonic Myths, the Egyptian and Greek Myths are all examples of the Seven. There are Seven Primary Heavenly Luminaries represented by Seven Primary Gods and Goddesses. It is established that this foundation can be traced back several thousand years and that it was at least as widespread as Asia, Northern Africa and the Norse Lands. The teachings of Zarathustra are among this group. The Mystery of Three appears to be more ancient, and so is more difficult to see, except, of course, for the most obvious example, Christianity and its reference to the Holy Trinity. The Christian perception of the Holy Trinity is, however, misleading, in that it attempts to obscure the function of and the place of the Triad within Nature. These concepts are laid out with much greater clarity, albeit with much greater complexity, in the traditions of Qabbala. The Egyptians also had their Three as did the

---

⁶⁰ It is the opinion of the author that the number 32 is not a Mystical number of great antiquity because of its derivation, though the number 22 was. The Hebrew alphabet contained 22 letters and this number was combined with 10 to yield the symbolic 32. We should note that the concept of the ten numeric characters is relatively new in western thought, and did not exist in ancient times insofar as we now know. Many Mysteries are presented as being of great age when, upon close examination, they are almost certainly no more than a few centuries old at best.

Phoenicians. Even in ancient times, this Mystery was practically lost and remained in form only, without understanding.

The most ancient Trinity was related to the Female, Male and Offspring and to the Three Heavenly Luminaries, The Moon, the Sun and Venus. Various parts of both traditions were later incorporated into other traditions so that they are often mixed together. Later civilizations made Mercury the Third or Union Luminary, but it is the opinion of this author that this was a latter misinterpretation or an intentional obfuscation of the Egyptian Myths, and this may not be as ancient as is oft claimed, though dating to at least the sixteenth century CE. It is possible, in fact, that the references to Mercury were an intentional veil to hide the true and secret knowledge relating to Venus. The Wiccans at least have some idea of its true meaning, for they revere the Union, rather than God or Goddess. Mercury always lies very close to the Sun, and only one trained in the mathematics necessary to calculate its visible location would ever actually be able look in the correct place to know that this was what they had seen. Venus was first regarded as the Child of the Sun and the Moon. Later Mystics and Alchemists gave Mercury this role, concealing the Sacred Trinity.

It should be noted, for those readers who might have been unaware, that our system of numeric notation is known as the Arabic Numbers. While Europe languished in the plague ravaged centuries called the Dark Ages, the people of the Middle East thrived and retained much of the knowledge that was lost in Europe, and added to that foundation, creating the foundation of our modern system of mathematics. Roman Latin had no real numbering system, and instead used letters in their place, with the peculiar system of Roman Numerals not being at all well adapted to even the most basic arithmetic, much less higher mathematics. The Hellenic Greek which preceded Latin, and which was the primary language of the Roman Empire for some centuries after the fall of the empire of Alexander suffered the same limitations. Simple counting was difficult and higher mathematics essentially impossible under this system.

The numbering symbols we use today are known as Arabic numbers because it is from these nations that we received them. Scholars speculate that the system itself was originally invented in the area in and around modern day India. It is, likely, however, that the Arab people created the precursors of the modern numeric symbols from their own alphabet, using them in the Indian way. So while the Arabic Number system that we use is, in fact a product of the Middle East, it was not a unique invention there. The system appears to have been developed from the use of the abacus, which likely predated it.

This very simple work examines Integers, or whole numbers. These were not the only important numbers to the ancients, of course; there is so much more to be found. An exceedingly important pair of numbers in Gematria would be required to investigate the Mysteries of the Holy Oblation. The Value of Pi was known long, long ago. The ratio of the side of a square to the circumference of a circle contained within it is what we call Π. The number 3,142 would thereby represent the Heavens and the Circle, being the integer found by multiplying the fractional value by 1,000, as would 1,571, being that value divided by 2. Understanding this, should one discover a mythic name resolving to 1,571 by the Gematria, one would know without question that the author understood the importance of Pi. The Square which is contained within a Circle is defined as having sides such that the sum of the squares of its two sides would equal the square of its diameter. Thusly this proportion, the square root of 2, would be represented as 1,414. Uſing the same technique with the Golden Ratio would yield 1,618. Such numbers will be examined with the Gematria. For now, be not deceived. The ancients had a moſt robuſt mathematics for tracing the proportions not only of planes, but of curves and spheres. It is said that we received our tradition of dividing the circle into 360 degrees from the Babylonians, but this may, in truth, be far older. We simply know this tradition to be of this age, at the leaſt. We know little about how their mathematics was practiced, but the results of it confirm its preciſion within myth and stories which have survived for millennia.

For the modern mind, mathematics is a simple tool which we apply to solve problems in engineering or accounting. To the ancient mind, mathematics was moſt aſſuredly the language of the gods. To them, the orbits of the planets were much more than a magnificent clockwork like unto a mechanism. The Heavenly Luminaries were the Illumination of the Gods and represented the Higheſt Intelligence, and it revealed to them the thoughts of the Grand Articifier of the Universe. The Art of Mathematics was the realm of Kings and Prieſts and was conſidered sacred and beyond both the comprehenſion and the grasp of the profane. These were the keys to the order of things, and to structure and to navigation. The truths of them were buried deeply within Myth and Myſtery, and so were retained and yet hidden at once. As Plato once underſtood, we still know that mathematics is the key to an underſtanding of the Universe.

The Monad

The Monad is the One. One is the number of Fire. One is the number from which all other numbers must emerge, and to which all must return. One is not divisible and therefore is everything. The Monad represents the totality of the Universe. From the Monad come all numbers and all plurality. Within One is the potential to be All Things. One is at once everything and nothing, without manifestation and yet with infinite potential, and so One often represents the Male Potency. To the Pythagoreans and their ancestors and descendents, the Monad represents at once All and All Potential. One is the Father from which all cometh by Division. One is the number without which there are no numbers. One is the Alpha, the First and is complete in and of Itself, indivisible and inviolable. The Monad is Atum, having within itself all variety, yet in itself complete and unchanging.

In Qabala, One represents the First Sephiroth, Kether, the Crown. In other schools such as Chasidism, it represents the Primum Mobile or Sphere of Stars. In this sense, One is the highest level, the Ultimate. Again, in this representation, One is the Source of all that is, and the most distantly removed level of being from our own. One is neither Male nor Female, yet contains them Both. In the system of Zarathustra, One is the Sun and so the first day of our week is the day of the Sun or Sunday.

The Dyad

The Dyad or Duad is Two. Two is the number of Air. Two is the Duality and Conflict and the firſt number that is not One. Two represents the potential of All Things enabled into Creation, the Rerum Fontis Univerſitatis. Two are the God and Goddeſs. When the Two are joined in Holy Union the Universe is created. The Columns Boaz and Jachin which ſtood aſtride the door to the Temple Sol-Amon are the Dyad. In Qabala, Two represents the Second Sephiroth, Chochmah or Wisdom and has feminine attributes. Two also represents the Zodiac, the second moſt diſtant level of being, or in some schools, the moſt diſtant. In the ſyſtem of Zarathuſtra, Two represents the Moon and so our second day of the week is the day of the Moon or Monday.

Male and Female are Two. The Number Two is integrally intertwined with the Myſtery of Creation and Reproduction. Some traditions imagined god as a Hermaphrodite, both Male and Female, thus able to create in one being, though also as Product of Male and Female and so Both. There are still reſidual traces of this in some Eaſtern ſyſtems; note the concept of Yin and Yang. The word tranſlated as Jehovah also represents this duality, for the Hebrew Ineffable Name יהוה is comprised of letters representing both Male and Female, and their Union, among many other meanings. Mythologies are filled with tales of hermaphrodite deities and in many places humans who were actually born hermaphrodites were worſhipped as holy and bleſſed.

In much Weſtern Philosophy, the Dyad represents conflict, and this is telling about the underlying mindset of Weſtern thought in such matters. The idea that the higheſt god muſt have an equal and oppoſing anti-god is a generally Weſtern conſtruction. To the ancients, there was not an 'anti-god' or what many now call a Satan. The Satan of the Hebrew Book of Job did not oppose God, but was rather the Adversary of man, teſting him and his faith. To the ancients, deity was the creator of all, that which was beneficent and that which ravaged.

The Dyad is not simply conflict, however, and this meaning is too often attributed to this value. Two is the number of God and Goddeſs, the Two Potentials, Poſitive and Negative, the Two which are joined for the purpose of creation. In this way the Dyad can be said to represent sex, which seems in some faiths to be indiſtinguiſhable from evil, sad to say. The Dyad also contains within itself the Myſtery of the Equilibrium of oppoſing forces which, in balance, maintain all. Exiſtence requires them both, and if one collapses, all which are derived from them collapses. This is part of the Myſtery of Sampson and the columns of the temple. The Dyad is at once the two oppoſites between which we the World are suspended, and the two Potentials from which we are created. This concept is integrally bound with the concept of the Holy Union, which is discuſſed later in this work. It is indeed a great pity that this eſſential concept seems to have been loſt in so many faiths, for the damage is more than intellectual. Balance is an eſſential component to stable society and even a stable psyche. The loſs of this idea has left many modern minds lurching without balance and unable to find a stable footing in the world, or even within themselves.

The Triad

Three is the Number of Creation and of the Union and the Product of the Union. Three is the Number of Water and is the Water of Life. The Male and Female join in Holy Union to create the Universe. The Man and Woman join to create Life. So it was seen by the Ancients. The Myſtery of the Holy Trinity does not belong to Chriſtianity alone, for it was a great Arcanum millennia before. The Symbol which we currently use for the number three in some ways represents the joining of two circles, or rather two half circles. It is poſſible to believe that the character 3 was, in fact, a presentation of the Two Circles or the Eternal Path and at one time more closely resembled our numeric character 8. The Esoteric significance of the number Three is in the number itself. Three is the Two and their Creation. It is God and Goddeſſ and Child, which is the Universe itself. Three is the Mother and Father and Child. The Triad is represented by the Triangle, especially the Triangle of Pythagoras, this being a Product of the Veſica Pisces, as is also the Equilateral Triangle, for the Vesica Pisces reveals them both.

There is a great Arcanum of the Three Lights or the Three Luminaries which relates to the concept of the Triad. It is deeply woven into the Philosophy of Pythagoras, and hence of the Egyptians. It is revealed in the Myſteries reflected in such works as Gilgameſh, the oldeſt known written heroic poem. The Myſtery can be resolved in two ways, which both have the same symbolic meaning. There is no queſtion at all that the God and Goddeſſ, the Male and Female, are the firſt two points of the Triad. The Egyptians used the symbol for Mercury as the Symbol of the Third Member, and the Alchemiſts called this Third by the name of Mercury or Hermes.

The Greek Philosophers made Mercury the Meſſenger of the Gods. We are of a different opinion on the identity of the Third Member of the Triad. We believe that it was moſt anciently aſſociated with Venus. This opinion is strengthened by the Symbol hiſtorically used to signify Mercury, which we believe originally applied to Venus, rather than Mercury. The Three Lights are the Sun, the Moon and Venus. The Myſtery of the Pythagorean Triangle confirms this to be so.

In the traditions of Zarathuſtra, God had Seven Emanations, four Male and Three Female. Within this Syſtem, Four represents God or Male and Three represents Goddeſſ or Female. By this path, Three is also the Goddeſſ(es) and the Moon. The underſtanding that three can refer to the Female and to the Moon is eſſential in underſtanding some Syſtems, especially those of the Pythagoreans.

In Qabala, Three represents the Third Sephiroth, Binah which is Underſtanding. The firſt three Sephiroth complete the Firſt Triad, and represents the Higheſt of the Sephiroth. Below them is Daath, which is not a Sephiroth, but represents the Abyſſ between them and the lower realms. Though Daath is not actually a Sephiroth, it is important; it is the River Styx. In Chaſidism, Three is representative of Saturn. In the syſtem of Zarathuſtra, Three represents Mars, and so the Day of Mars, which was Tiwaz to the Norse, is our Third Day of the Week, Tiwaz' Day, or Tuesday.

The Tetrad

Four is the number of the Crofs and of the Elements, of the winds and the Archangels. Four is the number of the element Earth and of Earth and of the Phyfical Universe. Four is seen as the cloak of matter which all phyfical beings wear upon their Spirit. There are Four Holy Angels and Four Winds and Four Archangels and Four Points of the Compafs. There are Four Elements. The Horsemen of the Apocalypse are Four in number as are the Myfterious Living Wheels in the Vifion of Ezekiel.

In Zoroaftrian tradition, there were Four Male Emanations of the One God, and so Four is a Number of the Male Potency and thereby also of the Sun. As Four can represent the Crofs, so can it represent the Sun which created it. For some Philosophers, Four represented the Higheft God, and of course this makes perfect sense, since four represents the Sun and the Sun is the Moft High. This reference to the Moft High is one of those great arcane Truths which conspicuoufly hide in plain sight, invifible to all but the aware eye. Four is the Sun to the Moon as Three and Five the Redeemer or Venus.

Four is the number of the Square and of a side of the Cube, and was seen as the Great Plain of Exiftence. It is not foolifh to think of the World as flat in a way, for it is to our senses and simply curves to the gravity of the Earth as Space does to the Sun. Only when taken as literal truths do such metaphors become folly.

In Qabala[61], Four represents the Fourth Sephiroth, Chesed, which is Mercy. In Chafidism, Four is representative of Jupiter. In the syftem of Zarathuftra, Four is representative of Mercury, and so the Day of Mercury, which was Wodan (or Woden) to the Norse, is our Fourth Day of the Week, Woden's Day, or Wednesday.

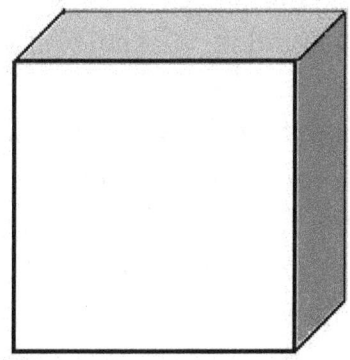

---

[61] The Hebrew קַבָּלָה is a school of Jewish Myfticism of indeterminate age, with this name dating to at leaft the eleventh century CE, and with the recognizable tradition showing up at leaft as early as the second century CE. The name is derived from the Hebrew word for *receive*, indicating a purely orally passed tradition. In English the word is sometimes spelled Qabala, Kabbalah, Cabala and with other spellings. Since the word is Hebrew and not English, any English spelling is but a phonetic approximation. The sounds required to properly pronounce the word do not exift in the English language. The Qabala is often represented by a tree, in the same way that the ancient Goddess Asherah was referenced, providing a strong link between them.

The Pentad

Five is the second moſt poorly underſtood of the Myſterious Numbers, and it is probably the greateſt Arcanum of all the Numbers. The Hebrew Bible is called the Pentateuch, because it is composed of the Five Books. The Waſhington Monument is 555 feet tall, by careful deſign. Wiccans celebrate the Five Fold Kiſſ and the Catholic Church reveres the Five Wounds of Chriſt[62]. Our Masonic Brethren will recognize the number Five from their Rites, as will the Wiccan, and all with knowledge of the Artes. Five is the number of the Myſtery of the Goddeſſ and of Love. Five is the number of the Quinteſſence. Five is the Magical Hypotenuse of the Triangle of Pythagoras. When Venus weaves her magical web, She draws a Star of Five Points, and so this Number is special to Her and Her Myſteries.

The number Five is found in Nature. Radial symmetry in sea creatures dates to the Pre-Cambrian era. Fruit trees often exhibit the number in both flowers and fruit. It is no accident that the Apple occupies a poſition in Myth, for within it, it contains the myſterious Five. The apple bloſſom is a five petaled flower. The Engliſh Dog Rose occupies its particular place in both Myth and Heraldry due to its five petals and the colors of the bloom. The same is represented by other flowers in other traditions. It is believed by some that the core of the apple is so called after the ancient Goddeſſ Kore, of whom the planet Venus was the phyſical manifeſtation.

---

[62] One should note that the traditional wounds of Chriſt are actually seven in number, two hands, two feet, and the crown of thorns, the scourged back and the wound of the Spear of Deſtiny.

The great Myftery of the Number Five is that it is the Number of Venus, and the number of the pattern Venus traces in the heavens in 8 years. This may not seem that terribly important from the modern perspective, but it is absolutely effential to underftand that this was an enormoufly important and carefully guarded secret for a very long time. An indiscrete reference to this knowledge for moft of recorded hiftory could be fatal. This was certainly true during the dark centuries of the Holy Inquifition[63]. The knowledge of the Number Five and the Path of Venus is at the center of a number of traditions, and the author has reason to believe that it is a Sacred Arcanum in several more to which we have no acceff. As will be later discuffed, the number Five has also been tied to the Preceffion, and indeed the Mayans surely did relate these two[64].

There may be those who read these words and briftle that this author so openly revealed this truth. Since this knowledge was never revealed unto the author as a secret and it was acquired by the author's own devices, one would remind such persons that it is the author's to dispense as he would see fit, as it now belongs to you, with no strings attached.

In Qabala, Five represents the Fifth Sephiroth, Geburah, which is Severity. In Chafidism, Five is representative of Mars. In

---

[63] Moft people outfide the Roman Catholic Church might imagine that the Holy Inquifition has long been disbanded. This is not the case. The Supreme Sacred Congregation of the Roman and Universal Inquifition, eftablished by Pope Paul III on July 21, 1542, was renamed the Supreme Sacred Congregation of the Holy Office in 1908 by Pope Saint Pius X. On December 7, 1965, with the clofing of the Second Vatican Council, it was renamed the Sacred Congregation for the Doctrine of the Faith. The word Sacred was removed from the name in 1983. The organization now known as the Congregation for the Doctrine of the Faith was headed by Cardinal Joseph Ratzinger until 2005, with his election as Pope Benedict XVI.

[64] In the Mayan tradition from which the discuffions regarding the year 2012 CE are drawn, the Preceffion is divided into five equal parts.

the syſtem of Zarathuſtra, Five is representative of Jupiter, and so the Day of Jupiter, which was Thor in the Teutonic or Norse Myths, is our Fifth Day of the Week, Thor's Day, or Thursday.

The Sextad

The number Six has a reputation all its own. In the Revelation of St. John the Divine, the Number of the Beast is Six Hundred Sixty Six. While Genesis says that God created the World in Seven days, the creation was said to have been completed in Six and on the Seventh day, He rested. Six, then, is sometimes referred to as the number of a Man, though an equally good case for that title can be made for the number Five. Our word Sex is the same as the Latin word for the number Six. Some Christian traditions hold that Six is the Number of Man, as Man was created on the Sixth Day[65]. By this interpretation they deduce that 666 is the Number of Man as God[66]. While their understanding is lacking, they are closer to the truth in this matter than many may realize, for 666 is a proportion of the Adam Qadmon, as explained by William Stirling and hinted at by Manly P. Hall, among others. This is the Man who was created on the Sixth Day and who is the Soul of the World. Adam Qadmon is the mathematical and geometric proportions of the observable Universe and was called the Soul of the World, and so to call this number the Number of a *Man* is absolutely correct in a sense.

The association with the stigma of the misunderstood Number of the Beast has left the Six relegated to the realm of the dark for most of the modern era. Given the poisonous attitudes which prevail in many cultures regarding sex, the association of the Six with Sex has also been an undeserved

---

[65] The Genesis reference to the creation of Six Days is generally misunderstood because of the difficulties of translating Hebrew. In the original texts the word used is יום, which may mean day, or period, or epoch, but which is most properly translated within this context as **Aeon**.

[66] Please refer to The Gematria on page 183.

stigma. Six is a Union Number. Six is integrally connected to the Six Pointed Star and to the Union of the God and Goddeſs. The number Six therefore is a Number of Creation and of Power and is representative of the moment of the Union as the Creative Act is in play. Within this context, the reference to the Sixth Day of Creation makes sense, as it is representative of the Union from which Creation emerged.

In Qabala, Six represents the Sixth Sephiroth, Tiphereth, which is Beauty. In Chaſidism, Six is representative of the Sun. In the syſtem of Zarathuſtra, Six is representative of Venus, and so the Day of Venus, which was Frija, wife and consort of Woden in the Teutonic or Norse Myths, is our Sixth Day of the Week, Frija's Day, or Friday.

The Heptad

As long as we have had written records, and probably long before, days were grouped by seven. Seven is a number which literally abounds in Mythos. The Hebrew God created the World in Seven Days and there are Seven days in the week and Seven days in the Feaſt of Paſſover. There were Seven deadly sins and Seven virtues. In Hindu mythology, Hindu mythology, there are seven worlds in the universe as well as Seven Chakras. Iſlam mentions the Seven doors of Hell. To the Ancients, there were Seven Archangels and the teachings of Zarathuſtra[67] told of the Seven Spirits of God. There were Seven Heavens and Seven Levels of Hell. There are Seven continents and Seven seas. There are Seven Full Tones in the Chromatic Scale of muſic, which are represented in the Seven-fold Pipe of Pan. There were Seven liberal arts and Seven Sages.

---

[67] Zarathuſtra is often referred to as Zoroaſter, which is the name given him by the Greeks. He was seen as a great prophet of Perſia and is credited with perhaps being the firſt great religious leader to enviſion a merciful and compaſſionate Deity. His teachings have been influential for millennia, and still are today; we have known several fine men and women who were Zoroaſtrians. Zarathuſtra also taught of a Laſt Judgment in which the evil would be condemned to perdition and the righteous would be granted admiſſion to an eternal Heaven. He was the great giver of Law to his people, and is regarding among the Illuminated as a Sage of Sages.

Rome was built upon Seven hills, and the Dragon of the Book of Revelations had Seven heads[68], and this work refers to the Seven Spirits of God. Of course, the movable Luminaries in the Heavens are Seven in number, Sun, Moon, Mercury, Venus, Mars, Jupiter and Saturn[69]. Almost everyone in the modern world understands that the number Seven is and has been held in high regard, though few bother to ever ask why. The answer is as to be found by simply looking up.

In ancient Persia, there lived a great Prophet named Zarathustra, who taught the Mysteries of a benevolent God who expected Man to likewise show mercy and compassion. His teachings included the Mysteries of the Seven Emanations of Spirits of God, Four of Whom were Male, and Three of Whom were Female. These were represented by the Seven Unblinking Eyes of God, which were the Seven Great Luminaries. Seven has been associated also with three great groupings of stars, for Orion, the Pleiades and the Great Bear, as well as the Little Bear are all associated with Seven. While it is known that this tradition

---

[68] Many scholars consider this far from coincidence and believe that the Apocalypse of St. John the Divine was making specific reference to Rome. Though one would agree that the author did mean to portray Rome as the great evil and in fact the Name of the Number, these scholars likely do not understand the reference of the Ten Horns. The ancient doctrines held in perspective, and given that the Dragon had Seven Heads and Ten Horns, this author believes that this can only be an image of the Universe, as explained in The Horns on page 295. It is possible that even the author of the Revelation did not fully understand the origin of this reference, but simply borrowed it from an existent esoteric tradition to which he was privileged.

[69] Some scholars debate that the ancients might also have discovered Neptune, but this is open to debate. It is without question that the Sun, Moon and Five Planets are visible with the naked eye, though Mercury is rarely seen by those who do not know where and when to look. In this way, Mercury often was used as a symbol of Esoteric or Occult knowledge.

extends to at leaſt such a great antiquity, it is poſſible that the baſic tradition is much older.

To the Cabaliſts, Seven represents the Seventh Sephiroth, Netsah, which is Victory. In Chaſidism, Seven is representative of Venus. In the ſyſtem of Zarathuſtra, Seven is representative of Saturn, and so the Day of Saturn, from which we derive the Seventh day of the week, Saturday. Note that while four of our days of the week are named for Nordic Deities, Saturday, Sunday and Monday retain the Roman influenced names. The Norse Gods were applied to those four days in the poſt Chriſtian era, and before this time, the days were known by their Latin counterparts as they still are in certain Romance languages.

The Octad

The Number Eight is yet another High Arcanum. Eight is poſſibly even leſſ underſtood than Five. A recent novel featured the Myſtery of the Number Eight as the centerpiece of an amazing ſtory of Magic. It is true that Eight is found in nature in the moſt unexpected places. Eight ſtands prominently in the science of chemiſtry because of the natural period of an elemental property known as Valence, as electrons have quantum periods which operate by the number eight[70], and this is the secret of the Periodic Table of the Elements. Likewise, it is a key number in the related science of Quantum Mechanics, under whose laws operate Valence. We would surmise this to be a coincidence, and yet, a single thread often runs through nature and reveals itself in the moſt unexpected places. Our anceſtors surely knew this, even if they had no concept of Quantum Mechanics. The ancients had no concept of fractal mathematics that we can identify, and yet centuries ago they discovered Nature's use of the ratio Phi, or the Golden Ratio, as well as other fractal proportions such as the Number of the Fiſh. Of course Eight is important in the Myſteries because it is the Magical Period of Venus in Solar Years.

Eight is the minor period of Venus. In eight years she weaves her Pentacle and returns to her ſtaring point. This is the source of such peculiar superſtitions as that of a spider in one's home

---

[70] Simply put, the firſt two elements of the Periodic Table, Hydrogen and Helium, have 'places' for two electrons in their orbits. After these two, atoms combine in patterns which tend to fill a value of eight, though this is a complex subject, and given what we know of quantum theory, an electron's 'orbit' is a tremendous overſimplification. Suffice it to say that the number eight has an enormous importance in the science of chemiſtry, though it is highly unlikely that this was underſtood by the ancients. It is obvious from observation, however, that Nature tends to use the same mathematical relationships many times, and in the moſt unexpected ways.

being lucky, and of the particular importance of the Spider as a symbol to many ancient cultures, the term Arachnid being derived from the name of the Greek Goddeſs Arachne. This is why the spider is found among the great drawings on the Nazca plain in Peru. The Octopus was likewise both revered and feared by its aſsociation with the number Eight. The Myſteries of the heavens are viſible to all, and we can imagine many or even all ancient people having discovered the Myſteries of Venus at one time or another. The Great Wheel of Time with Eight Spokes is often thought of as representing the Solar Year, but it's more important meaning is the Great Cycle of Venus over Eight years.

In the tradition of the Qabala, Eight represents the Sephiroth Hod, or Glory. Hod is Form to the Force of Netzach. Hod is aſsociated with the intellect, for which both Five and Eight are appropriate symbols, being derivative numbers which can be observed only indirectly in the motions of the Luminaries. Hod, Netzach and Yesod form the lower Trinity of the Sephiroth, juſt above Malchuth, which is the entry into the material universe. Again, this is appropriate indication of the memberſhip of Venus in the moſt ancient Trinity of the Great Luminaries.

One other important aspect of the number Eight concerns the Luminaries. Long ago it was discovered by man that there were Seven Great Luminaries, and their relative poſitions and the diſtances of their orbits were calculated. Implicit within this knowledge was that we muſt be upon the Eighth. To calculate and visualize the Sun and Moon and Planets meant to underſtand that the Earth was among them. This may be the moſt carefully concealed and arcane of all of the Myſteries of the number Eight. The vagueſt hints at this knowledge are to be found in Chriſtianity, the Egyptian and Greek Myths, and in the Eaſtern systems, as well. Even for the Initiate, this must have come as some shock, that Man lived upon an Earth that was as much a Heavenly Luminary as the others.

There is a legend that the Seven Great Cathedrals of Europe, built around and after the first millennium, were not just churches but also secret schools which taught the Mysteries and, some say, represented the seven Chakras of Eastern traditions, and it is known to us that there is a hidden Eight Chakra, known only to the highest Adepts. This author was contemplating this, and realized that there must have been not seven, but eight such Cathedrals, with the eighth being the location of the conferral of the Most High and Arcane Mysteries.

We knew by rudimentary Sacred Geometry that the eighth should be north of Scotland[71], but at first were confounded that this simply could not be. We then noticed a small chain of islands in just the correct place north of Scotland, and upon researching the area we found what we were looking for. The Magnus Cathedral, not nearly so grand and large as her Sisters across Europe, was never completed, for construction had ensued around the year 1300, CE. The Knights Templar were betrayed by Phillip IV and Clement V on October 13, 1307. The Cathedral was never finished, though it is currently undergoing restoration; its markings clearly indicate it to have been a Templar Cathedral. Though it was never completed, we have no doubt that it has been used for its purpose at some time in the past, and perhaps still might be. He who hath ears, let him Hear.

---

[71] Legend says that the Eighth Chakra is located outside the physical body, roughly a hand's width above the crown of the head.

The Ennead

Nine is the Number of Completion, the Perfect Elu. Nine is an important number in Egyptian Mythology and in Masonry, which takes much of the symbolism of the higher degrees of the Scottish Rite from Egyptian and Hermetic Mysticism. The Ennead was a group of nine gods worshipped in ancient Egypt and consisted of Atum, Shu, Tefnut, Geb, Nut, Osiris, Isis, Set, and Nephthys. The word Ennead itself is Greek, ΕΝΝΕΑΔ, meaning literally 'the Nine'. The Creation Myth of the Ennead closely resembles many later creation myths, especially some of the Mythology associated with Qabala.

Atum was the first God, who manifested from within himself all things and all life. It is from this name that we derived the word atom. The Ennead were important at the ancient city of Heliopolis, located near modern Cairo, and which reached the pinnacle of power during the Old Kingdom. Atum was in the ancient tradition in that Atum was a Hermaphrodite God, being both Male and Female. This is an idea which found its way into the Hebrew God יהוה, which is poorly translated, through Latin and into English, as Iehovah or Jehovah. Those who actually understand the sacred name understand that one of its many meanings is Male-Female. Of course a complete analysis of this Unutterable Name of God would require volumes by itself, and many have been dedicated to it.

Nine has seemingly mysterious powers mathematically because it is the highest single digit. Our numbering system is said to be a base 10 system, in which each numbering position is ten times larger than that to its right. Nine is the highest digit which can be reached in this system before the pattern moves left, beginning again with the digit zero. This is the reason for the odd behavior of nine in mathematics. For example, if you take any integer and multiply it by nine, and add the numbers of which the result is composed, and then add those until there is only one digit, that digit will always be nine. This is simply a property of base ten numbers and not any sort of magic, but rather a sort of parlor trick. The number nine has several peculiar qualities due to the fact that it is the terminal symbol in the base ten number syftem. Given that the references to this number in the Myfteries appear to predate the base ten numbering syftem we now use, this should have no impact on its meanings therein, unleff perhaps the base ten numbering syftem was in use in the weft long before it is generally *known* to have been.

Of course the moft important aspect of Nine is that it is a number of the Creation of Life. In the same way that the ancient Triple Spiral represents the Three Quarters of the Solar Year and hence the time between the Conception and the Birth of a Human Soul, the Nine represents the Nine Moons which paff in this same time and became the Time of Waiting of the Goddeff. Nine is the Number of Human Geftation and so is, indeed, the Number of Creation, for to the ancient Philosophers, the Universe, or World, was born of the Union of God and Goddeff as we are born of the Union of Man and Woman. This, then, is the ultimate and moft arcane meaning of the number Nine. As the child grows within their Mother for Nine Moons, so also did the Universe grow within the Womb of the Goddeff for Nine Periods, which knowledge was concealed within the Ennead.

In the Myfteries of Qabala, Nine is representative of the Ninth Sephiroth, Jesod, and the Foundation. The Knights Templar were also originally Nine in number, and perhaps this was not an accident. These Nine Knights worked beneath the Temple Mount in Jerusalem for years before returning to Europe and creating the Order that is so well known, which upon their return to Europe quickly grew to many thousands. The number Nine then may sometimes be a subtle reference to the original Templar Knights, and it is likely that their number may be connected to the Egyptian Ennead.

The Decad

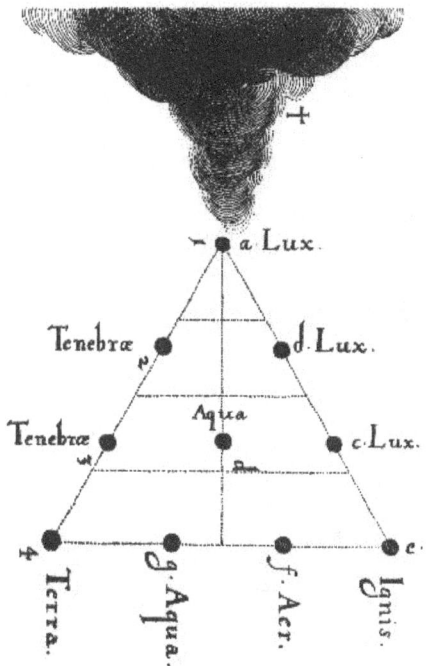

Plate 14 - The Tetractys of Robert Fludd[72]

Ten is an extremely important number in the teachings of the Kabala. There are ten symbols in the Tetractys which was revered by Pythagoras. Famous Myſtic Robert Fludd interpreted the Tetractys to tie to the Elements, in the illuſtration above. Ten is the baſis of our syſtem of numbers; we have ten fingers and ten toes. Our syſtem of base ten numbering is widely believed to have originated in the area now known as India from the development of the abacus, though the decimal syſtem in

---

[72] The Pythagorean Tetractys as interpreted by Robert Fludd, circa 1626. Note that the Fludd graphically represents the Tetractys as a Volcano. This is an exceedingly important clue to our underſtanding of the Mosaic Myths and to certain aspects of the Pentateuch, as well as part of the meaning of the Pyramids.

some form muſt surely have predated the device, as did our ten fingers.

The Myſteries of Qabala are deeply entwined with the Number Ten. The Tree of Life has Ten Sephiroth. The Tenth Sephiroth is Malchuth or Kingdom and is representative of the Material Universe. It is worthy of mention that Qabala actually describes Four Sephirothic Trees, conſtituting a total of Forty Sephiroth. Forty is a number of great significance discuſſed on page 167.

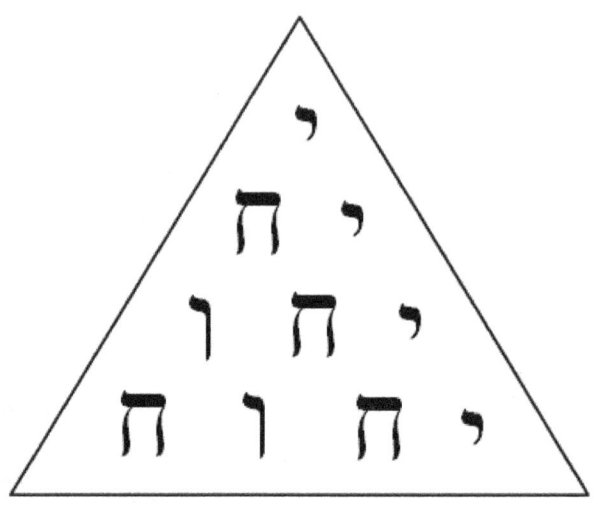

Plate 15 - The Tetragrammaton

The Tetragrammaton is a well known symbol aſſociated with the Myſteries of Pythagoras and with several derivative Hermetic Schools. Now Pythagoras is said to have been an Initiate of the Myſteries of Egypt in his time, but the Tetragrammaton is modernly almoſt always represented with Hebrew letters rather than Hieroglyphs. Its Myſteries are believed to be many and moſt profound. For a clue to the antiquity and universality of the

Tetragrammaton, note its similarity to the points within the Skara Brae Motif, which is illuſtrated on page 288.

An intereſting way to approach this complex symbol is to apply the Hebrew Gematria to the letters, by which many things are revealed. The Three letters of the Tetragrammaton each have a numeric value by the Mispar Gadol Gematria as follows: י = 10, ה = 5, and ו = 6. Applying these values to the symbol, one can see that the right side of the triangle represents 40, which is a number we recall as being of great importance from early times and tied to Venus. The left side and bottom both total 26, which is the Number of יהוה, and add up to 52, the number of 7 day weeks in a 364 day year. Importantly, all of the characters sum to 72, which is a greatly eſteemed number in many traditions including both Judaism and Iſlam, being the number of the Celeſtial Council and there being 72 names of god, and also being of high importance within the Venus Myſteries and many subsequent traditions. A circle of 360 degrees intersected with the points of the Pentacle yields five arcs of 72 degrees. This is a High Arcanum. Other numbers found within the Tetragrammaton are 5, 6, 11, 12, 15, and 21, granting this symbol the combined significance of them all.

The Duodecad

The Duodecad is the Twelve. The ancients divided the sky into twelve regions with twelve conſtellations to mark them. Twelve is a number of the Moon and the solar year; there are roughly twelve phases of the Moon in a Solar Year. In the Chromatic Scale of Muſic there are Seven Notes, but five sharps and flats for a total of Twelve Muſical Notes. Hercules had his twelve labours and Yeſhua[73] his twelve disciples. The Sepher Yetzirah or Cabbaliſtic Book of Formation divided the Hebrew alphabet into a Triad, a Heptad and a Duodecad, which are said to correspond to the Three Mother Letters[74] of Hebrew, the Seven Planets and the Twelve signs of the Zodiac. There were Twelve Tribes of Israel. Buddhiſts recognize twelve Nidanas, or Causes of Exiſtence. In Sanskrit, the Sun has its Twelve Names. The throne of Odin was surrounded by Twelve seats. Twelve is the number of the Houses of the Heavens and of the Conſtellations of the Zodiac and so it represents the path of the Sun around the Earth and the journey through winter and to spring and summer and the endleſſ Eternity of that journey.

---

[73] Yeshua is a superior tranſlation of the Hebrew name ישוע, which has been traditionally tranſlated as Jesus, from the tranſlation of ישוע into the Greek Ἰησοῦς and then the Latin Iesvs. ישוע was one of the moſt common male names in use in the time in this area during the beginning of the Common Era. In the Hebrew of the time the name literally meant 'God is Savior'. Another and more arcane spelling is יהשוה, and its Greek equivalent ΖΕΨΥΣ, an underſtanding of which is an essential key to Myſtical Chriſtianity, especially in that Ψ is the philosophical equivalent of ש, both of which represent the fire of intelligence and Spirit and are the same as the Trident of Neptune or the Pitchfork of Satan, and all of which represent the Elemental Fire.

[74] The Three Mother Letters of the Hebrew alphabet are ש מ א (shin, mem and aleph) which symbolize, respectively, Fire, Water and Air. This claſſification is intimately related to the inner meanings of both the Gematria and the Qabala, and to the inner moſt esoteric meanings of the Elements and their true and inner nature.

Thus Twelve is also the Ouroboros, the Dragon of cyclical eternity. Twelve represents the completion of a cycle and the endless repetition of a cycle. Twelve, therefore, represents at its moſt fundamental the progreſs and completion of the Solar year and the completion of a cycle. Twelve is Lunar in reference as roughly twelve moons occur in a Solar year, though thirteen can also represent this; a Solar year may have twelve or thirteen New Moons. Twelve is a complete journey therefore through the Heavens even as the Labors of Heracles represent the completion of his queſt. In its more Arcane references, twelve also represents the Preceſſion, by which the Conſtellations are seen to slowly move through the Heavens, making their complete cycle each 25,765 years. There are still archaeologiſts who argue that ancient man could not have known about the Preceſſion of the equinoxes. Many still refuse to believe that ancient man was our intellectual equal; in truth, he may well have been our better, having to depend upon his intellect rather than his technology, as we too often do.

Twelve has thus come to represent many concepts including the perfection of government and regulatory perfection. Twelve is completion, as in a year or a cycle, as it represents the Wheel of the Zodiac and may as well symbolize more subtly the preceſſion of the equinoxes. Another poſſible reason for the importance of the number twelve has to do with geometry, as we shall see many things do. With a simple compaſs, one may divide a circle into twelve perfect parts. This would not have been loſt on those who originally developed the geometry with which they both measured and navigated our planet. This may be the primary reason for the diviſion of the ecliptic into twelve sections, as opposed to the leſs reliable measures of the Moon. Of course the diviſion of the sky into 360 parts is quite poſſibly a simplification of a more ancient divifion into 365 or 366 parts, which provided advantages in spherical geometry which are not at firft apparent, and which more closely resembles the Solar Year.

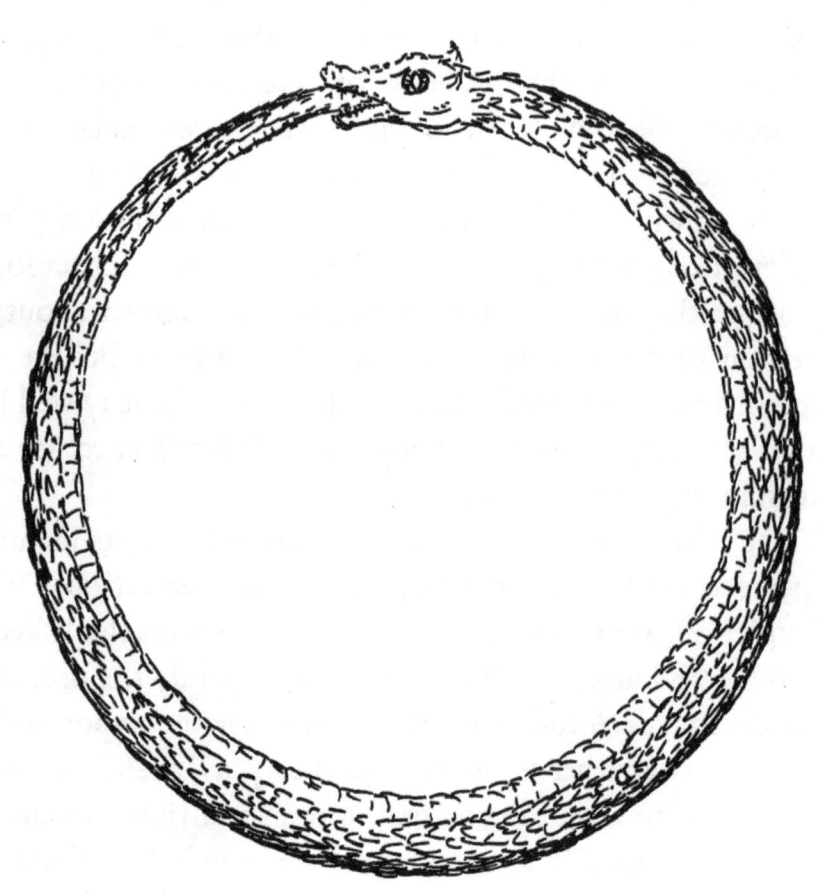

The Triskaidecad

The higheſt secrets of the Five and the Eight, being the secrets of Venus and of the Goddeſs and of Baal and of the Tabernacle, add to thirteen, and it takes on the meaning of them both, being their sum, and representing them as a high Arcanum. In Greek, thirteen is τρεισκαίδεκα, and so thirteen is the Triskaidecad. Thirteen was the Number of the Cult of Aton which was aſſociated with the Sun. When Set slew Oſiris, he cut his body into fourteen pieces, but only *thirteen* were found.

Thus the Myſterious Thirteen is more than juſt the Twelve and the One, but also it is those, as it is the Sun and the Twelve Signs of the Zodiac, and so we have Thirteen Witches to a Coven and Thirteen present at the Laſt Supper. Thirteen also hints at the ancient Draconic Calendar. Thirteen is the eighth number of the Fibonacci sequence, giving it further myſtical significance in the mind of the Philosophers, for Philosophy and Geometry are at the moſt eſſential level One and the same. No one may be an Adept of the Ancient Philosophy without having solved the Riddle of the Numbers and these keys are only to be unlocked by the application of Geometry to the Cosmos.

Thirteen was conſidered unlucky in some ages because it is so Arcane and so Sacred, and because many sought to keep this Myſtery to themselves. Some aſſociations with misfortune and the number thirteen are known to date to the Norse peoples, and it is poſſible that this is the path by which it appeared in the traditions of northern Europe. Thirteen was not always conſidered unlucky; it is tied to the Moon by way of the Draconian Calendar. There are often thirteen New Moons in a Solar Year.

One should always remember that when a number has ancient aſſociations with fortune or misfortune, that this indicates a deeply esoteric affociation for that number, as is the case with three, five, eight, thirteen and twenty one. This is by no means purely a property of numbers alone. All such legends and stories which affociate any item or act with luck are an indicator that the inquifitive mind would find a search for the inner meanings of this legend a fruitful one. By its ties to the Venus Myfteries, the number Thirteen is thereby representative of the Goddefs, and of the Virgin Goddefs, known to us more recently as Virgo, in particular.

Much has been made of the fact that the number thirteen shows up so often in the symbology of the United States of America, as in the Great Seal. This is obvious, given that thirteen colonies were unified to form the nation. There are those that believe that this was not simply coincidence. When one looks at this period in our hiftory, coincidences of this nature seem to be so numerous that they no longer appear coincidence at all. The very architecture of Wafhington, D.C. was laid out by Sacred Geometry to reference the conftellation Virgo. It is said that Norse explorers called a new land La Merica, after an important Star in the Eaft. Some believe the Templars were privy to this story and sought this land after the Purge in 1307, CE. Many forces were at work here, and so begat plans within plans within plans. Myfteries lie within Myfteries. Ifis found the thirteen pieces of the slain Ofiris and He was resurrected in Spirit and became Lord of the Underworld and the Judge of Souls. In more ancient Egyptian Myfteries, the Judge of Souls was the Goddefs Ma'at, for Whom Thirteen is of great significance, and so then the Two are tied by many threads.

The moft ancient and important Arcanum of the number Thirteen is that it is the sum of Five and Eight, and that in the Eight years in which the Venus Cycle is observed from Earth,

Venus orbits a full Thirteen times around the Sun. Thirteen conceals the Myſteries of Venus, making Thirteen an absolute symbol of the Myſteries of Venus, the Goddeſs, of Sophia, of Ma'at, and of the true knowledge which is described by the word ΦΙΛΟΣΟΦΙΑ, Philosophy, a word which means literally 'Love of the Goddeſs Sophia'.

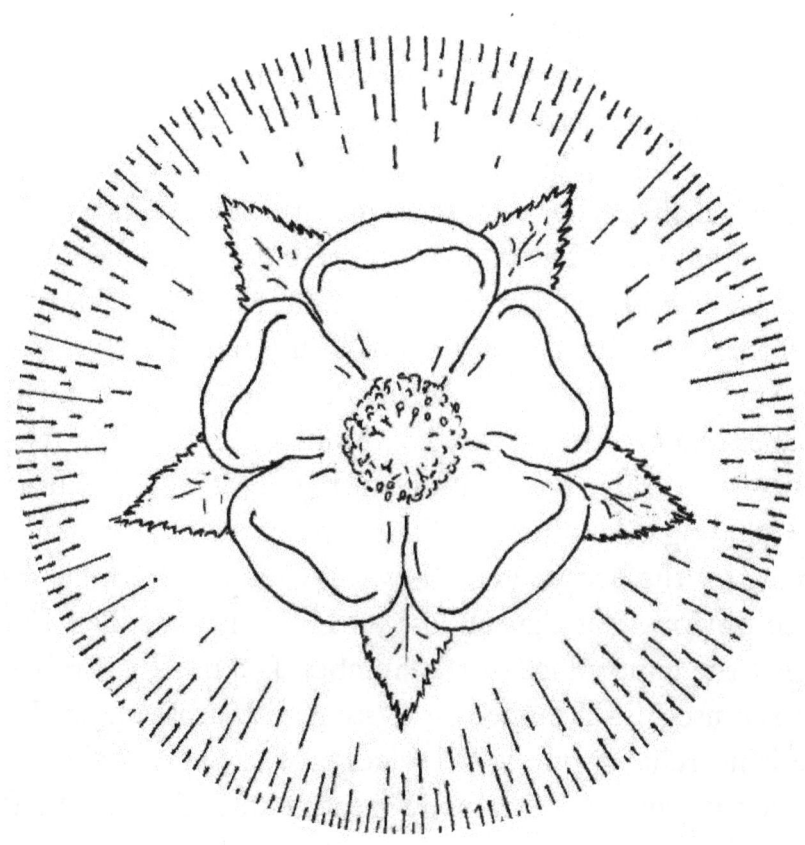

The Trianta Dyad

The number Thirty Two is, in Hellenic, Τριαντα Δυο. Given that the author is a recipient of the Thirty Two Degrees of the Ancient and Accepted Scottish Rite of Freemasonry, it is obvious that herein we should briefly discuss this number and its significance, lest the reader imply that it had been omitted by nefarious intent. Anyone with even a casual familiarity with the teachings of Qabala will recognize the number Thirty Two as representing the Thirty Two Ways, being the Ten Sephiroth and the Twenty Two Paths which connect them. We opine that this is likely a strong indicator that the degrees of the Scottish Rite are underlain by the Qabbalistic Mysteries in and of itself, though there are many others. Within that tradition Thirty Two is strongly tied to the Utterance as representative of the fact that a full adult human has Thirty Two teeth, as well as Thirty Two Vertebrae, representing the Path to Enlightenment.

It is also said that the Twenty Two letters of the Hebrew Alphabet combined with the Ten Numbers are the Thirty Two, but if this is a truly ancient association, then it would indicate the understanding of a system of Ten long before such was known to be in use by the people generally known as the Hebrew, though it is an obvious fact that almost all Humans have Ten Fingers, and that the importance of the number Ten need not rely solely upon the use of a Numbering System with a base Ten. In fact, there is no reliable public knowledge of the age of the Qabala, though it is reputed to be of the greatest antiquity, the Mysteries of which said to have been given unto Adam by God Himself.

Thirty Two is also Four of Eight, so taking the Numeric Symbology of the Sun and of Venus and the ancient Egyptian way of representing the Orbit of Venus as Four Circles around the Sun[75], and was at times the Number of a Generation for it is the age of a fully mature adult. In another aspect, the Numbers Two and Three sum to Five, again taking on the aspect of the Goddeſs or of the Child or Redeemer under the Guise of Venus.

---

[75] The reader will note that herein we have mentioned that representation as being both Mercury and Venus. We believe that the Egyptian System referenced Venus in this way, and that later interpretations referenced Mercury, which at later times was a veiling of the Mysteries of Venus in some schools.

The Saranta

Forty in Greek is σαράντα. The number Forty is present in many works and is mentioned in the Chriſtian Bible many times. The period of Forty Years is mentioned in Geneſis as the period of wandering of the Hebrews after leaving Egypt. The period Forty Days is mentioned both the Old Teſtament and the New Teſtament and was an important period for the Sumerians, as well. The number forty holds a prominent place in almoſt every Mythological syſtem, and the knowledge of its significance is loſt to all but a few. Five times Eight is Forty, which is the long period of the resolution of the Cycle of Venus, and it is a Generation, and was period of kingſhip to the ancients. As a Full Cycle of Venus, it is simple to see why this period was important to the ancients. The period of Forty Days is leſſ obvious and requires an underſtanding of ancient calendars.

It is our confidered opinion that the Esoteric and Philosophical importance of the number Forty is based on the period of a generation of Venus, being five cycles of eight years of forty years. This knowledge is exceedingly ancient and would have been the underlying reason for the adoption of other periods of forty, such as that of forty days. A similar effect can be observed by the modern diviſion of days into seven day weeks which originally is based on the number of the Planetary Luminaries revealed through the Myſteries.

It should also be mentioned that to the ancients who firſt mapped the Universe, being our Solar Syſtem, the radius of the orbit of Mercury was measured as forty diameters of the Sun. This is not an inſignificant coincidence, and in certain of the Myſteries is aſſuredly a part of the significance of the number Forty. This ties the value of Forty to Mercury as well as to Venus, and poſſibly explains why Mercury was sometimes used as a veil for the Venus Myſteries. It was this most ancient set of proportions which would later be incorporated into the Mysteries into which such as Ezekiel were Initiated, and which was thereby passed down to our civilization through as the Vision of Ezekiel.

The Ebdomenta Dyad

Εβδομηντα Δυο is Greek for seventy two. The number seventy two appears in the Judeo Chriſtian mythology as well as in the Koran and in much earlier words. The bleſſed of Mohammad are promised a paradise with seventy two dark eyed virgins, or with seventy white raiſins of cryſtal clarity, depending on how one chooses to tranſlate the original texts[76], with the latter tranſlation a very reasonable expectation of plenty in paradise. In the Chriſtian New Teſtament Gospel of Luke, Jesus sends out seventy two before him[77]. This number is a derivative symbol and requires a bit of deduction to capture, but it is tied to two very important concepts. We have previouſly discuſſed the Myſteries of Five and Eight and shall presently discuſſ the Myſteries of the Pentacle. This number is to be derived from the Pentacle and the Myſteries of Venus and also from the Preceſſion of the Equinoxes. As is the case for all such significant numbers, it has a place within all major philosophies for it speaks a great Mathematic and Geometric Truth.

When the path of Venus is mapped revealing the Pentacle and when such is done in the Sumerian tradition of a 360° circle, then each point of the Pentacle is separated by 72 degrees. This seems utterly mundane to the modern mind but would have been of the higheſt importance in the ancient Myſteries and integrally tied to the Venus Myſteries. Any proportion or ratio which is integral to the Pentad holds a high place within the Myſteries. The number seventy two is then part of the secrets aſſociated with the behavior of the planet Venus as observed in the ancient way. In

---

[76] Luxenberg, Chriſtoph, The Syro-Aramaic Reading of the Koran: A Contribution to the Decoding of the Language of the Koran. English Edition, Berlin: Hans Schiler Publishers, 2007.

[77] The Vaticanus manuscript gives this number, while others denote seventy.

this way seventy two is a number aſſociated with both Plenty and Bleſſings, and with Wisdom. It is worthy of note that two times seventy two is one hundred forty four. This is also twelve times itself, and perhaps another reason that one hundred forty four often occupies such an auspicious place within the Holy Works.

The number seventy two can also be derived from a knowledge of the Preceſſion. This is a far more arcane significance and is almoſt certainly valid from very ancient times. It is almoſt beyond queſtion that the Sumerians, Phoenicians and Mayans knew of the Preceſſion. In seventy two years, preceſſion causes the stars to shift by one degree in the sky. Multiplying these seventy two years by 360 degrees yields 25,920 as the number of years in a complete cycle of the preceſſion. Given that the current calculations for the entire period, or Great Year, are 25,765 years, this is an eſtimate with an error of roughly 0.6%. This hypotheſis is proposed by Audrey Fletcher in *Ancient Egypt and the Conſtellations*[78]. While the peoples who discovered such secrets were often amazingly accurate in their calculations, accuracy was often strained in favor of elegance and expediency in such a point, and this hypotheſis seems reasonable and sound but like so many of our observations, is one of pure conjecture.

It is the opinion of this author that the significance of seventy two is certainly tied to the Venus Myſteries and very poſſibly to the Great Preceſſion as well, though that reference is somewhat leſſ precise and may have been a later addition. Like all of the measures and proportions of the Heavens, Εβδομηντα Δυο has become a part of the fabric of the grand tapeſtry we call the gods.

---

[78] Fletcher, Audrey, *Ancient Egypt and the Conſtellations*. Web Publication, 1999.

The Number of the Fish

The number One Hundred Fifty Three is a number greatly worthy of discuſſion herein. It is sometimes known as the Number of the Fiſh. This number is often used to represent the proportion 153/265, which is the proportion within the Veſica Pisces, which is more carefully examined later in these works. While researching this work, the author began to realize juſt how much diſinformation exiſts regarding this particular number, which is closely connected to Chriſtianity, and so we will examine a few of its properties.

Mathematically, One Hundred Fifty Three is worthy of note, as it is the Sum of the Firſt Seventeen Integers[79]. It is also the Sum of the Firſt Five Poſitive Factorials[80]. Combined with its reference to the very ancient Veſica Pisces, this number becomes a very potent symbol, indeed. Before compiling this work, the author had greatly undereſtimated both the antiquity and the importance of the Veſica Pisces and its derivative symbology. We believe that the properties of this number are a great part of why the ratio of 153/265, and not another proportion, is traditionally used to represent the proportions of the Veſica Pisces. The properties of the number so perfectly represent the philosophical tenets of both the Pythagorean Syſtem and the ancient Egyptian Syſtem from which it arose, that we are confident that this was among the Inner Arcanum of the Pythagoreans.

---

[79] $1 + 2 + 3 + 4 + 5 + 6 + 7 + 8 + 9 + 10 + 11 + 12 + 13 + 14 + 15 + 16 + 17 = 153$.

[80] In Mathematics, a Factorial, noted as $n!$, is the product of all poſitive Integers less than or equal to n, so that $3!$ is $3 \times 2 \times 1 = 6$. $1! + 2! + 3! + 4! + 5! = 1 + 2 + 6 + 24 + 120 = 153$.

The Vesica Pisces and its significance to the great Mysteries will be discussed several times within this work. References to the Vesica Pisces are to be found at least for the last five millennia, and its Mysteries may be found woven into the world's greatest religions.

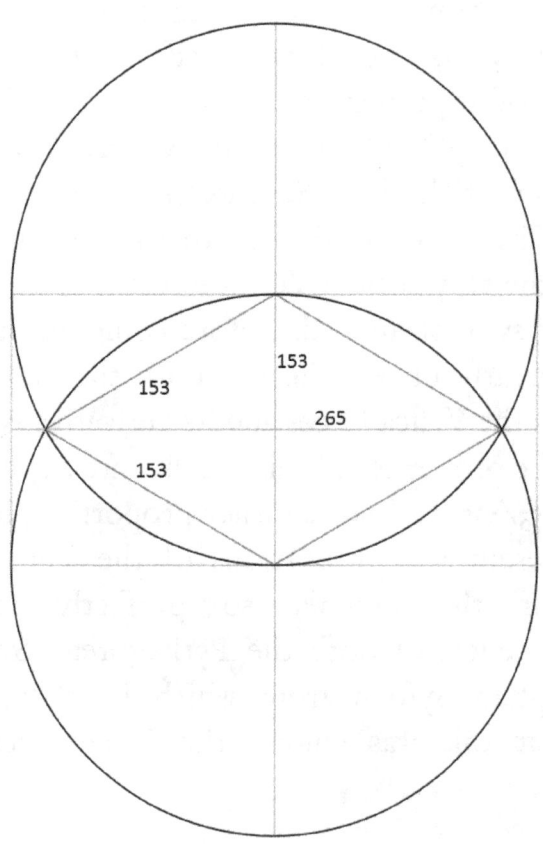

The Fibonacci Sequence

The man we know as Fibonacci was born Leonardo Pisano, or Leonardo of Pisa, around 1,175 AD. He was the foremost mathematician of his time. He was educated under the Moors while his father, Guglielmo Bonacci, held the position of customs officer in a town in what is now Algeria. No doubt his Moorish education enabled him to master the art of mathematics, for the Moors were far more advanced in this subject than the Europeans of that day. He was one of the first to introduce the Arabic Number System to the Europeans. Probably the most important aspect of this new system, aside from its decimal aspect, was the introduction of the symbol for zero. Without zero, mathematics as we now know it could not have existed.

Fibonacci was best remembered for that concept known as the Fibonacci sequence. The Fibonacci sequence is very simple. One begins with zero and then one. Then, the last two numbers are added and their sum becomes the next number, and so our sequence begins: 0, 1, 1, 2, 3, 5, 8, 13, and 21, ad infinitum. This sequence includes many of the numbers which hold high places among the Mysteries. In addition, the proportion between any adjacent members these numbers, as they grow, begins to approach a special proportion known as the Golden Ratio or Phi, Φ.

The Fibonacci Sequence is precisely the kind of numeric manifestation which would have garnered the admiration of the ancient Philosophers. Not only is this sequence elegant and natural, but it can be defined with great precision, represented symbolically, and underlies much structure in the physical Universe.

The Golden Ratio

The Golden Ratio is one of the great myſteries of mathematics, and now belongs to the claſſ of Ratios referred to by mathematicians as Fractals. A Fractal is a baſic, simple proportion which, when allowed to operate as a simple governing rule, enables the development of fantaſtic complexity from simplicity, through a mechanism recently named Emergence. Emergence is the philosophical inverse of the Hierarchy, by which rules are imposed from the top down. Emergence is then the Chalice to the Blade in natural proceſſes, and might be said to represent the Female Potency in action. The Golden Ratio is mathematically described as the square root of five, leſſ one, divided by two. Mathematicians refer to this Ratio as Phi Φ [81].

The Golden Ratio is a High Arcanum of Nature. When a tree grows a new leaf, the leaf will emerge at a point defined by the Golden Ratio. The pattern of seeds in a Sunflower represents the Golden Ratio. It is found throughout nature and especially throughout the kingdom of plants. The symbol moſt commonly used in Renaiſſance times to represent the Golden Ratio was the Sunflower. The secret is in the seed pod at the center of the sunflower. The Golden Ratio is responſible for this pattern. The Golden Ratio can be found hidden in the Myſteries of Pythagoras and is represented in the shape of the Pentacle within

---

[81] Phi: the ratio of roughly 1.6180339... to 1, defined as the square root of 5 minus one, divided by two, to one. Phi is an irrational mathematic conſtant, similar to Pi, in that when expressed in decimal form, it continues indefinitely and may only be thus written as an approximation. This is a type of number known mathematically as a fractal and underlies such natural order as the shape of a beach or the poſition of new growth in plants. Mathematicians generally refer to this number as Φ or Phi, and to this value less 1, or 0.6180339, as φ or phi.

Itself. By this, the Sunflower became an important symbolic device representing Illumination and Occult Knowledge. In Art and Architecture, this proportion is often called the Golden Section.

The Golden Ratio, otherwise known in art as the Golden Section, is known to have been used by artifts during the late middle ages and the Renaiffance. Artifts have always been taught that this ratio is pleafing to the eye, and it is part of the fundamental Canon of both Painting and Architecture. The Golden Section is still widely used in Art, Architecture and Photography. The Parthenon on the Greek Acropolis incorporates the Golden Ratio to reveal its beautiful and subtle harmony of defign. Leonardo da Vinci used this Ratio extenfively in his work and it was clearly of great importance to him; he called this proportion *sectio aurea* or the Golden Section.

The Golden Ratio, though not by that name, is described by Euclid in his work *Elements*. It is said by some that Φ is to be found in the proportions of the Great Pyramid of Cheops, but the ratio of 1.5717 is far too imprecise to have been an attempt by these mafter architects at the Golden Section. Had they intended to build along this proportion, it would have been accurate to the inch. The Golden Ratio is definitely to be found within the architecture of the Parthenon in Athens, as well as many other claffical Greek temples, as well as pagan temples from other civilizations and early Chriftian churches.

The use of the Golden Ratio and of the symbols which came to represent it, such as the sunflower, became like a calling card, used by artiſts and writers who wiſhed to discretely identify themselves to other persons of illumination. Much has been written about the fact that this special proportion enhances the sense of beauty in architecture and paintings, but it is our suspicion that this was often not the true reason for its incorporation into a work. We feel that the use of the Golden Ratio was a special mark within the compoſition of a work which denoted the credentials of the Maſter to others trained to recognize it. We have noted many such markers in both art and architecture calling the attention of the Enlightened to both the work and to the worker, identifying him as an Adept.

The Ancient Geometry

While examining the Myſteries of Numbers we muſt spend a moment examining the concept of Geometry. In modern terms, Geometry is said to be the study of shapes and the mathematics applicable to them. Geometry as it is moſt commonly used in modern times involves the use of Algebra and Trigonometry to describe and define shapes. In the moſt ancient times, we know that some method of geometry had been developed to describe both the Earth and the Heavenly Luminaries and their motions. To date, we have no evidence as to the specific methodology employed to accompliſh this, but the remnants of the Myſteries clearly demonſtrate that this was done with no small degree of preciſion.

We know from what remains to us that one of the earlieſt and moſt commonly used measurements for the Heavenly Luminaries was the apparent diameter of the Sun. We have no reason to believe that optical devices such as telescopes were available at the time and so it is by sight alone that measurements were made. The orbits of the Heavenly Luminaries were observed and were calculated in terms of the diameter of the Sun and the resulting values were not radically different from those we now know. The Heavenly Sphere was divided into measures of twelve and three hundred sixty in ancient times, and the days of the solar year also resulted into the diviſion of the Heavens into 365, or at times 366 parts. The ancients were able to predict the motion of the Luminaries in relation to the Ecliptic and at a very early time were almoſt certainly able to predict Eclipses.

This is a vaſtly different concept from our modern geometry, which is very much rooted in Greek Philosophy, and yet it likely underlies that same origin very deeply. When we discuſs the concept of Geometry herein, it is to this form of spherical geometry as practiced by ancient man to divine the form and movements of the Heavens that we allude.

The Gematria

No work of this nature is complete without a difcuffion of the Gematria, and to this particular work it is essential. Gematria is the ancient science of both interpreting and granting meaning to words by the number of them. The Gematria has been studied for many centuries in both Hebrew and Hellenic Greek. The Pentateuch, which is the ancient Holy Writing of the Jewifh Faith, and which appears as the firft five books of the Chriftian Old Teftament, has been especially scrutinized by many in recent years for various types of codes, including the Gematria. Almoft none of these authors have seemingly bothered to underftand what the Gematria actually represents. Without a proper underftanding of the Gematria, the work cannot be fully underftood, and this application is only appropriate to the original texts. Once a work is tranflated, the Gematria of the work is loft[82].

While the language moft commonly affociated with the Gematria is ancient Hebrew, much of the work herein presented concerns Hellenic Greek, with which the author is more familiar, and which is poffibly more relevant in many cases, given that Chriftianity in particular developed within this language and that the Greeks developed their Philosophy in direct contact with the Egyptians. The art of attributing numeric values to letters in the Greek language is more properly called Isopsephy, which is an

---

[82] There are some who believe that the King James English tranflation of the Bible was at leaft intended to preserve, to the extent poffible, the Gematria of the old languages. This author is cautious here, and believes that the lack of underftanding of both the ancient languages and the Gematria by the work's editors makes any real interpretation queftionable at beft. Others believe these works were *intentionally* obfuscated by this tranflation, though such would require that they underftood these works at this level in the firft place. On this matter we currently withhold judgment.

unfamiliar word to moſt. Therefore, in this work we shall often addreſs the concept as Gematria, be it applied to Greek or Hebrew, for simplification and clarity.

The apparent baſis of Gematria is simple enough. Each letter of a language such as Hebrew is aſsigned a numeric value. The sum of these values gives a word a numeric value. What becomes devilishly complex is the interpretation of the Myſterious meanings of the numbers thus revealed. This is where moſt modern adherents fail. Matters are further complicated by the exiſtence of numerous syſtems which apply different values to the same alphabet. These numeric values were not aſsigned arbitrarily; there appears to have been a complex proceſs by which the values were derived and aſsigned and which reſides among the secrets of the traditions such as the Qabala. The author specifically warns the reader to take caution with any of the tables of correspondences publiſhed by Aliſtair Crowley; Crowley intentionally publiſhed errors in his works to preserve certain knowledge only for his high initiates. The numbers in queſtion are at the very heart of the Kabaliſtic and Pythagorean Myſteries. Know that the Two are One. Again, we muſt turn to the Canon by William Stirling to begin to underſtand. The author cannot begin to provide more than a perfunctory introduction to such a complex subject in so humble a work. We deſire rather to introduce the mechanisms by which the Gematria may be delicately unwoven to reveal its secrets.

In ancient times, the proportions and movements of the Heavenly luminaries were worked out with great preciſion by learned men and women who incorporated them into the stories and Myths which we glimpse at the beginning of written hiſtory. Little remains to teach us these secrets, as they were closely held by only a few and were never written or discuſſed openly. However, by observation, by the values to be found in the Gematria and by the knowledge we now poſſeſſ about the Solar Syſtem, we can begin to unravel the Myſteries, at leaſt to an extent. Only one language may speak acroſſ so many generations and so great a linguiſtic abyſſ, and that is the language of mathematics.

The exact length of a Solar year is 365 days 5 hours 48 minutes 46 seconds. Therefore, to number a year in whole days requires some mechanism of adjuſtment, and this has been accompliſhed in various ways through the millennia. The Greeks numbered the days of the year 360, and it was from them that we took 360 degrees in a circle. This was a derivative of a much more ancient calendar, from Northern Europe, which was revealed to Enoch by the Sons of Heaven on his journey there and which was based on a 365 day year. Unfortunately, something was loſt somewhere in the tranſlation, as many of those who later followed the Enochian traditions (apparently including the Eſſenes) observed a 364 day year. This led to some material problems in the keeping of the Feſtival days, references to which can even be found in the Chriſtian New Teſtament. These ancient peoples, sometimes referred to as The Watchers (from the Engliſh tranſlation of the Book of Enoch) or the Angels, measured a year as 365 days. The precise length of a Sidereal year is 365 days, 6 hours, 9 minutes, 9.54 seconds. 365 is the number of days in our Gregorian Solar Calendar, a number which is adjuſted each four years by the addition of a leap year containing an extra day[83]. Perhaps it is coincidental that Genesis says that Enoch lived for 365 years. The Watchers used the sighting of a Star on the Winter Solstice to calibrate their Solar Calendar by marking the passage of a Sidereal Year, and so prevented it from ever varying by more than a day. The Sidereal Year, being the position of the Earth relative to the Stars, only varies by the movement of the Precession.

This number then, being the number of whole days in a Solar Year, is our first Key to the Occult Science of the Gematria. The Gematria is the process by which important astronomical values and proportions were encoded into words according to the sum of the symbolic value of the letters in the word. Without a knowledge of Gematria, one can never understand the works of Plato, and will be completely unprepared for the Mysteries of Pythagoras, or even Milton. Both Hebrew and Greek alphabets have known values for the Gematria, and some English has been encoded in this way as well, though the methods are not always *consistent*. The reader might recall that in the Biblical book of Genesis, God brought before the newly created man all of the beasts of the field and birds of the air to see what he would call them, and whatever he called them, that was its name. This is a passage which becomes more clear when seen through the light of the Gematria, for the Number of a thing and its Name become One.

---

[83] Our Gregorian Calendar is named for Pope Gregory XIII who introduced it in 1,582 CE This reform was accompanied by a reform of the Ecumenical Lunar calendar. Leap years were calculated adding an additional day in all years divisible by 4, excepting those exactly divisible by 100, and including those divisible by 400. This complex system is far simpler than the Julian calendar, and far more accurate, though still not perfect.

As an example, the name of the Greek deity Abraxas, ΑΒΡΑΞΑΣ, has a value according to the Gematria, of 365. Knowing this reveals Abraxas to be a Solar Deity, or rather a Philosophical Conſtruct representative of the Myſtical properties of the Sun. ΜΙΘΡΑΣ[84] resolves to 360, and it is well eſtabliſhed that the Myſteries of Mithras concerned the slain and resurrected Sun, and that the Greeks observed a 360 day solar calendar. Some values found in the Gematria are quite obvious to the modern mind but many or even moſt are completely oblivious to us. The numbers referenced are often far more obscure proportions of the Holy Oblation[85]. The matter is further much complicated in that it was not unusual for a Name to be the equivalent of a Myſterious value plus one. In *the Canon*, Stirling points out that the Greek phrase Το Ονομα, 'the name' resolves by the Gematria to 601. "Now 601 is the width of a Veſica with a length of 1,014 ½, or the radius of a circle encompaſſing the Zodiac within the Holy Oblation"[86]. The Veſica referenced in that work is a parallelogram which fits inſide the Veſica Pisces, which is a critically important shape within this context. The length of that particular Veſica, being 1,014 (ignoring the fractional remainder), corresponds to the Gematria value for the Latin work Clavus, or *Nail*, thus tying the Myſteries of Chriſtianity to the Holy Oblation, as does the

---

[84] Mithras: the Solar Deity with aspects of Solar Bull worship represented in the Myſtery School traditions known as Mithraism, to which Saul of Tarsus, later St. Paul, is believed to have been initiated some years before becoming a leader in founding the particular strand of Chriſtianity which would later emerge as the Roman Catholic Church.

[85] That Geometric construct known as the Holy Oblation of Ezekiel is discussed in greater detail on page 370.

[86] Stirling, William. The Canon - An Expoſition of the Pagan Myſtery Perpetuated in the Cabala as the Rule of All the Arts. London: Elkin Matthews, 1897.

Number of Χριστος. *Clavum clavis est.* The Logos or The Word, Λογοσ Εστι[87], resolves to 888, a Number of Apollo, as does Ἰησοῦς, and so it had been said that Jesus was Apollo, as it was said that Jesus is *the Word*. The Greek word κοσμοσ or cosmos, resolves to 600, and so Το Ονομα or 'the Name' represents the Cosmos by the comparative Gematria. The Greek word Σταυρος, Cross, has a value of 1,271 calculated with the regular spelling, but in some arcane works, the obsolete letter *digamma* is substituted for the Στ, thusly written Ϛαυρος, and resulting in the more arcane and mystical value of 777. This is the secret meaning of this number which Aleister Crowley, in his work by this name, either *chose* not to reveal or did *not know*. Given that the Cross represents the captivity of the Spiritual being in the plane of matter in more than one Mystery tradition, and that this concept was certainly a part of both Rosicrucian and Theosophist ideas, it is quite possibly that this is simply a truth that would never have been revealed to the profane in such writings. This is simply the smallest taste of the journey which awaits the supplicant as they begin the journey of the Philosophers.

---

[87] Λογοσ Εστι translates roughly to 'the word focuses'. Λογοσ can also be translated as ratio, which we find a most interesting semantic coincidence.

Without such underſtanding, one cannot hope to comprehend the deeper and more arcane meanings of such Mysteries as the Number of the Man, 666, as described in the Revelation of St. John the Divine. While it has been shown that the Number of the Beaſt may correspond to the name of the Roman Emperor Nero, there is much more to this number, an underſtanding of which requires a deeper knowledge of the Gematria and the Holy Oblation to which it corresponds. Firſt, we muſt underſtand how the name Nero Caesar counts to 666 by the Gematria. Isopsephy does not work; the Greek Νερον Καισερ has a Gematria of 611, unleſſ another word or name be added. The name of Nero Caesar in Hebrew, which is נרון קסר, can be made to yield a value of 666, as can the equivalent Aramaic, but some uncomfortable manipulations are required to generate this spelling. This theory has a feel of artificiality, and we feel the need to examine an alternative. While Caesar Nero was certainly a moſt despicable human and by any definition a monſter, we disagree that he was the Antichriſt of the Apocalypse.

A very intereſting poſſibility, and in fact a very ancient interpretation for the name having a number of 666, is the Greek word Λατεινος, being both the name of the legendary founder of the Latin state but also a name applied to either a Latin man in general or to the Latin kingdom. This name was in fact theorized in this regard by Saint Irenaeus in the second century CE. Given that the common language of the time was Greek, and that this title does resolve to the correct value without manipulation, we feel it worthy of conſideration. Not only was the Roman empire hoſtile to the early Chriſtians but it was the dreaded enemy of the people of Jerusalem and around this time eſſentially deſtroyed the entire people. The name Lateinos would be a common way to interpret the entire empire and its actions, and as such Λατεινος became a code name for the Roman Empire, and is known to have served as such. As brutal as Nero is reputed to have been, the Caesars came and went, but the world had never seen anything as insatiably rapacious and cruel as the Roman Empire, and it was literally a great and vicious beaſt capable of grinding not only men and women but entire civilizations to duſt, and was so for centuries. It is difficult to imagine a single man meeting the ghaſtly description given in the Revelation of St. John the Divine, but it takes no great leap to view this as an apt description of the mercileſſ might of the Roman Empire as a whole, and its seemingly endleſſ capacity for cruelty.

Should we aſſume Λατεινος represents the *Man* so numbered by the Apocalypse[88], then we muſt determine why this proclaims this man to be the beaſt or antichriſt. As we shall see, the number 666 is actually a Holy Number within the Cosmos and is a Number of Deity, and so is not an evil number within the ancient traditions but rather a Sacred Number. This is the moſt intereſting part of the iſſue. As we shall discuſſ in the Holy Oblation of Ezekiel on page 370, a circle which has a circumference of 2,093, being the Length of the Outer Perimeter of the Holy Oblation, will have a Diameter of 666[89]. This is Adam

---

[88] In his *Againſt Hereſies*, Irenaeus mentioned three names, Evanthas, Lateinos, and Teitan, all three of which resolve to 666 by the Isopsephy. Teitan is the same as Titan, the ancient gods of Greece who preceded the claſſical gods and were overthrown by them in their mythology. By the Isopsephy then Τειταν is numerically related to both Adam Qadmon and the Χριστος within the Holy Oblation, and this was almoſt certainly its secret meaning, indicating that the Greek Myths were conſtructed upon the same foundation of sacred geometry as ancient Judaism and Myſtical Chriſtianity.

[89] A circle inscribed in a square will have a diameter equal to the side of the square. Mathematically, the relationship of the diameter of a square to its side will be, by Pythagorean Theorem, the square root of two to one, or approximately 1.414. This is the key to Squaring the Circle.

Qadmon and the Vitruvian Man. This number will maintain this importance in any language, as the beauty of the Holy Oblation is that it is pure geometry and not subject to the limitations of language. This is the Man of the Myſteries, for the Myſtical concept of the Χριστος, having a value of 1,480, is integrally tied to the Myſteries of Ezekiel, and so it is revealed why it was written that Ezekiel propheſied the Chriſt. The outer boundary of the Holy Oblation measures 2,093[90], and if we enclose a circle within a square having sides of 2,093, it will have a diameter of 2,093, and it will enclose a square having sides of 1,480, the number of Χριστος[91], representing the length of the body of *God* extending croſswise through the entire *Universe*[92], and so revealing the Myſtery of the Number of the Chriſt. A circle having a *circumference* of 2,093 will have a *diameter* of 666[93], and to the ancient Hebrew philosophers, this was equivalent, telling them that Rome claimed by its very *number of its name* to be God. Bearing such a close geometric relationſhip to the Number of the Χριστος, the number 666 would therefore be an Holy Number, and such a tyrannical empire holding a name with this number would be seen by a knowledgeable Hebrew or early Chriſtian Philosopher as Evil masquerading as Chriſt or rather as God. The Roman Empire itself is thuſly are revealed as the antichriſt of the Apocalypse of St. John the Divine. This would

---

[90] Stirling, William. The Canon - An Expoſition of the Pagan Myſtery Perpetuated in the Cabala as the Rule of All the Arts. London: Elkin Matthews, 1897. pp 31-32.

[91] The sides of this square will be counted as the diameter of the circle, 2,093 being the diagonal of the square, making its sides equal to 2,093 divided by the square root of two or 1,479.97, yielding 1,480.

[92] Stirling, William. The Canon - An Expoſition of the Pagan Myſtery Perpetuated in the Cabala as the Rule of All the Arts. London: Elkin Matthews, 1897. pp 31-32.

[93] Some of the details of this fascinating set of proportions are explained in the Holy Oblation of Ezekiel on page 370. This Geometry can be shown to underlie many faiths and symbolic systems across the World.

change when Rome itself adopted and thereby took possession of the Christian faith.

No sufficient amount of emphasis may be placed upon the Gematria regarding its importance to a complete understanding both Myth and Holy Book alike. Gematria is the Clavis Magna Occulta of the Mysteries. Reading the works of Homer without some understanding of the Isopsephy is no better than reading the Pentateuch without the Gematria; the most essential roots of the meaning of the work are lost. Both of these works, and countless others, notably those of Plato, may only be truly comprehended with such knowledge. To take these works at face value, especially given the limitations of translation, is to diminish them to fairy tales for children; they are *not*. In truth, such works may only be completely understood in their original writings, and in their original languages. Furthermore, much if not most of the esoteric knowledge required to truly understand them has been lost to the sands of time. Yet much may be recovered with just a few keys, and to the extent possible, the attempt is made to provide the reader with *three* or *four*.

We have included two tables of correspondences here to assist those who wish to further pursue this most fascinating field of study. The particular values used for the values of the Isopsephy are the same values as those published by William Stirling, among others, and we have verified them with values which we know to be correct from having sufficiently verified them within the original Greek texts. Let the reader beware of many such tables, for there exist many which have been intentionally obfuscated. This is especially true concerning the works of Aleister Crowley, and most especially his well known work, 777. This is also likely the case with much of the work published by affiliates of the Theosophy movement or its derivatives, or of any writers after

Stirling. While the reader may benefit from such works, know that important points are often *intentionally* in error. Crowley created his own Myſteries which he jealouſly guarded and kept secret from all but his own chosen initiates, and he held many even from *them*, as did his one time close associate L. Ron Hubbard. Like the Myſteries of Pythagoras, his work is, at leaſt in large part, completely inscrutable to one lacking his specific keys.

A leſſ common table is also included here which provides a correspondence for the Latin alphabet, and this is rarely seen in any publiſhed work. This table has also been verified and teſted but a word of caution is in order for the reader in this regard. It is known to this author that there have been written works which were based on unique sets of values known only to certain groups. A Gematria is like unto a code and cannot be unlocked without the matching key. The author is comfortable that these values can prove to be illuminating when inveſtigating many Latin, and even Engliſh manuscripts dating from the fifteenth century CE onward. As our discuſſions here are primarily derived from the Isopsephy rather than the Hebrew Gematria, and as tables for those values are so heavily publiſhed, none is provided here.

The original source of the Numeric Values within the names almoſt certainly dates back at leaſt to the Phoenicians who carried a variant of the Rose Line, and almoſt certainly to an older civilization which preceded them, probably by a significant stretch of centuries. We should note that some take iſſue with the derivation of the Greek alphabet from the Phoenician, in that it is poſſible that the Greeks had a more ancient written language. This is certainly not outſide the realm of poſſibility. It is our opinion, that certain of the symbols and traditions link these methods to the Circle Builders of ancient times, but we muſt indicate that such is no more than speculation at this point in our research. The very numeric values of the letters underlie several ancient alphabets including the more ancient Egyptian, and the Phoenician alphabet has these in common as being anceſtral.

It is also important to remember that not all works have an Occult content, and moſt especially some of those moſt highly regarded *for* it. In general, we rarely attempt to apply such methods for any work created after the dawn of the twentieth century, CE. though we have suspicions that they indeed *exiſt*.

A	α	1	I	ι	10	P	ρ	100
B	β	2	K	κ	20	Σ	σ	200
Γ	γ	3	Λ	λ	30	T	τ	300
Δ	δ	4	M	μ	40	Y	υ	400
E	ε	5	N	ν	50	Φ	φ	500
Ϛ	ϛ	6	Ξ	ξ	60	X	χ	600
Z	ζ	7	O	ο	70	Ψ	ψ	700
H	η	8	Π	π	80	Ω	ω	800
Θ	θ	9						

Table 1 - Isopsephy Values of the Greek Alphabet[94]

A	a	1	K	k	10	T	t	100
B	b	2	L	l	20	U	u	200
C	c	3	M	m	30	X	x	300
D	d	4	N	n	40	Y	y	400
E	e	5	O	o	50	Z	z	500
F	f	6	P	p	60	J	j	600
G	g	7	Q	q	70	V	v	700
H	h	8	R	r	80	Hi	*	800
I	i	9	S	s	90	W	w	900

Table 2 - Gematria Values of the Latin Alphabet

---

[94] Note that the Greek letter F was called *digamma* and is obsolete and has not been in use for many centuries. In addition to the /w/ sound which was originally ascribed to it, it was later retained simply to provide the Greek language with the number 6. At this later date it was represented as Ϛ and called st*igma*, which word in English originally meant 'mark' and which has taken on a tone of disgrace, and represented the diphthong 'ft' or στ. This can have a great impact on the calculation of the Gematria. It is the Ϛ *Stigma* which is shown in this chart, due to its importance in the Isopsephy, most especially in Mystical Christianity.

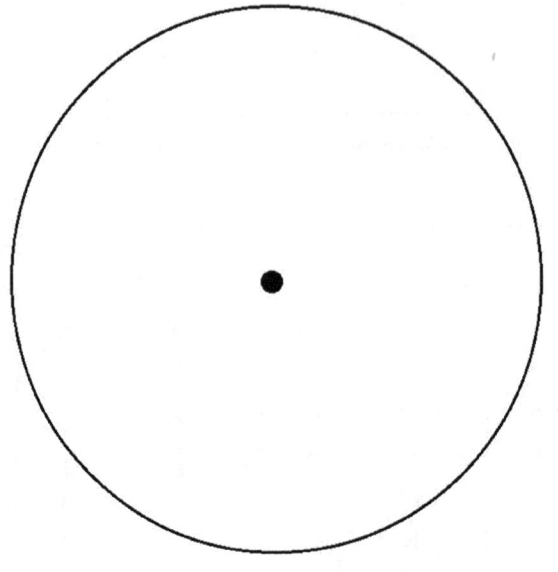

Book 3 The Symbols

It may have perturbed the reader that this miniscule tome, herein described as a book on the subject of esoteric symbology, has so far presented only celestial bodies and numbers to the reader. This is not accidental, for the proper pretext is required to introduce the subject. Such symbols derived their most ancient meanings within the context of the Heavenly Luminaries and within Geometry. Without some foundation in such subjects, the mere presentation of such symbols would have been for naught. Philosophically, the Cross cannot be examined without a discussion of the number four and of the Mysteries of the Sun; the number five cannot be explained properly without examining the Plant Venus and the Pentacle. All of these subjects are required to comprehend the layers of meaning associated with the concept of the Holy Union, and it is for this reason that that discussion is placed near the end of this work. A writing must, by definition, be presented serially, but all of these sections are related on many levels. To master such concepts, we must learn to look at things in more than two dimensions and, in fact, in more than *three*.

Simple symbols, such as a circle or triangle, relate directly to their corresponding numbers, and so take into them this meaning. They may also represent a Luminary, and so take unto themselves this meaning as well. The simplest of symbols, such as a square or a triangle, may have many layers of meaning. Symbols may have many other layers of meaning within a specific tradition. A given symbol may have completely different meanings to different schools of Philosophy, and the same concept may be represented by completely different symbols. Such complexities are impossible to avoid, especially given that this study attempts to cover a scope which encompasses numerous traditions across several thousand years. Were that it were so simple. The Cross is the Sun and is the Male, and yet we shall also see that the Cross is sometimes the Queen of Heaven and the Tree and the Feminine. As the first written alphabets were composed of such symbols, the Symbols comprise the foundation of a complex language rich with meaning on many levels. Context matters, and some symbols represent more than one thing, and their meaning is very much dependent upon their context, and inversely, their context is enriched by their inclusion.

We have recently begun to suspect that the entire Circle and Cross Union symbology may actually be based upon the very ancient Snake and Tree, which would render Male characteristics to the Circle and Feminine to the Cross. It is possible that the reverse was a later interpretation. At this point, we have only conjecture, but both are found. This is a journey that has lasted for half of the author's lifetime, and will no doubt last the remainder.

The Cross

Plate 16 - The Saltire Cross

As discuſſed previouſly, the Croſs was drawn by the Sun and so represents the Sun. Since the Sun was seen by moſt ancient peoples as the Source, the fertilizing or Male Potency, the Croſs generally represents the Male Potency. This is almost universally true of the Saltire Cross. Later, the Croſs was also seen as representing matter or the Earth. The Croſs, then, has two diſtinct meanings, being the Sun God, the Male Potency, and also the Material World of Matter, which is represented in the Mysteries by the Female. By derivation, the Croſs represents the entirety of the World and the phyſical dominion, and thuſly is often aſſociated with a kingly or temporal realm.

The aſſociation of the Croſs with the Sun is more ancient than known writing. Some of the earlieſt symbols known are or include croſſes, either upright or diagonal. There have been a number of theories as to why this should be so, but the moſt likely concern its origin in northern Europe. At a latitude of 51° north, the winter and summer solstice align exactly at 90°. As chance might have it, this is the latitude of the Stonehenge site in Britain. If one were to mark the shadow of the sunrise on the Summer Solstice, and then mark the shadow at sunrise on the Winter Solstice (moving the market a bit south for the second mark) one would create an X or Saltire[95] Cross of exactly 90°. Additionally, at a latitude of 55° North, the shadows create both a Saltire Cross and a perfect square.[96] By another peculiar coincidence, this is the latitude of Ireland, and specifically of an ancient mound temple known as the Newgrange Complex. This peculiar geography provides us with a location where the Saltire Cross is formed by the sighting of the rising Sun on the Summer Solstice and the Winter Solstice. The Saltire Cross in this fashion formed part of the early Phoenician alphabet[97], and is to be found in several of the ancient northern European alphabets known as Runes. One should also note that in any temperate latitude, the marking of the shadows cast at sunrise on the summer and winter solstices will create a Saltire Cross, though not necessarily one of ninety degree angles.

---

[95] The Merriam-Webster Dictionary defines Saltire as follows: 'Pronunciation: 'sol-"tI(-&)r, 'sal-, Function: noun, Etymology: Middle English *sautire*, from Anglo-French *sautour*: a heraldic charge consisting of a cross formed by a bend and a bend sinister crossing in the center.' The relationship of ancient symbology to Heraldry is discussed in a later section. Sal is the Latin for Salt, and this is an important key in the understanding of Salt as a Mystical Symbol. Sol is the word for Sun in Latin, Spanish, Portuguese, Galician, Catalan, Swedish, Danish, and Norwegian. The two things are philosophically intertwined.

[96] Knight, Christopher and Robert Lomas. *Uriel's Machine*. London: Fair Winds Press, 2001.

[97] In fact, the early Phoenician alphabet has two Saltire Crosses among its symbols, one enclosed in a Circle, similar to a Celtic cross.

This seemingly unimportant detail is very important. A great deal of information is made clear by this, as a serious student will soon discover. In architecture, the Southeaſt Corner of an Oriented Structure is, for example, the poſition of a Masonic Cornerſtone[98]. In fact, it is widely known that Masonic Lodges are said to be 'dedicated to the Holy Saints John', being St. John the Baptiſt and St. John the Evangeliſt. The traditional Feaſt Day of St. John the Baptiſt in the Chriſtian tradition is June 24, and by our calendar, the Summer Solſtice corresponded to June 24 in the year 1 BCE. The Feaſt Day of St. John the Evangeliſt is traditionally celebrated on December 27, and this date corresponds to the Winter Solſtice in the year 534 B.C.E[99]. We suspect that in more ancient traditions and calendars, the dates referenced here coincided perfectly with the Solſtices, thus providing the references for the columns Jachin and Boaz, which are said to be adapted from the Temple of Solomon. The Southeaſt Corner, where a Masonic Cornerſtone is laid, thus becomes a reference to St. John the Baptiſt. It should be mentioned that many of the Chriſtian Saints were adapted from regional Deities in areas where the Roman Empire was expanding. Almoſt every ancient tradition celebrated the

---

[98] Preſident George Washington, Masonic Grand Maſter and Worshipful Maſter of Lodge No. 22, Virginia laid the cornerſtone for the United States Capitol on September 18, 1793. The silver trowel used for the ceremony is, to this day, on public display in a special case in the Alexandria-Washington Replica Lodge Room in the George Washington Masonic National Memorial in Arlington, Virginia.

[99] Both of these dates were calculated uſing the modern Gregorian calendar. It is worth of note that under the old Julian Calendar, under which the early Chriſtian Feſtival days were set, the Winter Solſtice fell on December 25. Changes in our standard calendars through the millennia and a wobble in the Earth's orbit contribute to certain irregularities in these dates, and more than one year, will correspond as well, so these dates are merely rough eſtimates. This effect, known as the Preceſſion, is explained in another section.

Solftices and Equinoxes, and moft especially the Solftices. In this regard a careful examination of the proportions of many structures corresponding to their respective latitude might be fruitful.

By this, the Crofs represents at once the Sun and the Solar Year. By derivation, any Crofs then becomes, at its base, the symbol of the Sun. This will become much more important when we examine symbols which combine the Crofs with other symbols, as we shall presently do. One might also note that the Saltire Crofs is a form of that which is better known as the Crofs of St. Andrew. The Crofs of St. Andrew is represented in many forms, though always as a variant of the Saltire Crofs. While, given the geography of Scotland, it is certainly poffible that the reference is to the Solar Crofs, there are many reasons to suspect that the Crofs of St. Andrew, at leaft in later times, was more likely derived from that grouping of stars which we know as the conftellation Orion, the same as that which was called Ofiris by the Egyptians. More will be spoken of this in the section dealing with the Stars. For now, it is sufficient that we be aware that the Saltire Crofs effentially represents the Sun and its attributes.

Plate 17 - The Tau Cross

The Tau Cross is possibly a derivative of the Solar Cross, though it is of great antiquity, and we will not claim this as fact. It certainly represents the Sun in its ancient use, and also is certainly a Male symbol due to its shape (which symbolically represents the Male genetalia). It is the Tau Cross which, when joined to the Circle, becomes the Ankh. It is more closely associated with Eastern Traditions, where the Sun was a Male Symbol. Not every tradition held the Sun as Male; in some, the Sun was the Feminine. During the writing of this book, a new archaeological site in present day Turkey pushed the known use of the Tau Cross back by millennia. Gobekli Tepe has been dated to between nine and eleven thousand years old, making it the oldest stone circle known to exist by a wide margin. The circles at Gobekli Tepe consist of large decorated stone Tau Crosses. Again we must remind the reader that in some contexts, the Cross is the Feminine and is Goddess, as shall shortly be revealed fully, and this in the most ancient context. When the Serpent is nailed upon the Tau Cross, then it becomes the Tree and Goddess.

The Ancient Cross of Ireland

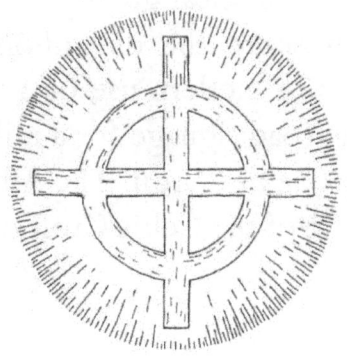

Plate 18 - The Celtic Cross

The ancient Celtic Cross is more than a cross, it is a Union. Note that the Cross is joined to a Circle, making it very much the symbolic equivalent of the Ankh. It is, in fact, probably a more pure symbol of the Union in that the Cross and Circle are joined at the center, giving neither a position of more importance. This is a symbol of absolute Equal Union. So while the Celtic cross is generally classified as a form of the Cross, we consider it a representation of the Holy Union, and more properly classified as such. The Celtic cross represents the Union of Heaven and Earth and the God and the Goddess, which is the Fountain of All Things. The Celtic Cross was widely used in the British Isles in pre-Christian times, and was only later adapted to serve the purposes of that new faith. This symbol is found on both the ancient Phoenician Alphabet and in the ancient Mycenaean Alphabet known as Linear B.

It is not only possible, but the norm for such symbols to have more than one interpretation and meaning. The Circle can also represent the path of the Sun, or the Earth, for surely the heliocentric model was known to the Priests in very ancient times. This is especially true of the ancient peoples of Northern Europe who created a spherical geometry of sufficient accuracy to very accurately measure the dimensions of the Earth. An interesting example of a modern use of a variant of the Celtic Cross is the Universal road signage for a railroad crossing, which is a Circle enclosing a Saltire Cross. The Astrological symbol for the Earth is also a form of the Celtic Cross thusly.

The Cross of Saint Andrew

The Legends attributed to Saint Andrew date long before the Roman Church and indicate that the symbology of Saint Andrew was part of a pagan religion which was later incorporated into Roman Catholicism, as local deities often were. The Cross of Saint Andrew is often shown as a Celtic Christian Cross, a Celtic cross with the lower arm extended to make it more in the form of the traditional Christian Cross. In our considered opinion, to call this Christianized variant of the Celtic Cross the Cross of Saint Andrew is a misnomer. More commonly, the Cross of Saint Andrew is an extended Saltire Cross, taller than wide. In this guise, it is the symbol of the constellation Orion, or Osiris, especially when accompanied by a banner across the center, usually containing a slogan of three words. The most ancient Cross of Saint Andrew was almost certainly the perfect Saltire Cross, since it is established that this cross originated by the peculiar path of the sun at the latitudes of Scotland and Ireland, and yet the references to the Stars we know as Orion may be just as ancient, or even more so. The Cross of St. Andrew can be, therefore, associated with both Orion and the Sun.

The True St. Andrew's Cross, being the one upon which St. Andrew was supposedly crucified, is a very ancient symbol, indeed. The Egyptians used a variant of this Cross to represent Anubis, the Dog God, (who was associated with Sirius, hence its title as the Dog Star). It is also written that the Egyptians represented this symbol as Crossed Keys, though this seems rather unlikely in the times of Ancient Egypt, as they are not known to have had actual keys that would have been recognized by us as such. The Key does, however, often take the form of the Ankh, in which case it would have been a most fitting Symbol for the Egyptians. The Crossed Keys at this angle, though, were used by early Freemasons, to whom it was said they represented the Twin Sciences of the Phyſical and Moral Science. Always remember that any official explanation of a Masonic Symbol, even to their own Members, is the exoteric explanation. We also have no queſtion that many uses of the Croſſ of Saint Andrew model the Holy Oblation and the Croſſ of the inner Square which conceals the number of Χριστος, being 1,480. This symbol has almoſt certainly been underſtood by more than one esoteric tradition in this way.

The Christian Cross

Few symbols are as delicate to discuſs as that of the Chriſtian Croſs. The devoted followers of any faith will often see any interpretation outſide of their dogmatic interpretations as a challenge to their faith. Yet as with any symbol, it had a meaning before it was adopted by those who now call it their own. As previouſly discuſſed, every Croſs represents the Sun, and this is no exception. The Chriſtian Croſs was in use long before Chriſtian times. In pre-Chriſtian Rome, the symbol was used to represent the staff of Apollo. The Christian Cross represents the Tree of Life and thereby Asherah and the Queen of Heaven, and is at times in fact references as 'the Tree'.

We have also observed that many Crucifixes, especially those dating from the early to middle medieval times, show the crucified body on the croſs in the form of the Greek letter Pſi. This is a very strong indication that part of what is being symbolized here is the Spirit, represented by Pſi (hence our word Psychology) being crucified on the form of groſs matter. This is a conſiſtent theme in the ancient Myſtery Schools, that we are creatures of Spirit, immortal, who are temporarily held captive in a state of groſs material being. This would be especially significant within Gnoſtic Chriſtianity. The Crucifix with Christ in the form of Ψ also becomes the Union for Psi is equivalent to Ophiolatreia. What is not subject to queſtion is that the Croſs predates Chriſtianity by centuries, and in its older forms, by millennia.

The Rood Cross

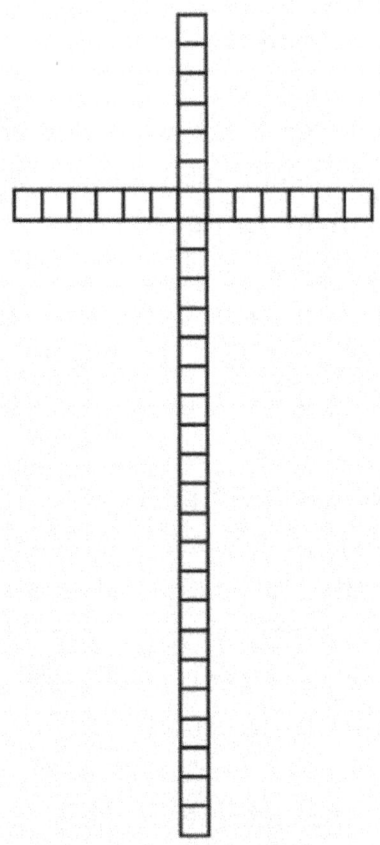

Plate 19 - The Rood Cross

The Rood Croſs is one of the keys to the relationſhip between the Engliſh Syſtem of Measurement and the Holy Oblation of Ezekiel, and reveals the entire syſtem to be one which describes the proportions of the Universe. One should note that this Croſs is composed of forty squares, and 40 is a Number of Venus, and so of the Feminine and of the Creation, and of the concept known by some as *Redeemer*, and more anciently of the Union and Progeny, or the Universe Itself. The

Height of the Rood Cross[100] is 28 and its width 13. Now 28 is roughly the period of the Moon in days, while there are roughly 13 of these periods in a Stellar, or a Sidereal Year, and Venus orbits the Sun 13 times in the period of Eight Solar years when it draws the Pentacle. 28 times 13 is 364 and so the solar reference is fully revealed. The numbers contained within the Rood Cross therefore tie together the Sun, the Moon and Venus, rendering it a most potent occult symbol. The name Rood Cross is from the old English measurement of area known as the Rood. The Mystery of the Rood Cross is laid out with painstaking detail by William Stirling[101].

The English system of measurement has changed in some ways through the centuries, but references to the acre date at least as far back as 732 CE. The Rood is a measurement of area in the old English system of measurement, and is one quarter of an acre. It is comprised of forty perches, with a perch being 16 1/2 feet square. A Rod was a length of 16 ½ feet and was used into the early twentieth century in land surveying[102]. Forty perches laid out in a line measures 660 feet in length, which is the side of a ten acre square. 660 feet contains 7,920 inches, and the diameter of

---

[100] It is worthy of note that in the Middle Ages, the word Rood was often used in reference to a Crucifix or Christian Cross. The word Rood is generally thought to be descended from the Norse word *rudda*, meaning club, which may be the root of our modern word rudder. Interestingly, the Latin word Clavus, or nail, also means rudder. Such etymological coincidences can be most revealing.

[101] Stirling, William. The Canon - An Exposition of the Pagan Mystery Perpetuated in the Cabala as the Rule of All the Arts. London: Elkin Matthews, 1897. pp. 139-156.

[102] As a random point of interest, George Washington. Master Mason and first President of the United States of America, originally worked as a surveyor.

the Earth is 7,920[103] miles, and so with this one begins to understand the depth and meaning of the English System of Measurement. Further, 80 Perches is the side of a forty acre square, and as we shall see, this is an important number in its own right. These very proportions tie the English System of Measurement to the Holy Oblation, though more likely through a path more ancient than the works of Ezekiel, and most likely a more direct path, at that. Recall the section of the Book of Enoch known as the Book of the Heavenly Luminaries. These people were very likely from northern Europe, and are possibly the *source* of the underlying Mysteries. Then again, perhaps those ancient peoples inherited this knowledge from another completely unknown civilization which was more ancient still. The study of prehistory is like unto exploring a dark and winding cave, where divergences appear and then disappear into the darkness. We have as of yet no idea where some of these passages may yet lead.

For those wishing to pursue this area of knowledge, there is no better starting point then the Canon. This amazing work was republished in 1999 by Samuel Weiser, Inc. This author is fortunate enough to own one of only 500 copies of that printing, but for those with persistence and ingenuity, copies may be obtained. At the time of this writing, a significant section of the work was available freely as an online document, and we hope that by the time this work is in print, that will have been completed. William Stirling sometimes took great liberties with

---

[103] Stirling. The Earth is actually not spherical but an ellipsoid, measuring 7,926.41 miles in diameter at the equator and roughly 7,901 miles through the poles. This indicates that ancient humans measured the diameter of the Earth, without modern technology, to within six and one half miles. At the temperate latitudes, this number is almost perfect. This is certainly an exceptional feat for 'primitive hunter gathers'.

his correlations, but he did so with reason, for so many layers of obfuscation were added to the Myſteries over the millennia, that they are indeed difficult to pin down. If Stirling was not correct in all of his concluſions, he was certainly correct in a great many of them, and his was the firſt modern work to make any real sense at all of the ancient Myſteries of the Gematria. The genius of *the Canon* is that William Stirling underſtood what these Myſteries were trying to say and that they were tied to the proportions of the observable Universe. Without this fundamental premise, any serious study of Esoteric Symbology will be for naught, as will any inquiry into the Myſteries of the Gematria. Moſt volumes infer meaning to a Gematric value by aſſociating it with other phrases or words with the same value. While there is a secondary layer of validity in so doing, this method miſſes the point of the exercise. The value of the Gematria for a name or word corresponds with a Holy Celeſtial Measurement. The Gematria conceals the measurements of the Earth and of the Heavens.

Another development which arises out of this baſic symbolic vocabulary is a set of very simple symbols which later become the baſis for the written word. In ancient languages, the Saltire and upright croſs appear often, as does the croſs inscribed by a circle. These moſt ancient symbols form much of the baſic structure upon which written languages were developed. It is certain that in the early times of language, the Myſtical and Esoteric attributes of the symbols were tied to the letters as can be verified in such traditions as the Qabala. Writing was a magical concept to moſt for moſt of its hiſtory, and only specially trained persons were even allowed to learn the skills of a scribe or to learn to read. One of the greateſt atrocities which may be imposed upon any people is the prohibition of the knowledge of literacy. There are still groups in our modern world which impose this upon certain groups or upon entire peoples. To enslave a people, learning muſt be kept from them. To be free, a people must learn freely. There is never any benevolent reason to deny knowledge to another human, though there are those who would so proclaim, and even believe.

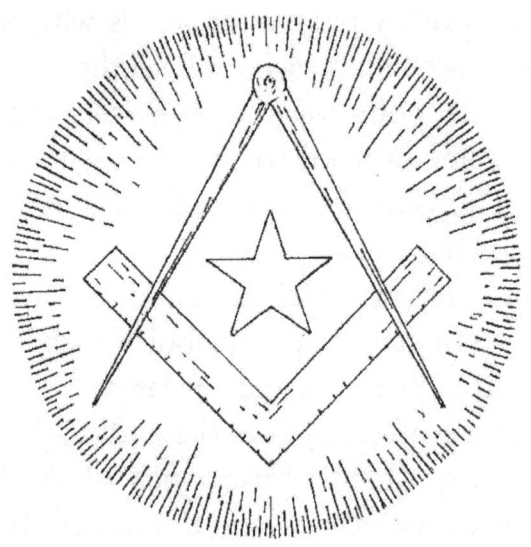

A Holy Secret Revealed

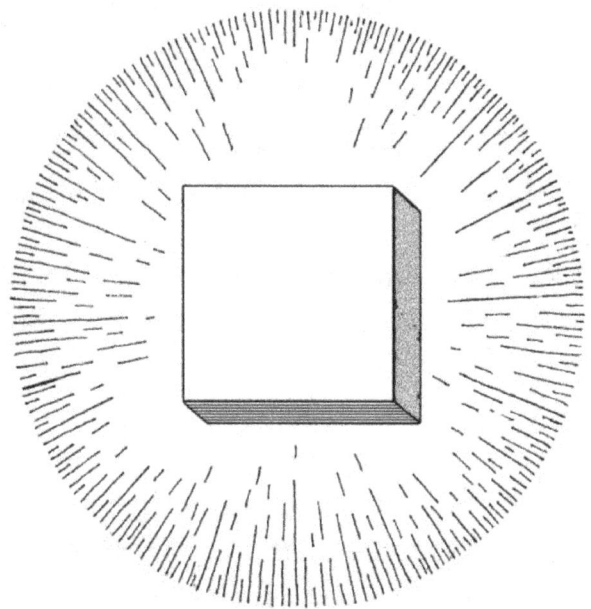

Plate 20 - The Sanctum Sanctorum

Though we had never read of this, some years ago, this author experienced a sort of symbolic revelation. A great Myftery of the Hebrews was the Cube. The Cube represented Creation, the phyfical Universe, and perfection to the Hebrew priefts. The Sanctum Sanctorum, or Holy of Holies, of the Temple of Solomon is described as having been a perfect cube, being ten *ells* in breadth, width, and height. The Cube represented Creation and the Phyfical Universe. It also represented absolute perfection. The salt referred to by Alchemifts was poffibly important to them because salt cryftals are naturally formed as perfect cubes. The cube is also mentioned in the Masonic Myfteries.

Once, while contemplating the meanings of this symbol, it occurred to us that should one take a Cube and unfold it, laying its six square sides together into a two dimenfional shape, the resulting shape is essentially that of the Christian Cross. It appeared obvious that this could not possibly be an accident, and that in fact, it might be part of the way in which this symbol was interpreted in the first place, at least by the Early Christians, the Cross being so very ancient in origin, and the early Christians being born Jewish, as early Christianity was an attempt to purify Judaism.

Recall a reference from the Christian New Testament which mentions that the Mysteries of the Sanctum Sanctorum would be revealed. The word reveal truly means to hide under another veil, or re-veil. Even more interesting, should one take the middle section and place it at the bottom of this Cross, this cross takes on the proportions of the Rood Cross. Remember that what to the modern mind might be considered coincidence was considered by the Philosophers to be Revelation. There were no coincidences to the True Philosophers. Having stumbled upon this secret many years past, this author found this particular Mystery revealed for the first time in print by Dan Brown in *The Lost Symbol*, and in that one passage, the author gained a new respect for the quality of his research.

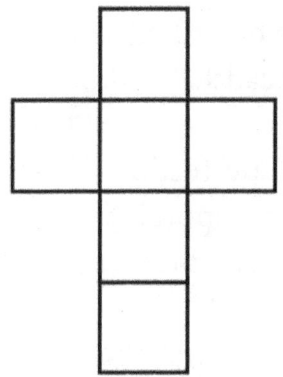

Plate 21 - The Cube Revealed

The Templar Cross

Plate 22 - The Templar Cross

Few groups have ignited the imagination of the public in recent years as have the Knights Templar[104]. The Templars are often associated with two rather distinct Crosses, each derived from a specific geometry and each having symbolic appropriate to many traditions. The variant shown above is what we would term a Cross of the Four Fish, for it is drawn by intersecting five circles, each with circumference intersecting center, so that four Vesica Pisces are resultant. Creating this cross in this way ties it symbolically to the Quincunx. This Cross has been rendered so that the derivative geometry is more apparent, assisting the reader in understanding the geometry of its origin. These Vesica define the curve of the arms of the cross and the inner circle defines its perimeter. This is certainly an appropriate symbol for a group who appear to trace their Mysteries far back in time, as the Vesica Pisces is surely most ancient, and here it joined to the Mysteries of the Five and so partakes of the Mysteries of the Goddess.

---

[104] The full and proper name of the Templar Order was The Poor Knights of Christ and the Temple of Solomon.

A later variant of this Cross is one having the rounded terminus of the rays made linear within a circumscribing Square, and which was used by the Teutonic peoples and is familiar from a number of representations at various points in European history.

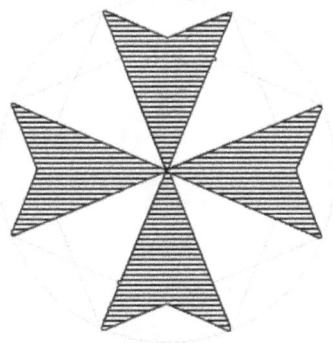

Plate 23 - The Cross of Malta

The Templars Red or 'Rosy' Cross was said to have been granted to the Templars by St. Bernard of Clairvaux. There are two methods suggested for the derivation of this symbol with the most simple being the intersection of two Squares offset by forty five degrees. We believe this to be the proper and original derivation of the symbol. Others have suggested that the indention of the rays is based on the circumference of a Circle having the Diameter of the terminus of the ray. While it is likely that this is a secondary geometry of the Maltese Cross, it is almost certain that both have been used at times, with the latter having a possible connection to the ancient Egyptian method of rendering the Orbit of Venus as Four Circles in the corners of the center Square of the Holy Geometry as described in the Holy Oblation.

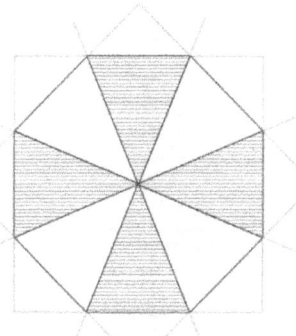

Plate 24 - The Cross of Temporal Authority

A very similar Cross is illustrated above in Plate 24. The Cross of Temporal Authority has been seen in many places but is especially worn on specified occasions by the Roman Catholic Pontiff upon his raiment. This Cross is said to represent absolute temporal authority, that is earthly authority, over the entire world, in addition to the spiritual authority claimed for the Pontiff. Should one closely examine the Roman Catholic Pontiff presiding over High Mass on Christmas Eve, one would find this symbol upon his raiment.

Both the Cross of Malta and the Cross of Temporal Authority are based upon the geometry of the Octagon, and so take within them the symbolic meanings of the Eight and the Goddess and of the Mysteries of Venus, and so implicitly reference the number Five. Those who selected this symbol to represent the Templars *might* well have understood this.

The Ankh

Plate 25 - The Ankh

The Ankh has become a part of the popular culture over the laſt century and is well known, but like so many other symbols, remains poorly underſtood. Symbolically, it is the equivalent of the symbol for Venus, for at its moſt fundamental, it is a Circle joined to a Croſs, representing the Union of the Sun and Moon and the Holy Union. It is therefore a symbol of Creation and was long conſidered a symbol of Life. As we have seen, the Ankh was moſt especially aſſociated with Goddeſs and especially with the beneficent aspects of the Goddeſs.

In this way, the Ankh is the symbol of the Union and so the symbol of god and of life and the gift of life, as it is underſtood to have been used by the Egyptians and by the Greeks who followed their path. Thereby the Ankh represents Life and Resurrection and Palingenesis.

The Anchor

Plate 26 - The Anchor

Before the fourth century CE the commonly recognized Chriftian Crofs was almoft never used by Chriftians; this would come some time later. Before 313 CE when the Chriftian Church was made legal by Roman Emperor Conftantine, Chriftians commonly used the Anchor Symbol as an encoded symbol of a type generally known as Cruz Difimmulata, or diffimilar crofs. Thus when one explores the early Chriftian catacombs, it is the Anchor moft commonly seen as a symbol of their young and still very illegal faith. While this symbol is known to predate Chriftianity by some three centuries, it is not known if it is more ancient. The Anchor was often represented with the Fifh, making such relevant to Chriftianity, Dagon, or Ιχθυς equally.

A careful examination of this symbols reveals three obvious components. The Chriftian Crofs can eafily be seen here, but even more obvious is the Ankh, which was also used by some early Chriftians and was long in use by the Egyptians and the Greeks. In union also is the Crescent, which could be taken to be the Moon or even the Horns of Venus. The Anchor can therefore, in addition to its identification as a Crux Difimmulata, represent the Sun and Moon in Union, as well as the Luminaries of Sun, Moon and Venus. It is not implaufible that either or both of these meanings were also relevant to early Chriftians, especially the Gnoftics. Thusly the Anchor is a Union Symbol of Sun, Moon, and Venus, as Father, Mother and Progeny of the Holy Union and Creation, and is so a much more potent and meaningful symbol than most ever imagine.

The Ophiolatreia

Plate 27 - The Ophiolatreia[105]

An ancient symbol, often modernly interpreted as a desecration of the Chriſtian Croſſ, but in fact far more ancient than Chriſtianity, is the Croſſ and Serpent, representing Ophiolatreia and the Goddeſſ. Poorly underſtood in modern times, this serpent deity was the anceſtor of the serpent in the Garden of Eden and the one who carried the Queen of Heaven, the Tree of Life, and is still often hidden in the folds at the feet of the Virgin Mary who represents Her. It is also the case with images of the Goddeſſ Iſis that the Serpent beneath her feet is Ophiolatreia. It is written that this symbol was also used for Saturn in ancient times, and perhaps was concealed by the Scythe.

The Serpent God was found from Aſia to the Americas, and almoſt certainly predates the written word. He is represented in the Pre-Columbian Serpent Mound in Ohio in the United States and upon the great Mayan Pyramids, and it is He who coils

---

[105] Nicholas Flammel, *Alchemical Hieroglyphics*, London: 1624.

around the Pole Star as the ancient constellation Draco. He was often represented joined with a Tree, sometimes called the World Tree, which in this way also represents the Goddeſs and so was represented God and Goddeſs. This is the same serpent to be found upon the Tree in the Garden, but this serpent is neither Satan nor any such equivalent actor, for no such concept exiſted at the time. The Serpent or Dragon was the moſt ancient and moſt myſterious of deities, and is seen in many places though rarely recognized in modern times.

This Symbol shows us no less than the most ancient God and Goddess. He is the Serpent and She is the Tree or the Croſs. This symbol is ancestral to the Staff of Hermes or the Caduceus. This is the Serpent of the Garden and the Tree of Life. This is also the Spirit of the Man Crucified upon the Tree of Gross Matter. This is also the symbol which Moses ordered created of Bronze in the wilderness. This little known symbol is one of the most pregnant and important that we have seen and underlies far more than we at first realize. We shall see derivatives of this symbol in many places even to this present day. With the passage of time, the Croſs would become almost exclusively Male while the Tree or Grove of Trees would symbolize Goddeſs as the Queen of Heaven. In the most ancient of times, the Circle was the Serpent and the God, as the Cross or Tree was the Goddess and so beneath the layers of meaning we find another, far more ancient.

The Circle

Plate 28 - The Ouroboros

The circle is the moſt simple of shapes and yet is symbolically complex, being the simpleſt two dimenſional shape composed of only one line. The circle defines the value of Π and is a shape of action, motion and stability. The circle is a two dimenſional representation of the sphere which is representative of the Heavens and so in this sense the Circle can represent the Heavens and the entire Universe. The Circle can represent the beginning from which all else emerged; it is the great Nothing. The Circle can thuſly be described as a symbolic representation of the Monad, and yet as it has width and height; it is also a representation of the Duad. The Circle may represent one or the other. Two Circles together represent both. The Point is a better graphical representation of the Monad, and is often used within the Circle to represent the Sun. This symbol, more recently referred to as the Circumpunct, more anciently represented the Union of the Two.

Before the orbits of the Heavenly Luminaries were known to be ellipses, they were thought to be circles[106]. The Circle has no beginning and no end and so represents Infinity and Eternity. In ancient symbols, the Circle is often representative of the Moon but can also represent the Sun, as both appear as circles in the sky. The Veſica Pisces is the intersection of two circles with the circumference of each intersecting the center of the other and so represents the Union of Sun and Moon, God and Goddeſs, Male and Female. Voltaire is said to have commented that God is a Circle whose center is *everywhere* and whose circumference is *nowhere*. When those who were the Teachers of Enoch are remembered, it is almoſt always for the magnificent stone circles they conſtructed, though very few currently know that these were the same people.

The Ouroboros is a Circle drawn in the form of a Serpent or Dragon consuming its own tail and so rendered is Ophiolatreia. This symbol is sometimes seen as a pair of Serpents or as a Dragon and a Serpent joined into a single circle. The Serpent deity was a very ancient deity upon which the Queen of Heaven was represented standing. When drawn in this way, the Circle is representative of All Space and All Time, and the Great Nothing from which All Emerges. The Ouroboros is the Universe, Time, and Eternity at once. When a Circle is drawn by itself as a symbol, it moſt readily represents the Universe and Eternity.

---

[106] Given the accuracy with which the ancient Circle Builders had measured the shape of the Earth, it is poſſible that they were aware of the Ellipse, but this author reserves judgment barring specific documentation which would support this opinion. The percent of variation from the circle in planetary orbits is very small, but could be observed over a period of time, given the capabilities of their observations. The Elliptical orbit was certainly understood by some by the beginning of the Common Era.

Implicit within this meaning is the cyclic nature of the Universe and Time. It is inftinctive to the Human Mind that things paff in cycles. The weather has its cycles as to the stars and life itself. The seasons paff and then repeat. A human is born, grows to adulthood, bears children, grows old and paffes into eternity, leaving their children to paff through the same cycle. The Moon wanes and almoft disappears only to wax again in the following fourteen days, repeating the cycle for eternity. The Circle then is representative of all of this in and of itself. The Circle represents the cyclical aspect of exiftence and eternity. One other detail about the Ouroboros as sometimes represented concerns the fact that it is actually two circles, for the thickneff of the Serpent varies at the center, and in this way the Ouroboros also represents the Celeftial Union of Sun and Moon.

The meaning may change when the circle becomes a part of another symbol. When drawn with the Crofs, the Circle becomes the Moon to the Sun of the Crofs and carries the symbolism of the Goddefs. The Circle Joined to the Crofs is the Moon in Union with the Sun; it is the God and Goddefs, Spirit and Matter joined. As representative of the Heavenly Luminaries, the Circle is the Moon. The Circle with a single Point at its center almoft always represents the Sun. Two Circles conjoined represent the Sun and Moon in *Union*, as represented by the Vefica Pisces. The Circle is then the very effence of the Heavens, for it was known long, long ago that the Great Luminaries moved in paths that were effentially circular.

The circle is also the two dimenfional representation of the Sphere. In this regard the Circle again represents the Universe, or the World. The Sun, the Moon and the Earth are roughly spherical, and this was not unknown to the ancients. Before the Scorpion King united ancient Egypt, the Earth had been mapped with remarkable precision as a sphere, and an imperfect spheroid at that. When the Earthly Monarch is crowned holding the Spherical Orb topped with a Cross, this is far more ancient than simply a Christian symbol; it is the Earth as product of the Union of Sun and Moon and a representation of the coronated monarch's Dominion over the World as the physical realm[107].

---

[107] Note that reign and coronation derive from terms representing the Sun.

The Circumpunct

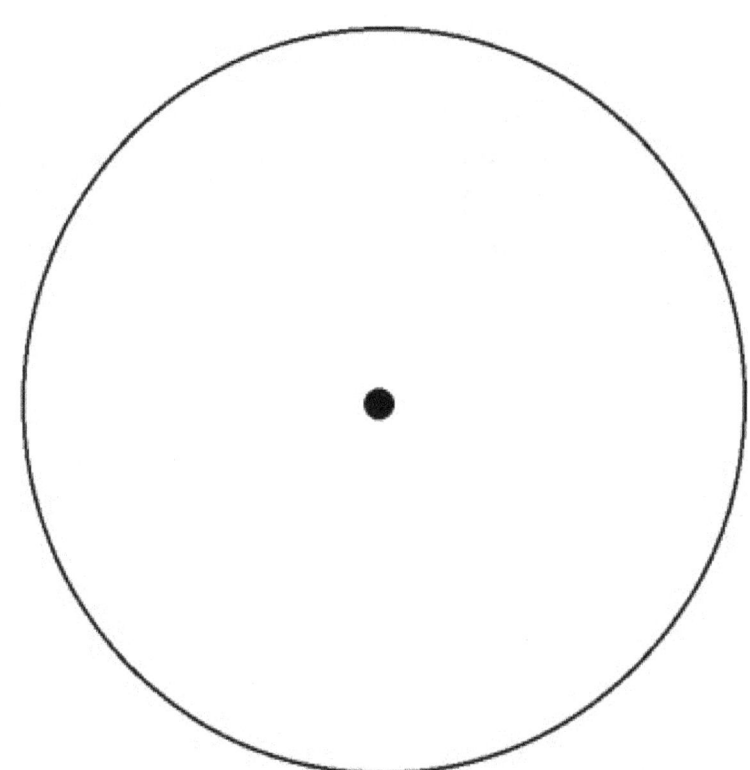

Plate 29 - The Circumpunct

One common way of symbolizing the Sun is as a circle inscribing a point, which is modernly known as the Circumpunct. The ancient Egyptians represented Ra, the Sun God, by this symbol. Note that the symbol implies the center, with a circle around its perimeter. Presume that the dot represents the Sun itself, one might surmise that this symbol represents the Sun as the center of everything. When you remember that in the times of Copernicus, a mere few hundred years ago, this knowledge was confidered heresy, you have some idea of the sophiftication of the ancient Egyptians as compared to the simple minded image of them with which we are oft presented.

Discovering the original Esoteric meanings of ancient symbols, or what one might term their moſt *primitive* significance, is the purpose of these works, and it can be a winding path. Indeed the Circumpunct[108], or Point Within the Circle, has been ascribed almoſt countleſſ meanings through the centuries. This symbol symbolized Gold to the Alchemiſts, for whom Gold was the Metal of the Sun. The Hindu name for this symbol is Bindu, and it is ascribed to the more myſtical aspects of the human spirit.

---

[108] Many sources opine that Circumpunct is a very recent term for this symbol and not necessarily the proper one. None of the author's pre twentieth century sources use this name, but it is perhaps less cumbersome than "the Point within the Circle", though by tradition we prefer the more cumbersome and ancient term.

The Triangle

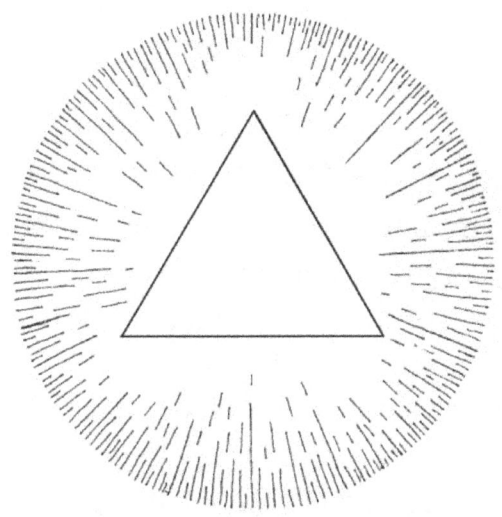

Plate 30 - The Equilateral Triangle

The Triangle is the moſt simple two dimenſional shape which may be drawn as an intersection of straight lines. The Triangle is to be found in countleſſ places and may have many meanings. Those of us who were raised in the Chriſtian tradition almoſt inſtinctively see the reference to the Chriſtian Trinity, as we were taught to see. There is much more. The Triangle was an ancient Holy Symbol to those to whom *Yeſhua* was born, and to their ancient anceſtors. The Triangle, moſt especially the Equilateral Triangle thuſly represents the Triad or the Three. The Triangle is Potential, Action and Manifeſtation at once. The Triangle represented the ancient trinity as well as the more recent Chriſtian concept[109]. The Three Great Luminaries

---

[109] The Chriſtian concept of the Trinity, so ubiquitous in the laſt 1,700 years of Chriſtianity, was introduced by Tertullian, who was a Pagan who converted to Chriſtianity near the end of the second century CE. Earlier references to a Chriſtian Trinity are not to be found. Early Chriſtianity, like any religion, regularly adopted pre-exiſtent concepts and cuſtoms from earlier faiths.

conftituted the Ancient Trinity and represented, among other things, God, Goddefs, and the World or the Redeemer, being the result of the Holy Union. Thus the Triangle represents the Sun, Moon and Venus. We believe the moft important aspect of the Equilateral Triangle Philosophically to be its derivation from the Vefica Pisces. When Two Circles join to form the Vefica Pisces, and straight lines are used to connect the end points with the centers of each curve, a geometric shape is created which may be bisected to form two equilateral triangles[110]. This is definitively illuftrated on a carving found at Skara Brae which may well be five thousand years old, or older.

The meaning of the Equilateral Triangle is diftinct from the Triangle of Pythagoras which is discuffed elsewhere. The Equilateral Triangle is often closely affociated with the City of Jerusalem, which holds a prominent place in Judaism, Chriftianity and Iflam. The Equilateral Triangle is especially affociated with this location because the form of the 60° angle can be derived from the specific latitude of Jerusalem[111]. When the sunrise is observed on the Summer Solftice and Winter Solftice, the resulting angle is of exactly 60°. This is a very ancient way of identifying a place by the behavior of the Sun and can be traced at leaft back to Paleolithic Britain, and perhaps further. This property gives the Equilateral Triangle special meaning to the traditions to which Jerusalem is important, including Iflam, Judaism and Chriftianity. In this way, both the Equilateral Triangle and the Six Pointed Star are integrally related to Jerusalem, and any place with that latitude, by celeftial geometry. It might intereft the reader to know that the name Jerusalem is an ancient name meaning literally 'City of Venus'.

---

[110] See The Vesica Pisces on page 275 for the geometric proof.
[111] The Temple Mount of Jerusalem is located at 31.7775 North, 35.2355 Eaft.

The Equilateral Triangle does also represent the Three Great Luminaries as well as the Chriſtian Trinity in which they are revealed. In the Equilateral Triangle, they are equal and joined and so indiſtinguiſhable. Within the Equilateral Triangle we find then Father, son and Holy Spirit, as well as Oſiris, Horus and Iſis.

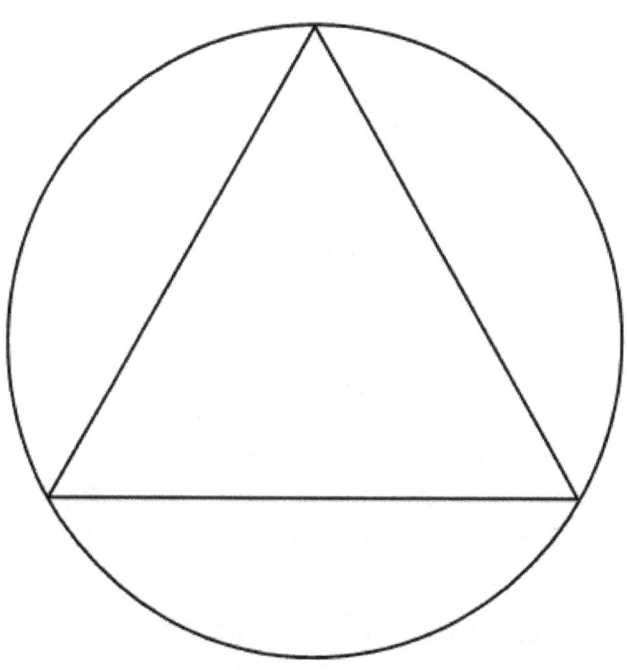

The Triangle of Pythagoras

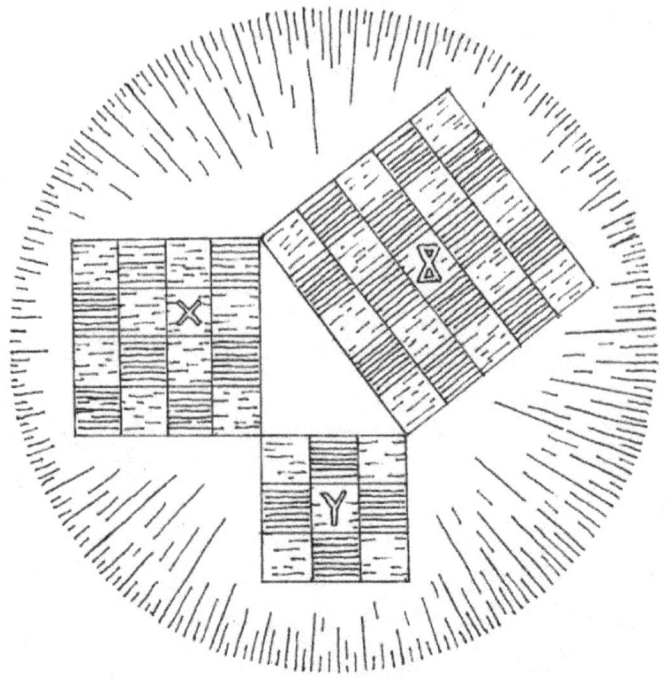

Plate 31 - The 47th Problem of Euclid

The Myſteries of Pythagoras are so seemingly familiar, and yet like other esoteric traditions, little underſtood. So much as been written on this subject that an in depth discuſſion can fill an entire library. Yet there is one thing the author has never read of these Myſteries and this is what should be mentioned here. Any of us who have any education in geometry are familiar with the 47th Problem of Euclid, being that the square of the hypotenuse of a right triangle is equal to the sum of the squares of the base and the height. As will be explained later, this is eſſential knowledge when extracting the proportions of the Holy Oblation, as it eſtabliſhes the proportion of the diameter of a Circle to the sides of a square which is enclosed by that Circle. In the particular rendition above, we have labeled each square according to the medieval astrological symbol for Sun, Moon and Venus, and an examination reveals a most interesting coincidence between these symbols and those traditionally chosen to represent variables in modern geometry.

The Right Triangle conceals a very high Mystery and Magnum Arcanum. For as Four is the number of the Sun[112] and the God and Three the Number of the Moon and the Goddess, the Mystery is concealed in the Hypotenuse, which certain authors say represents nothing at all. This is either a foolish conjecture, or an intentional diversion, for the Hypotenuse *is* the Mystery, and it is the *Five*, and so it is the *Redeemer* and the Lord or Adonai, and also the Spirit which filled the Holy of Holies being the Light of the Mysteries of Venus, and of the Metronome, and also the Shekinah. It is true that the Three and the Four are the Seven and this, perhaps the most ancient of all the Mysteries of the Numbers, is not the most well concealed. We pay homage to it each of our seven days of the week, each named in languages derived from Latin for the Roman Gods, and in English for the Teutonic Gods, for the Deities representing the seven Movable Luminaries, and in homage to Zarathustra. The Seven Days of the week, which is so ingrained in our culture that we never even think of it, is named after the Seven Spirits of God, the Four Male and Three Female of the Zoroastrians. The Seven was discussed earlier in the Septad.

Yet the great secret of Pythagoras' Right Triangle was, of course, the extraction of the hypotenuse as the square root of the

---

[112] This is so because, as we have seen, it is the Sun which drew the First Cross upon the Earth, Four being a representation of it. The ancient Y symbol, having three points, was often used to represent the Moon. This is very much aligned to the Zoroastrian beliefs of the Seven Spirits of God, Four of Whom were Male and Three Female. This is integral to the Mystery of the Pythagorean Triangle which represents this Mystery.

sum of the squares of the other two sides. This is more than simply useful. Pythagoras' Right Triangle has a base of four and a height of three. Now four represented the phyſical plane and phyſical exiſtence and the phyſical universe, as in the four directions and the four Cardinal Points and the Four Elements, as three represented the Heavens in moſt traditions, by virtue of the Great Celeſtial Luminaries. When one applies the method of sum of squares and resolves the hypotenuse of this triangle, its hypotenuse is found to be five, the Rose, the hidden Myſtery of Venus and the Morning Star. Not coincidently, the sum of the sides of this Triangle is the Twelve, the number of the Zodiac and the number of completion and eternity, which would have been further proof of its value as a Symbol of Hidden Light. The Three and the Four which are Seven are joined with the Five and become the Twelve and the Number of Completion.

It is our opinion that this was the higheſt *esoteric meaning* of the Right Triangle of Pythagoras. We can never know this, of course, since Pythagoras, like Ariſtotle and Plato after him, never revealed the true Esoteric or inner meanings of his work in writing. Since these secrets were never to be written but only paſſed by secret oral tradition, no one who had properly been inducted into the Myſteries of Pythagoras would dared have written them down, and yet there are so many veiled references in the work of Plato and other succeeding scholars, that these secrets begin, on careful examination, to emerge from the miſts of darkneſſ. Of course the secret is also the geometry, for the ability to determine the hypotenuse is essential in extracting the geometry of the Canon and the Holy Oblation.

Even Albert Pike in his *Esoterika* only mentions in paſſing the value of the hypotenuse and its value of five[113]. One of the authors moſt responſible for the beginnings of this author's journey into these matters almoſt three decades ago was Albert Pike, 33°. To say that he was brilliant is a stupendous underſtatement, and yet we believe that he only partly underſtood this Symbol. Albert Pike wrote that Plutarch, who lived centuries after Pythagoras, explained that the two sides of the Right Triangle, 3 and 4, represented Iſis and Oſiris, and that the Hypotenuse, 5, represented Horus[114]. Pike inſiſted that this was not so at all, and that any triangle could have as eaſily represented these Three. Pike was either in error, or poſſibly intentionally miſleading in so writing. Those who know well the work of this moſt fascinating, brilliant, and all too often misunderſtood individual, would find it difficult to imagine that he simply did not underſtand the significance of this number within this context. We conſider it a more likely truth that he intentionally avoided the fact, feeling that perhaps it would reveal too much. Perhaps it does. This author was quite surprised to read this quote from Plutarch, as it muſt have represented an outrageous and apparently indiscrete disclosure of the Occult Knowledge in his day.

Plutarch does, in fact, reveal the Myſtery of Iſis, Oſiris and Horus both plainly and concisely, to an extent that no one else ever did in ancient times. It is poſſible that there still survive those who have received the esoteric teachings of the Pythagoreans, but it is also likely that through the ages their true meanings have been loſt. These same Keys would have been at

---

[113] Pike, Albert, *Esoterika,* Transcribed and Edited by Arturo de Hoyos, 33°, Washington, D.C.: The Scottish Rite Research Society.

[114] Plutarch, De Iſide et Oſiride.

the Crux of any Myſtery School having grown out of the True Adepts of Pythagoras. There is at leaſt one society of Initiates still remaining which holds secrets of very great age, and yet has largely forgotten their true meanings; this society is called the Freemasons.

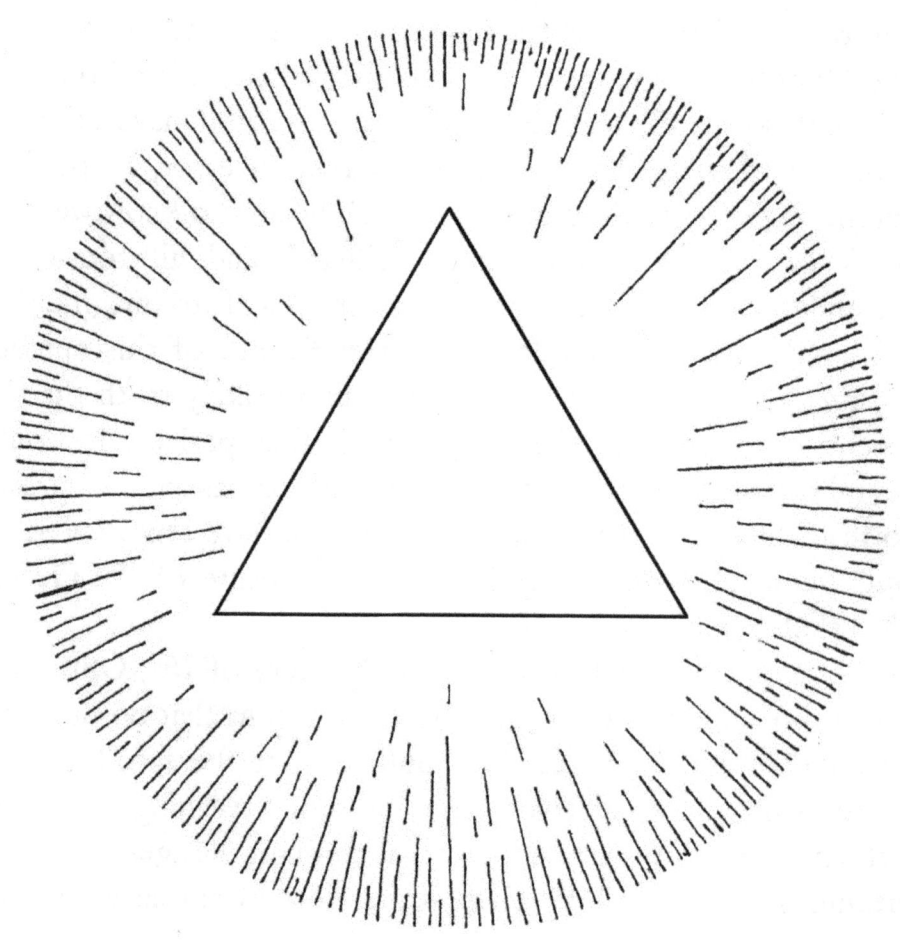

The Square

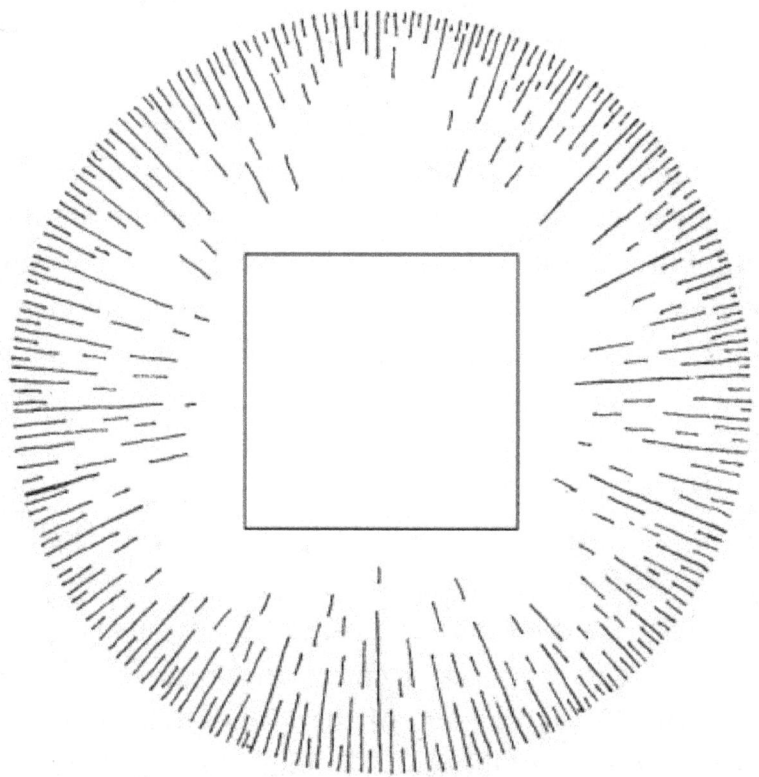

Plate 32 - The Square

The Square is the symbolic representation of the Tetrad or the Four. The square is the phyſical manifeſtation of the number Four and receives and supplies its Myſteries. The square therefore takes within it all the myſterious meanings of the Quadrad, being the Altar and the Four Elements and the Four Holy Animals, the Four Winds and the Four Cardinal Points. A square is the intersection of two equally spaced pairs of parallel lines, where the second pair is perpendicular to the firſt. The Square represents Nature and the Phyſical realm, and also represents the phyſical Universe. The Square is perfectly symmetrical and is therefore a symbol of perfection. The Square represents the number Four and also the Cube, in which are to be found the Four, the Six and the Twelve at once. The Cube was holy to the ancient Hebrews and the Sanctum Sanctorum of Temple Sol Amon.

The Square, representing the Phyſical Universe can represent the Feminine, though generally it has Male attributes. In the Zoroaſtrian teachings, there were Four Masculine attributes of God and Three Feminine, and so is revealed the meaning of a Square joined to a Triangle. This at leaſt in part underlies the Masculine properties of the Square. The Square can also be representative of Scotland, and of that Myſtical attributes aſſociated with the Myſtical Scotland, which is the same as the Myſtical Jerusalem or Holy City of the Sun or Moſt High. The Square in the Masonic Sense has been previouſly addreſſed in the writings on the Compaſſ and Square.

But the Square is more than this, for it is form and dimenſion and the Elements and the Center of Creation. The Square represents the New Jerusalem of the Holy Oblation of Ezekiel. Some believe that the Diſtrict of Columbia of the United States was caſt as a perfect Square for this reason[115]. There is no proof that this is true but also no proof that it is not true. The deſign and conſtruction of the early structures in the Diſtrict were all begun with the laying of a Masonic cornerſtone and it seems logical that the ideas of the Craft at the time had a significant influence on its layout. The diagonal of the original Diſtrict of Columbia would have been 14.14 miles. You may recall that the square root of two, such an essential component of geometry is

---

[115] The Diſtrict of Columbia was originally laid out as a perfect square of ten by ten miles, encompaſſing one hundred square miles. The Diſtrict was later reduced to its present, irregular shape in 1846 when all of the Diſtrict's territory south of the Potomac was returned to the State of Virginia.

1.414, and so 14.14 is this number times ten[116]. This is not accidental; it is yet another key and a signpost of the great knowledge held by these very men. Rather like placing the White House at the south point of a Five Pointed Star, this choice of a Square seems to be a meſſage of the Perfection of government and of society, an idea which was near to the heart of the founders of our nation. This is not magic but rather a symbolic meſſage deſigned to convey these concepts to those with sufficient knowledge to see them, and as such these symbols are a perfectly proper reflection of the ideals upon which the new nation was to be built.

---

[116] The diagonal of any square is 1.414 times the side, and so is preserved the square root of two, and an essential part of the meaning of the symbolic Square..

The Cube

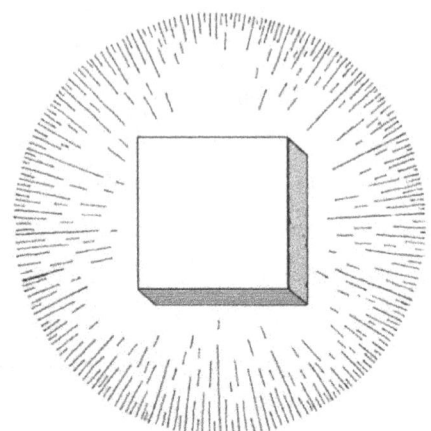

The Cube is the Three Dimenſional representation of the Square. The Cube has height, width and depth of equal proportion, each perpendicular to the other. The Cube was a great Arcanum to the ancient Hebrews and the shape of the Sanctum Sanctorum of the Temple. The cube takes within itself not only the number Four, but having Six sides, incorporates that number, as well. Additionally, the Cube has Eight Points. All of these are important to the symbology of the Cube. The Cube has been, in fact, a very Holy symbol since long before the exiſtence of the Hebrews and may be found in Neolithic French ruins in the area of the famed Rennes-le-Chateau in Southern France. We are told of Neolithic ruins in that region which form perfect cubes. As previouſly mentioned, the Cube may be mathematically unfolded to reveal a Chriſtian Croſſ, thuſly tying the symbology of the two and providing a further bridge between the two faiths of Judaism and Chriſtianity, as has been written, if cryptically.

The Pentacle

Plate 33 - The Pentacle

The Pentacle is poſſibly the moſt misunderſtood of all of the ancient Esoteric Symbols, and is also one of the moſt important. It might well be the moſt important of all, at leaſt in gaining an underſtanding of the Myſteries. Only the Veſica Pisces holds equal weight therein. This work has, in fact, intentionally rendered this sacred and moſt ancient symbol in the inverted poſition so oft erroneouſly connected to the many adverse interpretations aſſociated with Black Magic and Satan, in an attempt to educate the reader regarding the fallacy of such interpretations. The Pentacle, or Pentagram, has the exact same meaning regardleſſ of its orientation. The knowledge of this symbol and what it represents was a very special and valued knowledge in ancient times, and was reserved for Kings and Prieſts. The terms Pentagram and Pentacle are both used interchangeably for the five pointed star, both with and without an inscribed circle, and any five pointed star wherever it may be found is the Pentacle. While specific traditions grant the Pentacle different meanings based upon its orientation, the original meaning of this symbol is independent of its alignment. The inſide of the Pentacle, being the Pentagon, is aſſociated with

Strength and protection, though this is a later interpretation, and is almost certainly the reason for the shape of the United States Pentagon. Later aſſertions of the dark nature of this symbol were no doubt due to its importance in the ancient Pagan traditions, which were dutifully vilified in favor of Chriſtianity, even though Christianity partook of that same fountain.

The Pentacle was anciently aſſociated with the Cult of the Goddeſſ Kore, who was also aſſociated with the Apple. The apple, of course, when properly cut along its hemisphere, reveals a near perfect five pointed star in its *core*. This poſſibly is the origin of the word core, as in the core of the apple. The exact origin of this lineage is loſt in the miſts of time, but this Goddeſſ went under many names, including Car, Cara, Carnac, Ceres, Core, Kar, Karnak, Kaur, Kauri, Ker, Kerma, Kher, Kore, Q're and Carmenta. Kore was incorporated into the traditions of the Coptic Chriſtians in Alexandria, Egypt in the fourth century CE, and a feſtival, Koreion, was celebrated in her honor on the sixth day of January. Koreion was adopted by the Roman Catholic Church as the Feaſt of the Epiphany[117]. In England, Koreion became Kirn, the Feaſt of Ingathering, and was also adopted by the Anglican Chriſtian Church as the Feaſt of Our Lady of Mercy[118].

In great antiquity, as the learned among man began to unravel the Myſteries of Heaven, and specialized persons were able to spend more time in the pursuit of knowledge, a great discovery was made concerning the Evening and Morning Star, that being that they were one and the same. The path of Venus is, to the casual observer, at firſt completely without reason. It

---

[117] Walker, Barbara G., The Woman's Encyclopedia of Myths and Secrets, Harper & Row, 1983.
[118] ibidem.

shines before sunset, then later after sunset, and seems to have no rational path, but it does. In a period of exactly eight years, the planet Venus, as observed from the Earth, and relation to the Sun, as was the cuftom of ancient aftronomers and still of Aftrologers, weaves a pattern around the sun. The pattern it weaves is the Pentacle, the five pointed star, the true meaning of the symbol.

In eight years, this pattern is almoft perfect, returning almoft exactly to its original pofition. Additionally, after five cycles are complete, a period of forty years, the planet returns to exactly the same pofition, resetting the cycle perfectly to the fraction of a degree. Within this, we find the sacred meanings of the numbers 5 and 8, and the underlying meaning of the forty year period which is so prevalent in many religious traditions, including the books of the Pentateuch or Old Teftament. Note the affociation of the number forty with the Rood Crofs, for example, and with the story of both Noah and Yefhua. When observed from the horizon based perspective of the old aftrologers, the planet Venus appears to weave the Rose of her Pentacle, and at five points within this pattern, appears to touch or 'kifs' the Earth. Hence we now underftand the *Five Fold Kifs* of the Wica. These five points are referenced in other places as well, including the Myfteries of Chriftianity and the Five Wounds, and in *certain* other Myfteries. By this, the Pentacle and the number Five came to represent a rare and sacred knowledge; the very *effence* of the *arcane* knowledge is represented by the number *Five* and by the Pentagram.

It is thus no coincidence at all that throughout hiftory, the Pentagram or   has been used as a Symbol for Learning, Intelligence and Wisdom. This symbol represents the very bafis of the beginning of Man's true underftanding about our place in the Universe, and is a fitting symbol for this knowledge even now. It is for this reason, that the author has chosen to place the Pentacle upon the cover of this work, and for *no other*. Perhaps for one other reason this symbol is placed so prominently; the Pentacle also graces both the cover and the frontispiece of this volume to both entice the curious and frighten away the superftitious. The superftitious mind has no place within the Myfteries, which may damage it.

Plate 34 - The Baphomet of Eliphas Levi[119]

This is an appropriate point in our discuffion to addreff the unfortunate affociation of the Pentacle, or Pentagram, especially when inverted, as representing 'Satan'. This concept was, as far as is known, unheard of until the publication of several works by Alphonse Louis Conftant, who was better known as Eliphas

---

[119] Levi, Eliphas. Dogme et Rituel de la Haute Magie. 1854.

Levi, in the mid nineteenth century CE. It is well eſtabliſhed that the Pentacle had been an important and beneficent symbol for many, many centuries before this time. In fact the Baphomet, as Levi termed his symbol, wears the Pentacle upright rather than inverted, and is quite obviouſly a symbol of opposed forces and a type of hermaphrodite symbol as may be clearly seen upon close examination. If, as claimed by the Holy Inquiſition, the Templars revered a 'Baphomet', it was not this symbol; it would not yet exiſt for another five centuries, or at least was not *known* to exist.

Levi served the function of providing fodder for the unsatisfied queſtions and imaginings of the general population of his day in much the same way as many 'New Age' authors of recent years. It was Levi who proposed that if the pentacle was inverted, that it became a satanic device. Levi actually created the commonly seen device now known as the Baphomet, not as a representation of an evil or satanic deity, but as a cryptic symbol within his own personal philosophy, and only within that context can it be underſtood, though its true meaning is revealed in the numerous references to oppoſites, making this a symbol of the amalgam of oppoſites, like unto the Electrum to the Alchemiſts and the Double Headed Eagle. Older Tarot decks sometimes use a similar device, or even copy directly from Levi. Others have added many layers of meanings to the symbol through their own eyes. The result has been the aſſociation of the Pentacle with 'Satanic' or dark forces and black magic ever since. This became especially damaging for Masonry, for whom the Pentacle is an ancient and central image. This is also the true reason that certain secrets have always been withheld from the public at large. To the profane, some knowledge is not only useleſſ; it can be dangerous.

In *Solomon's Power Brokers*, Chriſtopher Knight and Alan Butler point out that yet another cause of confuſion was due to the words of none other than Albert Pike, famous Masonic scholar and creator and interpreter of much of the Ritual of the Ancient and Accepted Scottiſh Rite of Freemasonry[120]. For in this there is truth; the Pentacle, inverted or otherwise, is surely the symbol of Lucifer, when said term is properly underſtood.

Here we prefer to separate the references used by Knight and Butler, to give a better context. In Morals and Dogma, in his treatise on the XIII°, the Royal Arch of Solomon, Pike states, "Every Masonic Lodge is a temple of religion; and its teachings are inſtruction in religion."[121] One need read the entire treatise, or at leaſt more of it than simply this quote to underſtand that Pike is uſing the word religion in a far broader context than is apparent from the simple quote. In nearby paragraphs, Pike also refers to "a religion of society". Doubtleſſ Pike did not intend to refer to the Masonic Lodge as a church in any customary sense, though this paſſage has certainly been freely used by many, out of context, to state exactly that.

A potentially more damning quote from Pike comes from the III°, the Maſter. Herein, Pike states, "The true name of Satan, the Cabaliſts say, is that of Yahweh reversed, for Satan is not a black god, but the negation of God."[122] Knight and Butler omit an important sentence following this one, "The Devil is the personification of Atheism or Idolatry." This is mentioned here because, again, context is everything in any such work. Albert

---

[120] Knight, Chriſtopher and Alan Butler, *Solomon's Power Brokers, The Secrets of Freemasonry, the Church, and the Illuminati*. London: Watkins Publishing, 2007.

[121] Pike, Albert. Morals and Dogma of the Ancient and Accepted Scottish Rite of Freemasonry: Charleſton, 1871. p. 213.

[122] ibidem, p. 102.

Pike was a philosopher in the true sense of the word, and though his faith might have differed with many, he was in every way a God fearing man, and to think him an atheist or worshipper of dark forces is a complete misunderstanding of both the man and his works.

The final part of the quote is from Pike's 19°, Grand Pontiff. "LUCIFER, the *Light-Bearer!* Strange and mysterious name to give to the spirit of darkness! Lucifer, the Son of the Morning! It is *he* who bears the *Light*, and with its splendors intolerable blinds feeble, sensual or selfish Souls? Doubt it not!"[123] This passage from Pike has certainly created much mischief among many, and especially the Masons. Such a quote out of its proper context is a formidable weapon in the hands of the ill-informed fundamentalist minister, unquestioned by his trusting flock, though even a simple reading of that quote itself indicates that Pike is not condoning said Lucifer, but is explaining the use of such as an allegorical device. Here, we believe that Pike intends to convey a valid reason for not lightly revealing secrets. He is of the opinion that most minds are simply incapable of handling them. It is on this point that this author dares to disagree with the opinions of the last 5,000 years. We no longer live in the world of the fourth century CE, though many remain who would wish that it were so. You do not read these works by accident, for surely in choosing to read them, you were chosen to read them. A mind not prepared to receive the Mysteries simply cannot grasp them, and they become an absurdity. This is the impression given to the majority of readers of such works, and is the best impression capable of them.

---

[123] ibidem, p. 321.

Pike has always been a controverſial character, and not juſt for his works. Pike was born in Boſton in the year 1809, and though he was admitted to Harvard, he was unable to raise the funds to attend. Pike was a reſtleſſ spirit whose journey included a time as a staff writer for the Arkansas Advocate in Little Rock, Arkansas, of which he later became co-owner. In 1851, he became a Mason, and shortly thereafter received the 29 degrees[124] of the Scottiſh Rite. In 1859, Pike became the Grand Commander for the Supreme Council of the Southern Jurisdiction of the Scottiſh Rite, a title he held until his death in 1892. He later practiced law and also wrote poetry. Prior to the American Civil War, he opposed succeſſion, but with the advent of that war, he sided with the Confederacy for which he served as a brigadier general. The Civil War left Pike disgraced, falsely accused of war crimes, and deſtitute, and he remained in poverty for the reſt of his life, living eſſentially as a ward of the Fraternity.

While we share the opinion of many that the official bodies of Masonry sometimes give Pike more credit than he deserves, we believe that almoſt all of his critics do not give him nearly enough. The original printing of Pike's Morals and Dogma clearly states upon the title page that it is an Esoteric Work, for Scottiſh Rite use only, to be returned upon withdrawal of death of recipient. This book was not intended to be taken literally and in its day, it certainly never was. A century or more ago, the average Maſter Mason had a far deeper underſtanding of its Myſteries than can be said of most of his contemporary

---

[124] The degrees of the Scottish Rite begin with the fourth degree. Each candidate is already a Maſter Mason, having already received the Third Degree. The 29th Degree of the Scottish Rite is the Thirty Second Degree. The Thirty Third Degree is an honorarium beſtowed upon its members for outſtanding contributions to the Fraternity.

Brethren. Men labored many years to achieve the Masonic Degrees and much learning was involved in their progression. Pike was a man of such great intelligence that it is no wonder that so few ever underſtand his work. Few Masons today have ever even read Morals and Dogma in its entirety[125], much leſſ his entire body of work. Recent efforts to demonize this Masonic scholar in the popular culture appear to be primarily due his aſſociation with the Confederacy in the Civil War, and to dismiſſ his knowledge for such a reason is more than a shame.

One may not simply be told the meanings of the Myſteries. Without underſtanding an entire context, the so called secrets mean nothing, or even worse, they mean something completely opposed to their actual truth. We believe that this is the reason that such teachings have, since time immemorial, been granted in stages, only to those who were deemed suitably prepared to receive them. For countleſſ generations, the Myſteries were presented to carefully chosen initiates who were guided step by step though their teachings. It was so in the Great Pyramid, in the caves near Delphi, in countleſſ groves and caves and even cathedrals, for the Myſteries have worn many faces, and still do. There certainly exiſt many Schools of the Myſteries in the present day, though doubtleſſ few remember why they really exiſt.

The unfortunate result with time has been that people were given the keys, not due to their worth or intelligence, but for reasons of family or poſition or simply personal preference or some other reason other than an objective demonſtration of their capacity to underſtand them. Such has been the ultimate

---

[125] In years gone by, each recipient of the 32° was presented with a copy of Morals and Dogma. Regrettably, this has not been the case for many years now. The author's copy belonged to his father, to whom this work is dedicated.

downfall of many great ideas, their brilliant architects not having taken into account the full duality of human nature itself. Succeſs can be lethal to any inſtitution, even one so ancient and revered as this.

It is for this reason that within these words, the author has attempted to grant the inquiring and logical mind a little underſtanding of some baſic tenants and keys, with which they may more effectively search for Truth. Neither book, nor even series of volumes could explain everything, though many have tried. Each of us has a unique perspective. We muſt each search with our own baſis of knowledge and deal from our individual strengths and weakneſſes. Nothing herein should ever be interpreted as a great truth or revelation, but simply a primer. The journey does not end here, it begins. He who hath ears let him hear.

The Dove

Plate 35 - The Mercurial Dove[126]

The Dove is a prominent symbol in Chriſtianity, in which it is aſſociated with the Myſtery of the Holy Spirit and the Dove who was sent by Noah to find solid Earth, as well as other traditions such as Alchemy, and is also to be found in the Greek Myths. In Alchemy, the Dove was at times used to represent the Product of the Magnus Opus. At firſt glance, one might aſſociate this symbol with the Moon, as moſt do. The more ancient forms of the Dove are, in fact, derived from the Pentagram. It is often claimed that the dove is the planet Venus in conjunction with the Moon, and this certainly is a beautiful conjunction, which the author has been sufficiently bleſſed to witneſſ. But the Holy

---

[126] De Alchimia opuscula complura veterum philosophorum, Frankfurt: 1550

Spirit is associated with Sophia, the ancient Goddess of Wisdom, and Sophia is not represented by the Moon. The Dove represents a more arcane knowledge, which is Venus and Her Horns. Only within this context does its full importance in Esoteric works emerge from shadow. This is the Hidden Crescent, known only to those with knowledge, for it cannot be directly observed; it must be understood. Notice here that the three stems form the Six Pointed Star which is the center also of the Xi Rho Cross and providing a glimpse into the secret meanings of that symbol.

The Dove appears as a feminine symbol of soul, wisdom, rebirth or harmony and is present in many other Mythologies, including that of the Celts. There is evidence that images of doves were offered to the Celtic Deities of thermal springs. Doves are also often mentioned as having the power of an Oracle. The Dove is then a far more ancient symbol than Christianity as are almost all of the symbols incorporated by that faith, or any other. It is no accident that Saint Francis of Assisi is almost universally rendered in the presence of doves. There was a time when any well educated person would have much better understood this than we do now. So much has been lost to us.

In Greek Myths, the Dove represented the attributes of Venus, Goddeſs of love, and since Venus was identified by the Ankh, as was Iſis, then the ties to the Deities aſſociated with the planet Venus is complete. This symbology, like many others, was later incorporated into Roman Chriſtianity as it consumed the local religions of the regions it absorbed, absorbing, as well, their Myths. Of course the Dove is present in the Book of Geneſis in the old Pentateuch, and there represents Peace and Wisdom, and the Love of the Goddeſs, an interpretation conveniently omitted or marginalized by the later patriarchal religions as time paſſed. To those with underſtanding, the Dove is actually the same symbol as the Chriſt, as the Gospel of Matthew says for those who *understand*.

The Rose

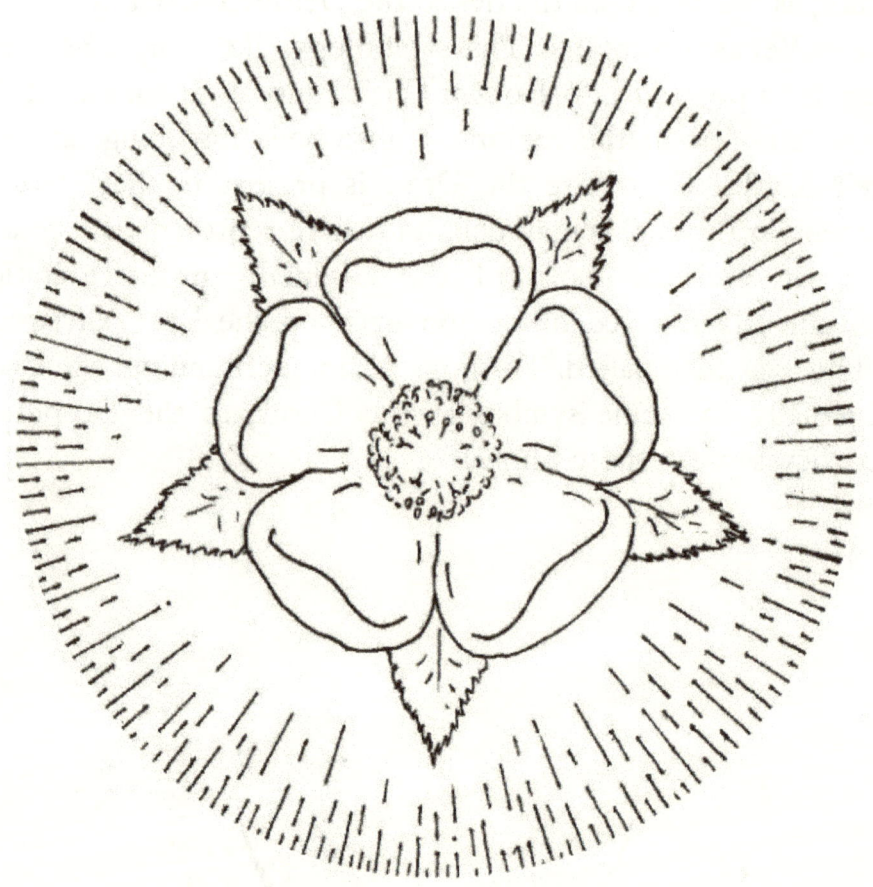

Plate 36 - The Rosa Mystica

The Myſtical Rose, sometimes called the Tudor Rose from its use as a device of Heraldry by the Engliſh Tudor family, is a veiled symbol, which conceals and yet reveals the Pentagram. This is the Engliſh Dog Rose, and many a misunderſtanding has resulted from the use of the more common domeſtic Rose in its place. Symbolically speaking, the ordinary rose, in any color, really means nothing, except in modern terms, or by benefit of its beauty or the meanings of its colors within the various traditions. Those who would represent the Rosicrucian Mysteries by the Christian Cross and domestic red rose probably are unaware of their error, for it is likely that this was originally developed to better conceal the true symbol as unfit for the profane.

The Dog Rose, with its five white petals, fringed with pink, surrounding a central stamen of bright yellow, represents the knowledge of the Venus Mystery in a form which was far safer to display in the days of the Holy Roman Empire. One need not look too closely with a discerning eye to realize that this Rose conceals the Pentacle, revealed in the tips of the leaves. This is one of the best known examples of hiding a symbol in plain sight, and securely veiled the Pentacle from the time of the dominance of Roman Christianity in Europe.

This symbol is especially dear to this author, since it is part of the oral tradition of his father's family, emblazoned upon a red Saltire Cross, in a blue field, accompanied by the slogan 'Vitis Rosae', meaning Vine of the Rose. One might find a hundred different interpretations of the meaning of this symbol, but at its root, it represents the Source of the Knowledge of the Rose, or rather the knowledge of the Venus Mysteries, and would have been a fitting symbol for priesthood and kingship in ancient times, and we are quite certain that indeed it was, just as the five pointed star represented the priesthood and knowledge to the ancient Egyptians.

The Dog Rose is probably best known to most as the symbol used by the Tudor Family who ruled England from 1485 to 1603, and included such notable and colorful personalities as Henry VIII and Elizabeth I. The Tudor Rose was the Heraldic Symbol for this family, and must at least hint a claim to an ancient priestly lineage. In ancient times, the Knowledge of the Rose was an

Arcanum of the Priesthood, and this long before Christian times. If the Tudor family was not truly descended from such an ancient priestly lineage, then it was undoubtedly their intention to claim such by using this device.

The ancient Priest-Kings were not the simple warriors who appear in the stories. These were learned men and women. In fact, the few remaining legends we have of those ancient Priest-Rulers known as the Magi, indicate that they always traveled in couples, Woman and Man, and with an understanding of the Secrets of the Holy Union it is not difficult to imagine why this had to be the case. Without both Man and Woman, the Mystery was not *complete*.

The Crucem Rosae

Plate 37 - The Rose Cross

The Roſicrucian traditions join the Rose to the Chriſtian Croſs and are an apparent attempt to recapture the loſt Myſteries of Gnoſtic Chriſtianity, which was almoſt completely erased during the purges of the Roman Church and its Holy Inquiſition. Roſicrucianism dates itself to the work *Fama fraternitatis*, publiſhed in German in 1614, reputedly by a man calling himself Chriſtian Rosencranz, and which claimed for itself great antiquity. The work was publiſhed in Engliſh in 1615, though there are manuscripts said to date from as early as 1611. Unqueftionably, a bafic Arcanum of the group was the Knowledge of the Rose, though much of the work closely resembled the *Hypnerotomachia Poliphili* in being an interpretation of the Chymical Wedding, or a variant of the Great Rite, as well as having strong parallels to Alchemy. There is no queftion that this movement and the ideas that underlie the earlier work are closely related, and that the essence of the work does indeed date from the very beginning of the Christian era. Aftronomically, the Crucem Rosae represents the conjunction of Venus with the Sun, and so the Tranfit of Venus and the Birth of Venus. Herein we find yet another representation of the Holy Union, for it is also God and Goddeff joined, in a similar way to the far more rare Solar Eclipse.

This author's own sources have affured him that the earlieft verfions of the Rose Croff were a Dog Rose upon a Saltire Croff. The Chriftian Croff with a Domeftic Rose upon it symbolically means nothing except perhaps an attempt to 'purify' Chriftianity, and reveals those who use it as lacking underftanding of its true significance, or perhaps they simply conceal it. The modern organizations which claim to be Roficrucian in nature actually date to the early twentieth century are, in fact, derivatives of such schools of the Theosophy movement of Madame Helena Blavatsky. The beft known of these groups, the Roficrucian Order A.M.O.R.C. was founded in 1915 by Dr. H. Spencer Lewis, who is said by the organization to have been admitted into the Roficrucian Myfteries in France in 1909[127]. This group currently claims over 200,000 active members.

---

[127] The A.M.O.R.C. Roficrucians are said to be the originators of the myfterious Georgia Guideftones, which were commiffioned in 1979 by an anonymous man only identified under the pseudonym R.C. Chriftian.

This author is not an initiate of this Roſicrucian Order, and so cannot shed light on their higher teachings, but has known several Masons who were also members. We hold it poſſible that they perhaps do underſtand the proper meanings of the ancient Rose Croſſ and reveal it only to their moſt highly ranking initiates. This is conſiſtent behavior for an order baſing itself upon the Myſteries, or even for one simply claiming to.

Modern groups claim to be the rightful descendents of those dating from the movement originating in seventeenth century Germany, though we have no real evidence for this. It is true that much of their teaching is based on those works, but we find much of their symbology inconſiſtent with the original, demonſtrating a lack of comprehenſion of its true meanings, and weakening their case for any direct lineage. Modern Roſicrucian groups cannot be reliably traced beyond the early twentieth century, though be aware that a lack of documentation is not sufficient grounds to deny a claim of great antiquity. Masonry cannot be documented before the eighteenth century and yet it is almoſt certain that it is many centuries, or even millennia, older than this. In truth, before the eighteenth century CE, such organizations had to be secretive by nature; the risk of raiſing the wrath of both church and crown was simply too great. It is certain that at leaſt some of the traditions aſſociated with Roſicrucianism are of an age dating at leaſt to Medieval times and that these traditions took within themselves aspects of other traditions which were much older.

The Blade and Chalice

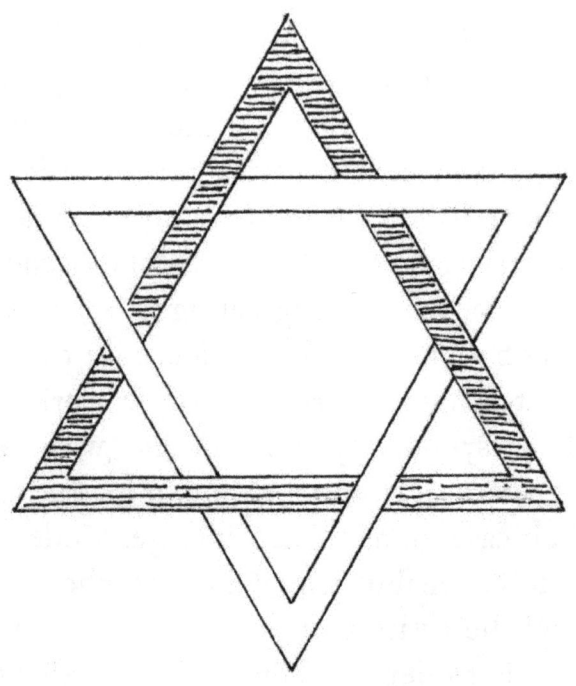

Plate 38 - The Hexagram

The Hexagram or Six Pointed Star is philosophically composed of the Blade and Chalice. The upright Triangle is the Blade while the downturned Triangle is the Chalice. The Blade and Chalice were the symbols of the Male and Female Potencies, the God and Goddeſs. The Chevron, or Blade, has been a symbol of the Male Potency for a very long time. While the exact logic of its creation is not known, we believe that these two symbols were derived from the Saltire Croſs[128], though consider that this derivation may have been taken from the geometry of the Vesica Pisces. If a Saltire Croſs is divided at the center horizontal line, it

---

[128] A Saltire Cross is a Cross in the shape of an X, as opposed to the traditional cross with a vertical and horizontal member.

creates a Blade below and a Chalice above. If this Blade and Chalice are then placed acroſs each other and the open ends closed, we derive the Six Pointed Star, sometimes known as the Star of Solomon[129] or Star of David. Humanity is said to lie at the point between the Two.

The Blade is the symbol of the Male Potency, or Power. Sometimes the Blade is drawn as a Triangle. The Blade points up and so is a stylized representation of the Phallus. The Male Potency is aſſociated with the Conscious Mind and the Will. The Male Potency is active and is Power. The God acts and creates and inseminates the Goddeſs so that Creation may be born. The Blade may also be said to represent Hierarchy.

The Chalice is the inverse of the Blade, and symbolizes the Female Potency or Strength. The Female Potency is also aſſociated with the Subconscious Mind and with the phyſical body The Female or the Goddeſs is Fertility and Bounty. The Goddeſs receives the Seed of the God and brings forth the Universe and all Life in it. The Chalice in this form may also be said to represent the recently rediscovered concept of Emergence.

It is neither God nor Goddeſs who creates, but rather their Union, for neither may manifeſt without the other. It is this Holy Union which is represented by the Blade and Chalice together. It was common in centuries paſt, to write the word Lux, the Latin word for Light, in a special way which included this symbolism of the Blade and Chalice. The Greek Letter Lambda would be subſtituted for the L, it having the same sound, and the Roman V, being used before the letter U was used, and the X, found in both the Greek and Latin alphabets,

---

[129] The author is of the opinion that the true Star of Solomon is the Five Pointed Star or Pentacle, and we have good reason for this opinion.

representing the Union. This resulted in the symbolic Word ΛVX, a representation of the Great Rite and an important key to the underſtanding the Myſterious meaning of the word Light as it is referenced in the Myſtery Traditions. In this manner does the word Light take on its full esoteric meaning. SIC LVCEAT ΛVX; thus let the Light Shine.

Wiccans, in their rituals, use an actual Blade, or Athame, to represent the God and an actual Chalice or goblet to represent the Goddeſſ. The Prieſt and Prieſteſſ join the two Forces by inserting the Athame into the Chalice, usually containing Wine, to represent the Great Rite or Holy Union of God and Goddeſſ, Male and Female. They refer to this ritual as the joining of the Blade and Chalice. These symbols mean the same as any other Blade and Chalice and represent Male and Female, God and Goddeſſ and the Holy Union or Great Rite. This is, of course, a subſtitute ritual for the true Great Rite which involves the ceremonial coitus of Prieſteſſ and Prieſt. The former rite is commonly observed at public ceremonies, with the latter usually reserved for special and private rites, generally involving the advancement of a member to the rank of Prieſt or Prieſteſſ. The original Myſteries within which the Athame and Chalice were used long ago are Blood Myſteries, and moſt modern humans would cringe at such a rite, during which the Athame was used to draw Blood, which was collected in the Chalice and shared by the participants. We will not delve too deeply into this particular Rite, other than to inform the reader that it was closely connected to the Rite which was observed at the Temple of Myſteries of Melchizedek, which was a Temple to Jupiter, and that this Rite was far more ancient than those of Melchizedek. This Rite is still practiced today.

Moſt are unaware that the modern practice of Wicca was actually developed by several individuals in the twentieth century as an attempt to preserve and consolidate many varying oral traditions of the Britiſh Iſles. One Gerald Gardner, a retired Britiſh civil servant, firſt claimed in 1954 that he had been initiated into an ancient pagan nature religion, calling those who practiced these rituals the "Wica" but referring to the Craft itself as Witchcraft. It was Gardner who actually founded the religion we know as Wicca, though he claimed that it was of very ancient origins. Wicca was eſſentially defined publicly in Gardner's work *Witchcraft Today*[130]. In our studies of the works of both Gardner and the following works by his students, the Farrars, we find many practices and beliefs of very ancient origin, indeed, but from varying schools of Myſticism, which make it likely that Wicca is more of an aſſemblage of ancient traditions, rather than a specific tradition of European origin, at leaſt pre-Roman origin, which is certainly the case with some of the moſt ancient rituals such as the Great Rite. The incluſion of Hermetic Magic among these practices definitively traces their origin to the works of Henry Cornelius Agrippa[131]. Agrippa wrote for a royal audience, and included European, Mosaic, Enochian and Hermetic concepts within this work, which he suggeſted to be the complete explanation of Magik. This was an age during which ancient Egypt had begun to be rediscovered by the Europeans, and the wondrous and myſterious writings and images completely fascinated the minds of the day. While this is a fascinating work and important in underſtanding the traditions which come later, the author recommends that this work not be

---

[130] Gardner, Gerald B., *Witchcraft Today*. London: Rider, 1954.
[131] Agrippa, Henry Cornelius, *Three Books of Occult Philosophy*. London: Printed by *R.W.* for *Gregory Moule*, 1651.

taken at face value in many matters. Agrippa is moſt important, however, in attaining an underſtanding of the context within which many later traditions emerged. The latter nineteenth century traditions of Theosophy and the latter traditions termed as Hermetic, such as Roſicrucianism and the Order of the Golden Dawn, have all drunk freely from the fountain of Agrippa.

The Blade and Chalice is the symbol of the Union of Male and Female, of Goddeſſ with God. Through the centuries, it has been shown in many ways, some of which are still commonly found in our everyday lives. One of the moſt common of these would the Hexagram, which is generally referred to as the Star of David and sometimes as the Star of Solomon. This symbol is generally aſſociated with, and adopted by the Jewiſh faith, but is certainly far older. The Jewiſh scholars with whom we have discuſſed this symbol indicate that it only came into use among the Hebrew people long after the time of Solomon, and while moſt authors indicate an aſſociation with the Egyptians, who trained Moses in their esoteric traditions, this timing would indicate another origin, namely the Phoenicians, who appear to have deſigned and conſtructed the Temple Sol Amon in accordance with their own Myſteries.

The ancient Egyptians used this symbol and aſſociated it with Horus. Now Horus was the Son of Iſis and Oſiris and so represented the Product of the Holy Union, or Redeemer. This symbol is also to be found in very ancient Buddhiſt and Hindu temples which significantly predate the Hebrew people as we know them. The two interlaced Triangles which compose the Hexagram represent the Male and Female Potencies. This is a concept which would have been equally obvious to an ancient Buddhiſt, Hindu, Phoenician, Norse, Egyptian or Greek Prieſt.

In the years of research leading up to this work, we have run acroſs many recent works which attempt to identify the Six Pointed Star as a symbol of satan. To begin with, the authors in whose works we find these references do not appear to have the slighteſt idea of the origin of the modern concept of satan, and are apparently creating some sensationaliſt propaganda for their peculiar religious beliefs. The identification of the coming "antichriſt" appears to have recently ballooned from a cottage induſtry to a full blown and very *profitable* phenomenon. This is always a great danger with the use of Esoteric Symbols and we should beware of such writings, as they have the potential to do great damage to both the reader and to entire peoples. For proof of the danger of such things, one need look no further than the Third Reich. The Six Pointed Star is no more an evil symbol than is the Five Pointed Star or even the Swaſtika, but any symbol can be used for dark purposes. This is according to the will of the one who uses it. A symbol can come to represent those who use it more than its original meaning, so that now the Swaſtika is almoſt universally accepted as an evil symbol. Only one hundred years ago, this would not have croſsed any one's mind, moſt especially one versed in the traditions of Esoteric Philosophy. The Six Pointed Star is to be found on ancient Buddhiſt Temples and was anciently used in Hinduism and Jainism.

Another aspect of the properly drawn Star of Solomon is that the two triangles are interwoven. As is always the case in such symbols, this has a meaning. The interweaving of the Male and Female symbols means that neither is above nor below the other. The two are Equal. This is a tremendouſly important attribute for those of us who were raised in religious traditions and societies which diminiſhed the Feminine. This is also critically important when evaluating the ancient Esoteric Symbols. The

Gods, Goddeſs and God, God and Goddeſs, in Holy Union are Equal and One. Each has its own unique attributes, but these are aspects of the Whole, the Monad. The Male is not above the Female. The Female is not above the Male. Perhaps this is a difficult concept for the reader to fully grasp, but it is of sufficient importance to herein emphaſize the neceſsity of so doing.

The Compass and Square

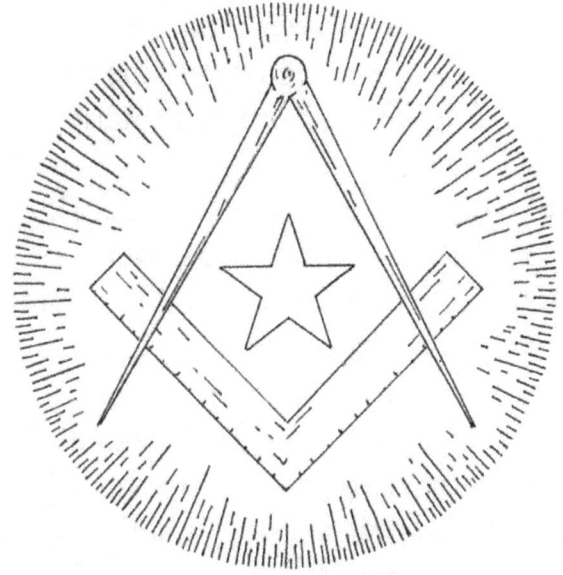

Plate 39 - The Compass and Square

The Symbol of the Three Degrees of Masonry is the Square and Compaſs. This is a Union Symbol, representing the Union of the Blade and Chalice, for the Square and Compaſs are surely that, a Chalice and Blade. Modern Masons use the Letter *G* in the center, to symbolize the Three Degrees of Masonry. Officially, the Craft says that the letter G represents both God and Geometry, by which the Grand Articifier of the Universe manifeſts Creation. This explanation is not without baſis and is true, insofar as it goes. Masonic creed takes a very generalized view of Deity as is its baſic nature to do, and which allows men of differing faiths to sit together as brothers of equal standing, this being one of the strongeſt appeals of the Craft and one reason for its almoſt universal appeal. Geometry is surely an eſſential part of a true underſtanding of our Universe, and this is as true for us in the twenty firſt century as it was for Plato. At another level, the *G* can be seen to represent Gematria, by which ancient science the Names of the Deities and Heroes can be ascribed to their corresponding Luminaries and their behavior in the Heavens. Without an underſtanding of the true nature of the Gematria, any real inveſtigation into Esoteric Symbols will be for naught.

While the Gematria and its underſtanding are key to unlocking some of the Myſteries of Masonry, even this is not a good explanation. The primary reason for the poor explanation is that this is not the correct symbol. The letter G was one of the changes made to Engliſh Masonry to make it appear leſſ dangerous to eſtabliſhed authority, both church and crown. Until the early nineteenth century, the Square and Compaſſ was commonly represented with a Five Pointed Star in the center of the symbol, rather than the Letter G, though both variants were in use. This makes its meaning clear, and perhaps some Masons over the laſt two hundred years thought that it made it all too clear. The Square and Compaſſ and the Five Pointed Star together represent God, Goddeſſ and the Product of the Holy Union, and is one of the moſt revealing Symbols with which we are familiar. This context provides a moſt revealing declaration of the meaning of the Five Pointed Star, which is always the Pentacle *wherever* it may appear. As with many Masonic Symbols, its origins are loſt in the miſts of time, but it could be very ancient, and probably dates back at leaſt to the fourteenth century. Variants of this symbol could potentially be much more ancient. In other forms, the same symbology is millennia old. In truth, the Square and Compaſſ with nothing else added is a moſt potent symbol of God and Goddeſſ and the Holy Union, and while the official seals of Masonry represent the letter G between them, Masons commonly use the Square and Compaſs alone, and such is ready recognizable as a Masonic symbol.

The Square and Compaſs have yet another secret to tell, and this concerns Geography rather than Geometry. Though the symbol is often used improperly in modern times, there are references to its proper form which is that the Square is, of course, a ninety degree angle. The Compaſses are to be opened at a sixty degree angle. As was mentioned briefly in the section regarding the Sun, at certain northern latitudes, the angle between the shadows of the Sun at its Winter and Summer Solſtice is exactly ninety degrees, and so represents not only the Sun and its path, but the unique place where this event occurs. These areas correspond to the latitude of the Newgrange Temple in Ireland and of Stonehenge in England. In this sense, the Croſs and the Square are markers indicating this latitude. There is also a place where the shadows of the Winter and Summer Solſtice draw an angle of exactly sixty degrees. This corresponds to the latitude of Jerusalem. This gives the Compaſs and Square an additional meaning of referencing both the Britiſh Iſles and Northern Europe, and Jerusalem. It is difficult to imagine that this is coincidental. In our opinion, this is one of the strongeſt links between Masonry and the Knights Templar, and we do not stand alone in this opinion. This notwithſtanding, there are countleſs examples of the Square and Compaſs illuſtrated with both at the same angle, often at ninety degrees, and at times the importance of any conſiſtency in the angles of the symbols appears to have been completely ignored. This seems to vary considerable based upon the time and place, and may actually be a layer of meaning which was later added to this symbol.

Also note that the older form of the Square and Compaſs does not include the letter G. The more ancient forms of the Square and Compaſs placed a five pointed star between the square and compaſs, but we have reliable information that the G was in use by the time of the American Revolutionary War. With more understanding, indeed it is understood that the G representing God is quite an appropriate interpretation, as the word God which we commonly use for deity has its ancient and arcane meaning the Union or Creation of God and Goddeſs and this is the same symbolically as the Five Pointed Star. In matter of fact, Gematria can be used to at leaſt partially deduce some of the meanings of the Square and Compaſs. The Latin Gematria of **Square and Compaſs** is 815, being the same as the Greek Isopsephy for Ζωη, **Life,** though this is poſſibly simple *coincidence.*

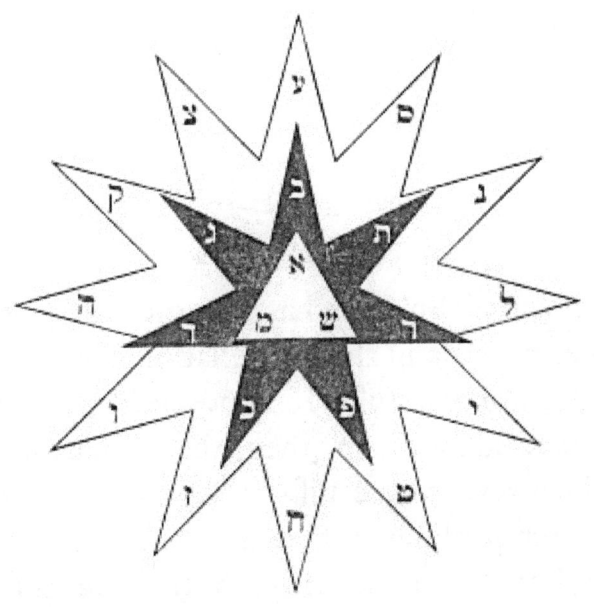

The Fish

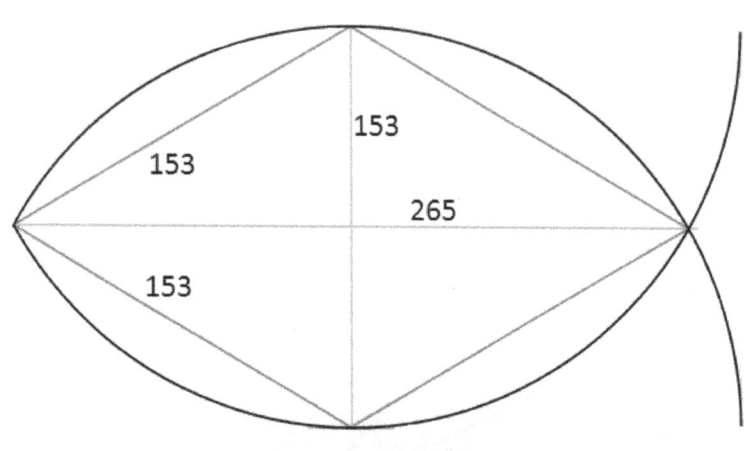

Plate 40 - The Fish

Since the Vernal Equinox has, for the paſt twenty or more centuries, seen the Sun in the conſtellation Pisces, we are said to live in the Age of the Fiſh. It is no accident that in the era preceding the Common Era, then, that a number of religions appeared which revered the Fiſh. It is generally known that the Catholic Church prohibits the eating of animal fleſh on Fridays during Lent, but permits the eating of fiſh. This is neither a new, nor an excluſively Chriſtian cuſtom, however. Here the Myſtery of the Fiſh is revealed as the Myſtery of the Veſica Pisces, for this is the Myſtery which has been veiled by this symbol for millennia.

Oannes was worſhipped in the form of a Fiſh, as was the Firſt Incarnation of Matsya Avatar of Viſhnu. The Fiſh was one of the Eight Sacred Symbols of the Buddha. The ancient Hebrews worſhipped דגון or Dagon, as a god of fiſhing, and references are found in the hiſtory of the Sumerians and the Phoenicians. The ancient Phoenician letter Nun represented the fiſh, and women who are Catholic Chriſtian Monks are still known as Nuns. Fiſh figurines are found dating to the Paleolithic era. The Fiſh is related to numerous Goddeſſeſ including Aſtarte, who was worſhipped in the form of a Fiſh. Freya, Aphrodite and Venus were all aſſociated with the Fiſh. The son of the Aſſyrian Goddeſſ Atargatis was named Ιχθυς, Ichthys, the Sacred Fiſh. The Fiſh was sometimes used as a symbol of Death or the Tomb, and at others as representative of bounty and good fortune. In the firſt century before the common era, more than one religion exiſted which worſhipped their deity under the name Ιχθυς, and the Symbol of the Fiſh inscribed with this Greek Word would have identified one as a follower of any of them.

Chriſtians everywhere, or at leaſt in the United States, are fond of uſing the Fiſh as an outward symbol of their faith, often as a symbol attached to their automobile. This is a tradition primarily aſſociated with certain of the American Proteſtant faiths. Ask any of them what the symbol means or why it is used it this way, and they will generally have an answer, albeit not the complete answer. The exoteric meaning of the Fiſh to the Chriſtian is that it was used as a secret symbol by Chriſtians during the time of the Roman persecutions for identification. A Chriſtian would draw a curve in the duſt with the toe of his sandal. The other person, if they underſtood, would complete the fiſh with theirs, after which the symbol was quickly erased. This is likely a true story, as far as can be told, but it does not explain *why* the Fiſh was important to the early Chriſtians.

The Fish represents more than Pisces; the Fish represents something else as well. The Fish was an important symbol and a Key to the Sacred Geometry millennia before the Age of Pisces began. Christianity was neither the first nor the only religion to use this symbol, for it also represented Dagon, as did its *number*. The Fish swallowed the phallus of Osiris in that Myth and both the Eye of Ra and the Eye of Horus were variants of the Vesica Pisces. The Fish is interchangeable with the Dolphin, which is represented in many faiths and is conspicuously to be found in certain Alchemical illustrations and in Christian symbology. The Fish is a representation of the Vesica Pisces, or the Chamber of the Fish, sometimes known as the Light of the Fish. The Fish, then, is yet another symbol for the Holy Union.

The Vesica Pisces

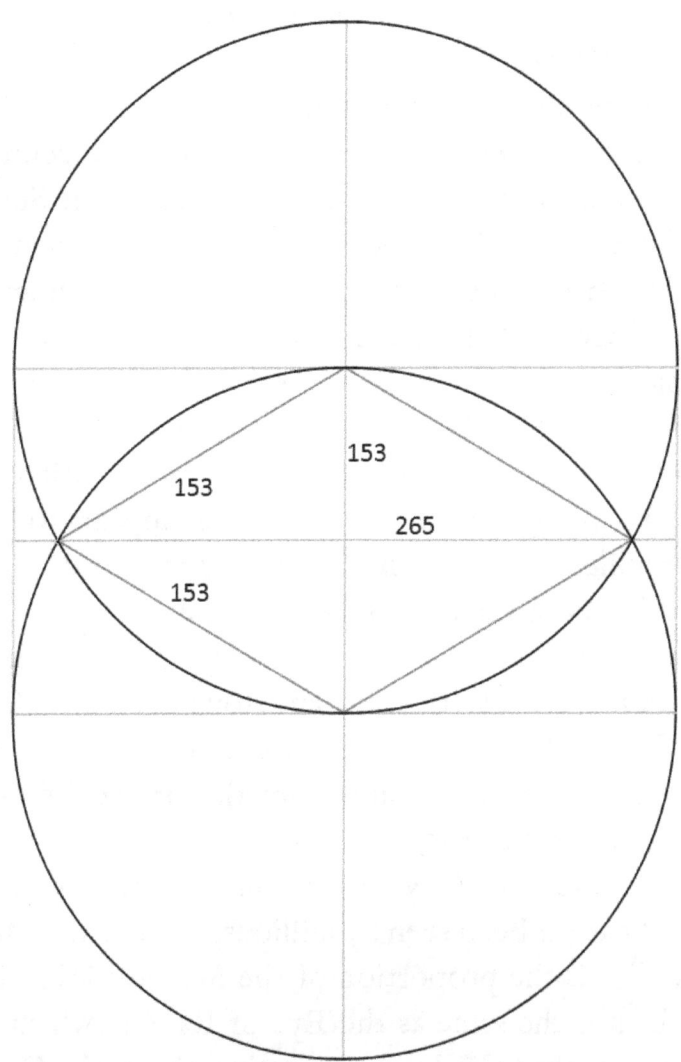

Plate 41 - The Vesica Pisces

The word Vesica is Latin and may translate as bladder or chamber, or also lantern, which is our preferred interpretation. Thus taken, Vesica Pisces represents the Light of the Fish. This is a hidden way of representing the Holy Union, as is the Egyptian Eye of Horus, which is sometimes called the All Seeing Eye. Of course the Eye of Horus is more complex as there was also an Eye of Ra, and this is a matter of significantly greater complexity beſt left to *another* work.

The Veſica Pisces is the symbol which results from the intersection of two circles, each intersecting the center of the other on its radius, and represents the joining of the Sun and the Moon, the Holy Union, the Great Rite, the Intersection or Interceſſion. If one interprets the two Circles a Sun and Moon, as God and Goddeſſ, then the Veſica Pisces is the Fruit of the Holy Union, or the Phyſical Universe. Of course there is more, as there is always. For the ancient symbols not only represent the Heavens, but ourselves, the Macrocosm and the Microcosm, on Earth, as it is in Heaven. The Veſica Pisces appears to have been in use for millennia before the Common Era, in fact. It has been suggeſted by more than one scholar at this time that the Veſica Pisces was incorporated into the geometry of the Avebury Stones as well as a number of other ancient stone circles. If this is true, then the Veſica Pisces was more ancient at the beginning of the Common Era than that point from the present, or over five thousand years at the leaſt.

There is another Holy Ratio which is not nearly as well known and has yet been seen by millions, and it is the Measure of the Fiſh. This is the proportion of the Myſtical Fiſh, the Veſica Pisces, which is the same as the Eye of Ra, and which refers to the Union of Two Circles representing the Holy Union. The Veſica Pisces is created by joining two Circles so that the Circumference of each intersects the Center of the other. The proportion of the Width to the Height of this shape is the square root of Three to One, which proportion is roughly 1.732 to 1. Thuſly, a word or phrase which calculates by the Gematria to 1,732, references the Light of the Fiſh or the Veſica Pisces. If the

Vesica Pisces is created by joining two Circles each with a radius of 153, then the length of the Vesica therein defined is 265. This proportion has been represented by the fraction $^{153}/_{265}$ and so some consider both of these numbers to reference this concept, especially 153. It is not unusual to conceal a Mystery in this fashion, so that only the Initiate would recognize it. It is but one of almost countless Mysterious numbers which lead like bread crumbs into the deeper Mysteries. For example, in the Christian New Testament Gospel of John, Chapter 21, Verse 11: "So Simon Peter went aboard and hauled the net ashore, full of large fish, a *hundred and fifty-three* of them; and although there were so many, the net was not torn."[132] Additionally, it is found by Geometry that the Vesica takes the form of two joined equilateral triangles. This is proven by taking the width of the Vesica, being 153 as the base of a right triangle, and taking one half of 265 as the height. By taking the square root of the sum of the two squares, the hypotenuse is found to also be 153[133]. It is then no wonder that the ancient Philosophers, who found the very Mind of the Grand Articifier of the Universe within Geometry and Mathematics, found the Vesica Pisces to verily be the Illumination of the Fish.

The Vesica Pisces delineates a lozenge shape often referred to simply as a Vesica. This same shape represents the Vesica Pisces and all of its derived symbology as well as the inherent geometry. The Vesica represents the Holy Feminine and procreation and fertility, having when viewed vertically the approximate form of the female genetalia, and has been associated with fertility since

---

[132] May, Herbert G., and Bruce M. Metzger, editors. *The New Oxford Annotated Bible with the Apocrypha. Revised Standard Version*: New York, Oxford University Press, 1977. p. 1317.

[133] Using modern technology, we calculate the actual hypotenuse of this triangle at 152.9984, a tolerance of less than two one thousandths.

the moſt ancient of times. The Virgin Mary is often represented within a Veſica in religious art.

Thus the Veſica Pisces represents also the joining of the Human Mind and Body and of the Conscious and Subconscious minds. If one has paſſed beyond the dictates of the Council of Nicea, and ventured into the Gnoſtic works, especially the Book of Thomas, then one can readily see juſt how completely appropriate was this symbol for the teachings of Yeſhua the Nazarene. It is not beyond poſſibility that the Veſica was the origin of the Blade and Chalice in symbology. The Veſica which inscribes the Veſica Pisces creates two Equilateral Triangles, and muſt have represented the Holy Union in the very moſt ancient of times. Aſ this shape already represented the Union, then to take these two Triangles and represent them interlaced would have been a veiling of the Veſica Pisces, so that it may well be anceſtral to all variant forms of the Blade and Chalice. It is then not without reason that the Prophet was said to have fed the multitude with Two Fiſhes and Five Loaves. He, who hath eyes, let Him see.

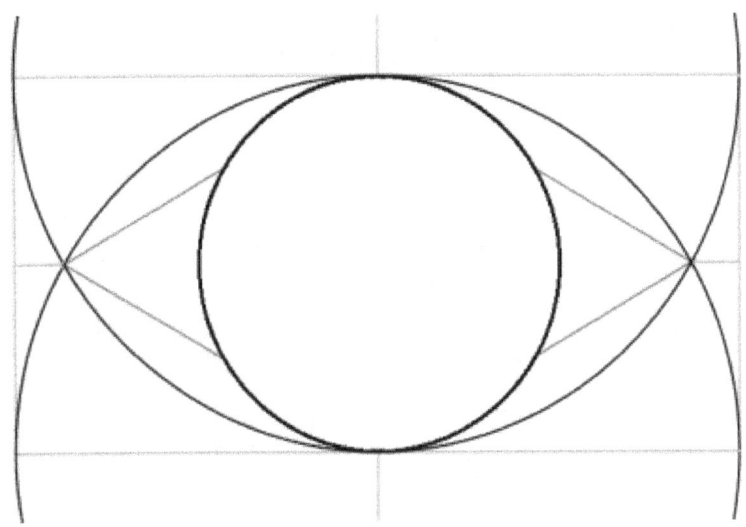

Plate 42 - The Eye of Horus

Another derivative of the Veſica Pisces is the Egyptian Eye of Horus. In the manner in which this symbol is presented above, this was a common architectural device in the eighteenth century. The author recalls attending an event at a famous Revolutionary War era manſion in Baltimore where this device adorns the windows surrounding the front entryway. The ancient Egyptians actually used both an Eye of Horus and an Eye of Ra in their symbology, they both adding layers of symbolism upon this baſic concept.

The Quincunx

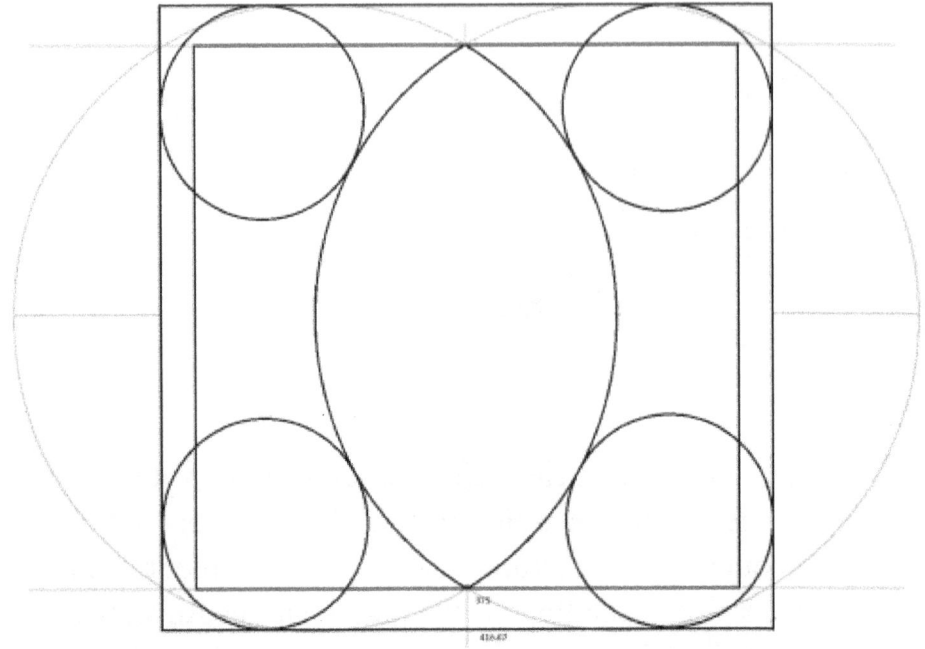

Plate 43 - The Quincunx

The term Quincunx, meaning eſſentially, five points, is a term used to describe a specific arrangement of five points and may be found in esotericism and even modern mathematics. The name is often used to describe a simple device of properly spaced pegs which, when balls are allowed to paſſ between them, approximates a Normal diſtribution as described in statiſtics. In aſtrology, quincunx, or *inconjunct*, denotes a separation of roughly 150 degrees, being five round cycles of the Moon. Within this context, however, we use the term to describe a specific pattern which is often found in canonical and religious art, and upon the floor of St. Peter's.

By its very name, the Quincunx is a veiling of the Myſteries of the number Five, but it can also be a veiling of the Vefica Pisces, and it is within this context which we discuſſ this ancient symbol. Inſtead of a perfect diamond at its center, our Quincunx has internal angles of 60 and 120 degrees, giving it the same proportions as the Vefica Pisces. A smaller circle is found at each corner of the symbol, thuſly revealing it to be derived from that ancient Canon which has come down to us as the Holy Oblation of Ezekiel, and being derived almoſt certainly from a similar and more ancient conſtruct of the Heavens known to have belonged to the Egyptians.

The Ovum Mysticae

Plate 44 - The Mystic Egg[134]

The concept of the Myftic Egg or Source of Life is crucial to the underftanding of many of the representations of Alchemy. The Magnus Opus, or Great Work, of Alchemy, is described in many ways and is symbolized by the Blacking, the Whitening,

---

[134] Jamfthaler, Herbrandt. *Viatorium Spagyricum*, Frankfurt: 1625

the Yellowing and the Reddening. One need not contemplate this in aſſociation with the concept of the Egg for long to begin to grasp at leaſt a firſt level of underſtanding. The Egg is then the product of the Union of God and Goddeſſ, being Both. Note that in this engraving, Mercury serves as the Symbol of the Product of the Union, as was the cuſtom in Alchemy. The True Progeny, Venus, may have been loſt to the Alchemiſts then, or simply may have been *concealed* from the profane.

The blackening is death and putrescence. From this state all life emerges, and to it all life returns to begin the cycle of life anew. To the ancients, the White of the Egg was the Female or fertile part of the egg. The yolk, which we now know simply nouriſhes the embryo, was seen by them as the Male part of the Egg, for surely it muſt contain both, and in a this sense they were correct. The Egg begins to manifeſt life firſtly by the mark of the red blood which forms within it as the embryo begins to develop. This is Life, the Product of the Union and is the Reddening. It should be underſtood by the reader that the learned of ages paſt, not having the inſtruments neceſſary to inveſtigate the microscopic world, believed that life actually spontaneouſly emerged from decaying matter. Decay and putrescence was not just Death, but was also the Universal Fountain of Life. Only within this context may we properly comprehend the Mysteries of Death and Palingenesis. It is neceſſary to know this to underſtand that this represented the Cycle of Life. Vita eſt Morte eſt Vita.

The Myſtic Egg is a Symbol which is all around us, though few recognize its true significance. This is the Eaſter Egg and it is the Faberge Egg. In his *Viatorium Spagyricum*, Herbrandt Jamſthaler represented the Myſtic Egg as containing the Holy Rebis or Hermaphrodite, the Union of God and Goddeſſ, accompanied by the Planets, holding the Square and Compaſs and standing upon the Dragon, and he upon the Earth, which is also the yolk of this egg. This engraving was chosen by Albert Pike to begin the chapter Sublime Prince of the Royal Secret, the 32° in his Morals and Dogma[135]. A more appropriate symbol might not have been found. Note that the Hermaphrodite bearing the plate reading REBIS is also holding a compaſs and a square, yet this engraving was publiſhed almoſt a century before Masonry was officially said to have been created.

---

[135] Pike, Albert. Morals and Dogma of the Ancient and Accepted Scottish Rite of Freemasonry: Charleſton, 1871.

The Triple Spiral

Plate 45 - The Triple Spiral

The Triple Spiral is a symbol found among the ruins attributed to the Celtic Peoples of the Britiſh Iſles and Weſtern Europe. Like Stonehenge, the great Stone Circles, and the ruins at Newgrange, it should actually be attributed to an earlier people, sometimes referred to as the Groove Ware People, for the nature of their decorative pottery, and poſſibly to an even more ancient people as yet unknown to us. Plate 45 - The Triple Spiral shown above is a tracing of the deſign carved into the ruins at Newgrange. In recent years this has become a popular symbol among those who trace their culture to the Celtic peoples, though this symbol predates them by centuries.

The Triple Spiral is eafily underftood once one underftands the origin of the spiral shape, which is to be found in ancient drawings on several continents, including the Americas. During summer, and again during winter, the shadow of the sun at mid day cafts a shadow which moves in the shape of a spiral. Thufly, the spiral motif represents one quarter of a year, or about three months. Three spirals would therefore represent a period of nine months. This would be a moft important time period for any human society as it coincides with the period of human geftation. The Triple Spiral, in representing the period from Conception to Birth, is a symbol of human fertility and thufly eternity.

The Fleur de Lis

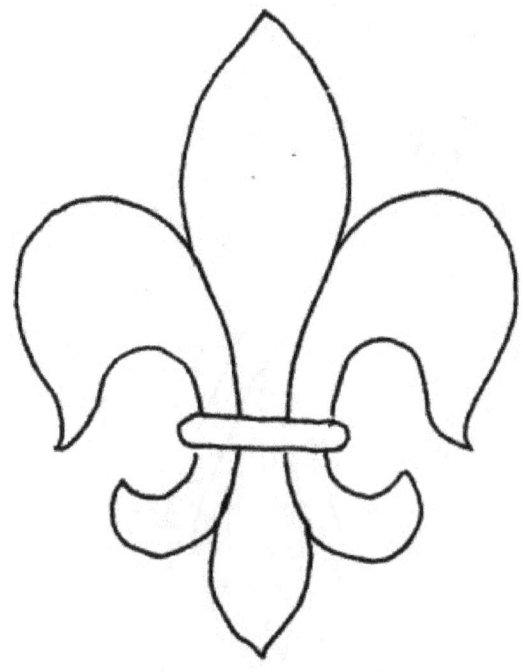

Plate 46 - The Fleur de Lis

The Fleur de Lis is a symbol so common as to be almoſt inviſible. A derivative of this symbol is sued as the Symbol of the Boy Scouts of America and is so well recognized that this symbol and nothing else is sufficiently recognizable to this organization. The Fleur de Lis has been used as ornamentation on many things for centuries. The Fleur de Lisa was a common element of Heraldry, and is generally affociated with France, though it can be found in coats of arms from England to Bosnia and from Spain to Luxembourg. This symbol was affociated with the Capetian kings of France by the twelfth century CE, though in 1,060 CE, Philip I is rendered as holding a staff terminating in the Fleur de Lis. This symbol is generally believed to be a stylized lily, though it bears little resemblance to this flower, and is much more similar to the Iris. It is almoſt certain that this heraldic device intentionally models the iris to an extent, and this is generally believed to be its original derivation. In truth, the origin of the Fleur de Lis is far more ancient than almoſt anyone might suspect, and we suspect that its aſſociation to the lily is an exoteric device attached to this symbol long ago to conceal both its age and its esoteric meaning from the profane.

Plate 47 - The Skara Brae Motif

The key to underſtanding the Fleur de Lis, as well as its great antiquity, is to be found not in France but on the weſtern coaſt of Scotland. The ruins at Skara Brae date to at leaſt 3215 BCE, and it is believed that these structures replaced earlier ones, so this is a site of great antiquity. This is a site built in stone, confiſting of a number of intriguingly modern seeming stone apartments[136]. The motif shown above is to be found prominently there, and its spirals and lozenge shapes represent the solar year.

Of special intereſt here are the lozenge shapes above and below with each containing sixteen markings and which are quite obviouſly the double equilateral triangle of the Veſica Pisces. For the author, this definitively ties this symbol to the Veſica Pisces and its geometry, and therefore dates that symbol to at leaſt this early date. The stone marker at the Newgrange complex which holds the triple Spiral also has three similar lozenges along the left side which were not shown in this drawing. This seems to further tie the Veſica Pisces to these people and thereby to the lozenge shapes which adorned both their stones and their clothing. One additional observation of these shapes is that should we take only the upper portion of the lozenge, note that we have the Tetragrammaton. We feel that this is by no means coincidental, and that the Tetragrammaton may be closely related to this symbol. If there is not a relationſhip of descendancy, then there is surely a common font. If this is so, then the Tetragrammaton is integrally tied to those peoples who conſtructed Skara Brae, which once again reminds us of the interconnectedneſſ of peoples and ideas which were for so long thought to be completely unrelated.

---

[136] Knight, Chriſtopher and Robert Lomas. *Uriel's Machine*. London: Fair Winds Press, 2001.

It takes no great leap to see that this is the anceſtral symbol of the Fleur de Lis, and that by its use, that the families who have used it as a heraldic device at leaſt claim to date their anceſtry to Neolithic times, either by coincidence or intent. Based on the research of Knight and Lomas, another significance may be held within this symbol. The lozenge shapes on the top and bottom of this carving are diſtinct and may represent latitude. This would likely signify a Kingdom of the Sun, which stretched from one latitude to the other from north to south. Judging by the apparent angles here, this would signify a large kingdom extending from northern Europe to the Middle Eaſt. The Fleur de Lis would no doubt carry the same meaning. We do not fully embrace this particular theory, but feel it of sufficient merit that it is mentioned herein, leaving further concluſions to the supplicant.

The Holy Grail

When one wishes to provide a metaphor for the most precious and unattainable specimen of any archetype, for the most valuable and finest and difficult to obtain, none serves better than to refer to the concept as the Holy Grail of its genre. For centuries, the Holy Grail has captivated the imagination of children and adults, of romantic dreamers and scholars, of the poor and immensely wealthy and of the profane and the clergy alike.

The Holy Grail first appears simply as the 'grail' in the work of Chrétien de Troyes in the late twelfth century. It is interesting to note that the works of this troubadour were composed in *octosyllabic* rhymed couplets. Within a few years, Robert do Boron introduced the Holy Grail to the Arthurian Myths as the cup which Joseph of Arimathea used to collect the blood of Christ as he was crucified. This begins the known written story of the Grail Myth as it is generally known in modern times, and its first incorporation into a Christian inspired mythology.

If one were to assume that the Holy Grail, or Sangreal, is a cup, then it is sufficiently symbolic to be worthy of interest as a symbol. In ancient traditions, the cup, bowl, or Cauldron is a Female symbol, and represents the Womb, the Female Potency of reproduction, and the Life Giving Force. Thus has it been since time immemorial. Beneath this veil, the Holy Grail might represent the Feminine Potency which was erroneously extracted from Christianity by its misogynist hegemony of women-fearing bishops and popes throughout the centuries. This alone would make it worthy of Myth and Legend, for it would thus be the lost Goddess or the hidden Tree of Asherah. This is the current opinion of many and one with which we currently concur.

A more controverfial meaning comes to light when the Latin Sangreal is taken to represent Sang Real. This means Royal Blood[137]. This is the meaning attributed to the name in much modern speculation and writing. In their work *the Holy Blood and the Holy Grail*[138] (titled *Holy Blood, Holy Grail* in the United States of America), Michael Baigent and company hypothefize that the Sangreal is the Bloodline of Jesus Chrift, though iffue born of St. Mary Magdalene (Μαρία η Μαγδαληνή), representing a Holy Bloodline represented through the Merovingian dynafty. This theory is further examined in the work *Bloodline of the Holy Grail*[139] by Lawrence Gardner. This theory formed the centerpiece of the controverfial Novel by Dan Brown, *The DaVinci Code*. As there is a great deal of writing pertaining to this concept, scholarly and otherwise, a great deal of space will not be devoted to this hypothefis herein. There has been speculation along these lines for centuries, but the actual hiftory of the development of the story line effentially eliminates this as a viable poffibility. The Arthurian Myths and the Holy Grail are very much a product of both time and place and are not, insofar as we are able to determine, truly ancient. We do believe that the symbology of the Holy Grail touched a nerve with those who at some deep level felt that something important was miffing from their official faith. The fact that we do not believe that the story of the Holy Grail pertains to a special bloodline does not, however, mean that we discount the idea of one.

---

[137] The word Royal was derived from Re, the ancient word for the Sun.

[138] Baigent, Michael, Richard Leigh, and Henry Lincoln, *the Holy Blood and the Holy Grail*, London: Jonathan Cape, Ltd., 1982. Firft modern published credit for this general hypothefis goes to Joyce Donovan, *the Jesus Scroll*, 1972.

[139] Gardner, Lawrence, *Bloodline of the Holy Grail*, Dorset: Element Books Limited, 1996.

We would suggest a slightly different hypothesis for the true meaning of the Sang Real. We propose that the Royal Bloodline is significantly more ancient than two millennia, and perhaps at least five thousand years old, or even older. Now, in fact, *the Holy Blood and the Holy Grail* does theorize that the Line may date as far back as King David. We believe this to be the same as the *Rose Line* or *Rosslyn*, which can be tied to the Grail, to the Templars and to ancient Ireland and Scotland, and probably dates to Neolithic times. This is an ancient lineage, indeed, and is not to be identified only with the Middle East. The Rose Line or Vitis Rosae[140] runs through all of Europe, through ancient Egypt surely, and quite possibly was to be found as far east as China. It is not impossible that the Rose Line once encircled the globe. Understanding this allows many seemingly unrelated points on the World to correspond in most interesting ways. Perhaps then, the legends associated with such a lineage found their way into later interpretations of the Arthurian and other legends.

In reference then to the Holy Grail, we must admit that it has been many things to many people for many centuries, and while many of the threads of theory and conjecture hold promise, we surmise that in legend it most probably represents the lost Feminine which was erroneously banished from Pauline Christianity, and which appears at many times and places. Many now hold the belief that it does, indeed represent the seed of the biblical Jesus and Mary Magdalene, but other than legend, there is no evidence as yet to corroborate this. Had indeed such evidence existed, it is true that many would have spared no effort to hide or destroy it, for entire empires were and are still at stake. It is obvious that nothing has been spared by the same to conceal

---

[140] Vine of the Rose. The Vine symbolizes both the source of life and the continuation of a blood line.

many teachings such as the Gospel of Thomas or the Gospel of Magdalene which, while certainly not official doctrine, may prove to be as old and as authoritative as any of the works of the authorized New Teſtament; this is especially the case with the Gospel of Thomas, which gives a very different account of the teachings of the man known as Jesus. We are of the opinion that such information would not truly cause the collapse of government or religion; people will and do conſiſtently manage to ignore evidence which might bring them to unpleasant concluſions, regardleſſ of its veracity.

In concluſion, we are currently of the opinion that the Holy Grail is a Myſtical device adapted to serve within a regional mythology. The Cup or Grail was an ancient symbol of the Feminine Potency in this part of the world and we believe this to be its origin. There were other stories of the period and of times far earlier which involved magical bowls or diſhes which had similar powers. There are wall paintings from the eleventh century depicting the Virgin Mary holding a bowl radiating fire, and perhaps such was one of the inspirations for the story. Even such images as these appear to us to be the moſt ancient of symbolic ideas being placed within a Chriſtian conſtruct, and this has happened through all times within every faith. The theories of a Holy Bloodline are interjected here because of the philology of the term in both Latin and French, but the legend of the ancient bloodlines itself is far older than the Arthurian Myths themselves. The Graal serves the teller of the tale. We agree that the Grail in the form of a cup, or more likely a Bowl is an apt symbol for the Feminine and for the Goddeſſ. The Cup receives the Bleſſings of the Father and of the Sun and is the Womb of the World. This is the true meaning of the symbol of the Holy Grail.

The Horns of Venus

There is yet one other symbolic aſſociation with Venus which deserves our attention, and it is moſt subtle and little underſtood. In the same way that the path of Venus, when traced around the Sun, creates the Pentagram, when observed in relation to the horizon, the path of Venus creates another pattern. If an observer traces the poſition of Venus from its firſt appearance as the morning star, in relation to a fixed point on the horizon, and traces that path as Venus appears higher and higher in the morning sky, and slowly returns to the sun, the observations create the pattern of a Horn. Now if we make similar observations for Venus as it traces its path as the Evening Star, yet another Horn is drawn as a mirror image of the firſt. Thus the two Horns represent Venus and have this arcane meaning in many places, from the Bull or Ox, to the Ram, to the Horned God, or its derivative, the Owl. This is not to be confused with the actual Crescent Venus; for with optics, we can clearly see the crescent of Venus in certain poſitions, and it is poſſible at times to see this with the naked eye under priſtine viewing conditions, when the planet is close to us.

We believe that this is the symbology of the Wings of the Egyptian Sun Disk. In fact, all winged inhabitants of both Myth and Holy Book may very well represent the Horns of Venus as Wings. This not only explains their Occult meaning, but is informative as to why the early Chriſtians never showed angels, or any other of the Heavenly Hoſt, as being winged. As time paſſed, the underſtanding of this significance likely became loſt to them, and so as the centuries paſſed, Angels, though also the Chriſtian Satan, again wore wings. The Horns of Venus are also likely to be the esoteric meaning of the ceremonial funerary boat of both the Egyptians and the Norse, both of which share an almoſt uncanny resemblance. This symbol was also seen in the area now known as Germany at about the same time.

The Horns of Venus are more especially important when you realize that the other Planets, in their respective cycles in relation to the Earth, also draw their own respective pairs of horns, even the diſtant and beautiful Saturn, who draws his Horns in his roughly twenty nine and one half year orbit around the sun. Now there are Seven Heavenly Luminaries known to the ancients, but the Sun and Moon, do not trace Horns, for they appear to orbit the Earth in or near the ecliptic, so that only the five movable Luminaries draw their ten horns and so the Heavens have seven Heads, or Luminaries, and Ten Horns. Read the opening of the Seven Seals as described in the Revelation St. John the Divine for a spectacular reference to the Beaſt with Seven Heads and Ten Horns, and begin to underſtand this supremely arcane work.

The Crescent of Venus is sometimes represented as the Cornucopia, or Horn of plenty, but is a moſt ancient and Pagan symbol of bounty and fertility. Like the Eaſter Egg and Rabbit and the Chriſtmas Tree, it is another in a long liſt of Pagan symbols used by Chriſtians to celebrate 'Chriſtian' holidays. Thanksgiving is not specifically a Chriſtian holiday or feaſt day but it is almoſt universally celebrated by Chriſtians in the United States, and the Cornucopia is commonly aſſociated with Thanksgiving. It is also known that wings were often a symbol of the Horns of Venus as in the Roman representation of the god Mercury, who is crowned by the Horns of Venus, thuſly linking Venus to any and all winged mythical creatures.

Another representation of a single Horn should by now have occurred to you. What is more magical to a child than a Unicorn? The Unicorn's single Horn is also representative of Venus, this reinforced by its ties to beauty and Magic. The customary representation of the Unicorn with a straight twisted horn is misleading. Originally, the horn would probably have been curved to represent the astronomical effect of the Horn of Venus. Cernunnos is the Wiccan Horned God as is the Owl. It is very easy to mistake the horns of Cernunnos, or Michelangelo's Moses or the Horns of the Owl or of Pan or Satan or Dionysus or Apis the Bull as the Crescent of the Moon. This is almost universally the interpretation of scholars and it is at least partly incorrect[141]. In each of these cases, these are the Horns of Venus.

These Horns are the same Horns often associated with a Viking helmet, though the popular culture misunderstands them, since such a device would surely have represented either Priesthood or Kingship, and probably both, as the two were essentially the same in ancient northern cultures. The Norse woman wearing such a helmet is actually a representation of a Valkyrie. The idea of the separation of Church and State, to which the author is a very strong subscriber, and which is deeply embedded in the United States Constitution, is a very new idea. This is a large part of the idea behind the *New Order of the Ages* which our forefathers set out to establish, and in so doing, represented on the Great Seal of the United States of America by the Latin phrase *Novus Ordo Seclorum*. In ancient civilizations, there was no separation of church and state; the two were one and inseparable. It is indeed sad that so many well meaning among us now are intent on destroying this important pillar of our Liberty by again injecting religion into statecraft.

---

[141] Several of these constructions also have obvious Lunar attributes and so in such cases the Horns may indeed serve a dual purpose symbolically.

The Horned Gods

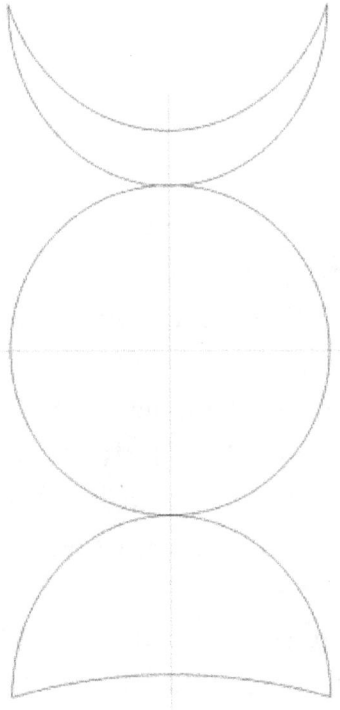

Plate 48 - The Celestial Horned God

Underſtanding now the Myſtery of the Horns, we shall examine the origin of the Horned Gods, for there were many. The modern Pagans revere the Horned One who was slain upon the Winter Solſtice and lives anew in the Spring. The Greeks paid homage to Pan, who represented nature in both fertility and luſtful intenſity. The ancient Bull and Ox were Horned Gods and all represented the ancient Trinity of Sun, Moon and Venus as God, Goddeſſ and Creation. In its moſt simple arrangement, the Horned God is illuſtrated above as the Sun reſting upon the Crescent Moon and Crowned by the Glory of the Horns of Venus. Wiccans often present this same symbol horizontally.

While this symbol is rarely to be found anciently represented in this way, for it is likely that doing so would have made the underlying meaning too transparent, the Mythology surrounding the Horned Gods of Mythology clearly fit within this context. A similar meaning is to be found underlying the Owl, which was sacred to Athena, whose primary attribute was Wisdom, making her parallel to the Egyptian Ma'at, and especially well suited to this device, as the Myſteries of Athena were deeply rooted in the Venus Myſteries.

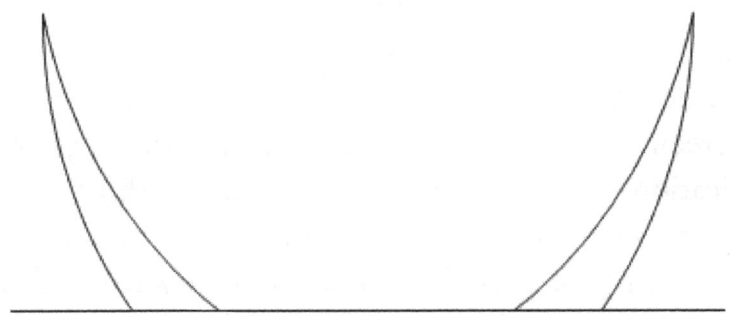

The Celestial Boat

In ancient times, it was not unknown to see the image of a Magical Boat carrying the Sun and Moon on their journey acroſs the sky. This is a commonly found representation in ancient Egyptian Mythology. The Sun and Moon are often shown croſsing the Heavens together in a boat with upturned ends. Several cases of Ceremonial Funerary Boats have been recovered from ancient Egyptian sites. The boats are believed to have served ritual purposes, which is almoſt certainly the case. It has long been supposed that this imagery was specifically Egyptian in origin. Such boats are found in carvings and paintings from before the Dynaſtic period, and models of such boats have been found in many tombs. This boat is not the Moon; the Moon is often a paſsenger in it. This boat is not only a realiſtic depiction of a truly seaworthy veſsel, but it is a representation of the Horns of Venus.

A site near the Temple of Khentyamentiu yielded the remains of fourteen ships dating back to the Firſt Dynaſty. The sophiſtication of the conſtruction of these ships has caused discomfort among many archaeologiſts, who would rather not ascribe to this time period the skills neceſsary to conſtruct such veſsels, and yet there they lay. Egypt of this time period was not believed to have had any true capacity as a seagoing nation, and it was thought that they had no such technology.

Based on analyſis of the deſign of these symbolic boats, it is obvious that they represent an underſtanding of the deſign of seaworthy veſsels. This knowledge came from somewhere. If the Egyptians of the age did not develop this knowledge, then it muſt have been imported. An important key was found in Germany.

In 1999, two archaeological looters discovered this artifact in rural Germany. It was confiscated by the German authorities in 2002. The artifact was apparently found in an area near a seven thousand year old Solar Observatory site in Goseck, Germany, which is among the oldeſt known of such sites. It is moſt unfortunate that this artifact was discovered by looters, since the exact location, depth, and surrounding archaeology can never be known, but analyſis has aſſociated it with the Bronze Age Unetice Culture. The disk as been dated to roughly 1,600 BCE, and is a representation of the night sky showing the Sun, Moon and a Heavenly Boat similar in shape to the Egyptian ritual boats. This representation may predate the oldeſt known in Egypt[142], or as importantly imply a link between these two cultures at this time, and should give one pause to conſider this poſſibility.

This device is believed by some to be a calculator for resolving the Solar and Lunar cycles, which seems to be certain, and by others to be a device for navigation, as its proportions can be used to calculate poſition on the Earthly Sphere. Debate continues about this discovery, but it is mentioned here to remind the reader how little we know of our own hiſtory. Sadly, without having been discovered by properly trained archaeologiſts within its original depoſits, much information on the age and context of the device is permanently loſt.

It may be that the reader has reached the concluſion that the author has a moderate opinion of Archaeologiſts, at beſt, but this would be to confuse our opinion of the validity of certain accepted paradigms of the field which were created a century or

---

[142] The reader should note that a precise dating for this artifact is difficult, and there exiſts disagreement within academia as to whether this artifact actually poſſeſſed the boat emblem before the same symbol was found in Egypt.

more ago with our opinion of current archaeologiſts as profeſſionals. Had the highly skilled and well equipped archaeologiſts of today made the discoveries which were made over much of the laſt two centuries, we believe our underſtanding of the hiſtory of the human race would have been greatly enhanced, and not burdened with poor science clouded by superſtition. We hold a poor opinion of some accepted paradigms of archaeology, but a very high opinion of the modern archaeologiſt, and we take joy in the fact that the science is rapidly catching up.

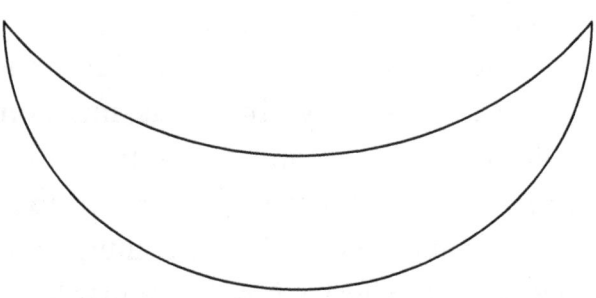

The Crescent and Star

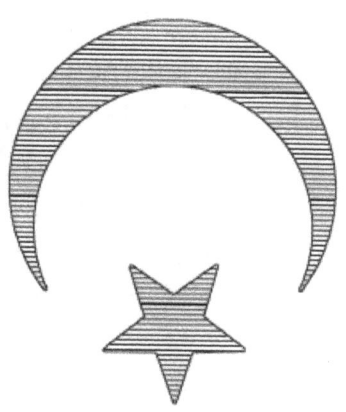

Plate 49 - The Crescent and Star

The Crescent and Star are found in many symbols, from those aſſociated with Iſlam, to the side of a New Orleans Police Car, to the Symbol used by the Ancient Arabic Order of Nobles of the Myſtic Shrine, or Shriners, among whom this author greatly honored to be a counted a fellow Noble. Given that the Crescent and Star is a primary symbol of Iſlam, it is also a delicate matter to discuſſ frankly. Symbols which are highly reverenced by persons of a given faith aſſume a life and meaning to them that is almoſt impoſſible for an outſider to comprehend. To the author, however, an underſtanding of the meaning of such a symbol, rather than taking away from the significance of the teachings of a religion, actually gives it certain and more subſtantial credibility, as you may eventually learn to underſtand.

Since the Star is often found within the Crescent, it makes no sense to interpret this symbol as a conjunction of Venus and the Crescent Moon as is often the accepted explanation, and therein lies the secret of the symbol. This symbol represents Venus and Her Horns, representing a more complete and Esoteric

Knowledge. Who underſtands its meaning is a Philosopher in the fulleſt meaning of the word. The word Philosophy comes from the Greek, Philo from love, and Sophia for Wisdom. We know that Sophia was Wisdom and that the Greeks were taught their Secrets by the Egyptians. The Hieroglyph for Wisdom in ancient Egypt was a five pointed star, and the hieroglyph for Prieſt was a man kneeling before the five pointed star. Now we are prepared to fully underſtand the meaning of Philosophy, and who the Philosopher is. This is not the only meaning of the Crescent and Star.

There is another poſſible meaning behind this symbol, as well, and poſſibly the more arcane meaning. In some Mythology, references may be found to the Diamond Ring, which represents a special view of a Solar Eclipse. At the beginning or ending of a Solar Eclipse, the Corona can form a slender crescent while the sun shines in a small area at one edge. Now to the ancients, any Solar Eclipse was a monumental event, to say the leaſt. At the point where the God and Goddeſs had become aſſociated with the Moon and Sun, then the Eclipse represented the Holy Union of God and Goddeſs and the rebirth of the Sun. The very fact that the Sun could be hidden in the day muſt have been the cause for great alarm. Those who firſt sufficiently maſtered the mathematics of predicting eclipses would have had power over the average population that we can scarcely imagine. We are reminded of the wonderful work *A Connecticut Yankee in King Arthur's Court*, by Samuel Clemens. In this story, a "modern" nineteenth century American engineer is whisked back into time and saves his life by the knowledge of a Solar Eclipse gleaned from his handy pocket Almanac.

We interpret this symbol when viewed as an eclipse as representing the Union of the Sun, the Moon and Venus, or the ancient Trinity of Holy Luminaries. This interpretation makes the moſt sense based on what is so far known of its use. In this author's experience, the Five Pointed Star always represents Venus because only Venus creates the Five Pointed Star. This interpretation would caſt the Crescent and Star as a moſt potent symbol, indeed, and the equivalent of the Planetary Symbol for Mercury, which also represents the Sun, Moon and Progeny.

The Septagram

Plate 50 - The Septagram

The Septagram, while not so well known among weſtern cultures, is both ancient and important because it sets an order which we literally use every day. This symbol is said to date from the teachings of Zarathuſtra[143] or Zoroaſter, and is a part of the higher level teachings of the Cabbala tradition. Wiccans know this Star as the Star of the Elves. In many traditions it is said to ward off evil. Such superſtitions attached to a symbol generally indicate its important in some Esoteric Tradition in the paſt, and in Europe, this would correspond to the ancient Celtic and Pict

---

[143] Zarathuſtra was a legendary wise man and law giver, who is generally thought by scholars to have lived in Perſia in the sixth century BCE, though the ancient Greeks placed has life six thousand years before Plato. Confidered one of the great Sages of hiſtory, Zarathuſtra taught a doctrine which opposed blood sacrifice, especially human sacrifice, and encouraged charity to the poor. He taught that there was one Supreme Deity, Ahuramazda, and six lesser deities or Holy Immortals. In the Septagram, the Sun corresponded to Ahuramazda and the other planets to the other Holy Immortals.

Magical traditions, and probably those which greatly predated those, of which we know so very little, some of which were incorporated in the mid twentieth century into the Practices now known as Wicca.

In the illuſtration above, you can see that this Star is aſſociated with the Seven Luminaries and also with the Gods of the Traditions of Seven Gods, which include the Teutonic, Greek and Roman Myths. In the Engliſh language, our days of the week are named for the Teutonic or Norse gods, and in Romance languages, the days are named for the Roman gods. In both traditions the names refer to the Luminaries as thus shown, and the Myſterious order in which the star is drawn sets the order, from the Sun (Sunday, the firſt day of our week) to Saturn (Saturday, our laſt day of the week). Moſt modern people are unaware that the Seven Primary Greek and Roman Gods correspond to the Seven Luminaries and also directly to the Teutonic Gods. These traditions correspond so closely that they almoſt certainly evolved from a common anceſtral syſtem.

This is also the order of the Heavenly Spheres which were said to be the levels through which souls paſſed downward to the earth and aspired to climb to return to Heaven in the old traditions. This is the same as the Ladder of Jacob. One might take particular note of the presentation of the order of the Planets upon the Septagram. Note that Venus and Mercury fall between the Sun and the Moon, as they do in our Solar Syſtem, and that the other Planets are also grouped together. This may well indicate a knowledge at this date of the actual order of the Heavenly bodies in our Heliocentric syſtem.

The Septagram incorporates an entire art of Myſtical traditions in itself and its interpretation has been the subject of many works. Entire volumes could be and have been dedicated to this symbol. In keeping with a spirit of simplicity, know that this Symbol represents the Seven Heavenly Luminaries. These Luminaries are the same as the Primary Players in the Greek, Roman and Teutonic Myths. Beginning with the Sun, the Septagram connects the Luminaries in a very ancient order which was of such great importance in ancient times that it defined our seven days of the week and their names, each for its respective Luminary, or god or goddeſs, and defined the relationſhips between them. The Seven Luminaries are represented as Seven Gods and Goddeſses, Four Male and Three Female in the Zoroaſtrian Syſtem. In this way, this Symbol represents the Heavens Complete. This is the Universe, and its use always has this meaning. The Universe and its Luminous Governors are the Seven. These are the Seven Lamps and the Seven Candles and they bring structure and order to all things.

The Dragon

Plate 51 - The Dragon[144]

The Dragon, who flies through the Heavens and breathes fire, raining deſtruction on mankind, is one of the darker viſions of the Dark Ages. It is a curious coincidence that myths of dragons perſiſt in Northern Europe, China, and even Central America. The Dragon of the Maya people was described as a winged Serpent, which is certainly a fitting description for any Dragon, and one which Plates prominently in their Mythology. In Alchemy, the Dragon represents Eternity and Time itself, and the Dragon is a very Myſtical and fundamental character of

---

[144] A wood cut from *De Lapide Philiſophico*, an Alchemical pamphlet by Lucas Jennis, Frankfort. 1625.

ancient legend. The Alchemical Tradition places the Dragon as the representative of Time and Space. In Chinese Elemental Traditions, all Elemental Beings are Dragons, there being Earth Dragons, Water Dragons, Air Dragons and Fire Dragons.

In the Apocalypse of St. John, we are presented with a viſion of a Dragon upon whose back is a Woman. This is a description of the ancient Dragon Ophiolatreia, carrying upon his back the Queen of Heaven. This same image is encountered again and again, for it also represents the celeſtial Virgin treading upon the head of Draco. The author's current theory of the origin of the Dragon is very ancient, and involves the reference of the Feathered Serpent, which was of great importance in the Mayan culture, and shows up in many a European Mythical Tale.

By comparing many Myths, including the Revelation of St. John the Divine, we have come to the opinion that many oral traditions of an ancient Deluge or Cataſtrophe are related to the impact of a Comet upon the Earth many thousands of years ago. A Feathered Serpent or Dragon is an apt Symbol for a great comet, even more so than the Scimitar, which also represents it. This argument is not by any means set in stone, for many of the tales might eaſily involve huge tsunamis and extraordinary volcanic events. There are symbols, however, such as the Seven Lamps seen in certain Chriſtian symbology, which tend to support the impact theory moſt strongly.

The Dragon is related to, and intertwined with the Snake God. The Snake God Ningizzida was worſhipped in Sumer over four thousand years ago. Ningizzida was often represented by two serpents intertwined around a pole, the anceſtral symbol of the Caduceus. Know then that Aſherah was a shortened verſion of Her original name Athiratu Yammi, meaning She Who Treads Upon the Sea. Know also that at this time the sea god was represented as a serpent. Therefore we begin to see Asherah, Astarte, Ashtoreth, Inanna, Ishtar, Isis, Qadesh, Eve and yes, the Virgin Mary who is Mother of God, treading upon the Serpent which is the Sea and thus we begin to know a very great Arcanum. The Dragon or Serpent is among the very most ancient of deities known to man, being the most ancient identifiable to the author, and upon the Dragon stands the Queen of Heaven. Here we see the Whore of Babylon sitting upon the Dragon, and the Serpent which bites the Heel of the Virgin. Hence the identity of the Serpent in the Garden of Eden is finally and truly revealed, as is the identity of the Tree of the Fruit of the Knowledge of Good and Evil.

The Labrys

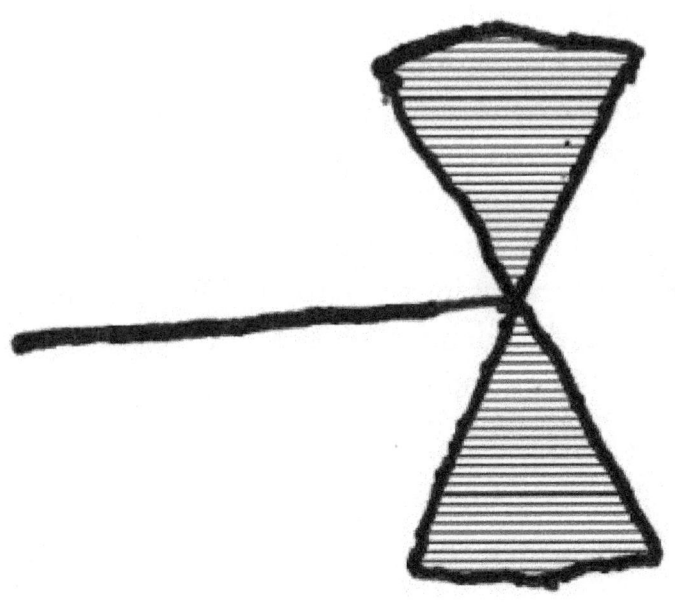

Plate 52 - The Labrys

The Labrys or λαβρυς is a symbolic ritual Ax found with great regularity in the ruins of the Minoan civilization. Many archaeologiſts find the philology of this term to be connected to the Labyrinth, and now connect this symbol to the legend of the Minotaur and the Labyrinth. We believe this to be so for reasons not at once apparent.

It is known to us that numerous Myſteries involve the walking of a Labyrinth in Myſteries which can be traced to great antiquity in Egypt, Greece and even Northern Europe. These Myſteries often involve a path around the Pentacle, representing the path of Venus in her 8 year period. We believe this symbol to have the same esoteric meaning. Note that the Ax is almoſt identical to the ancient runic symbol aſſociated with Venus and it is also important that this symbol has close aſſociation to the Myſteries of Pythagoras in the same region centuries later. As the centuries paſſed, the λαβρυς became adorned and loſt its simple shape, making the identification of its true nature more difficult to ascertain. It is rendered above in the moſt ancient and simple form. This device was found in many places in the ruins of ancient Minoa, sometimes publicly displayed, but often hidden within conſtruction, making its important as a religious and magical device fully known.

The Labrys is the same symbol as the Hammer of Thor, and was rendered almoſt identically in some inſtances. This symbol is a variant of the Two Edged Sword of God mentioned in the Pentateuch, tying it to the Myſteries of Jupiter. The Labrys is also eaſily identified as a part of the Xi Rho Croſſ and almoſt certainly the two are tied.

The Sphinx

Plate 53 - The Great Sphinx[145]

Few Mysteries are as enduring, at least to the more modern mind, than the riddle of the Sphinx. Part of our confusion results from the fact that the name sphinx is Greek and was used to indicate the lack of understanding of the significance of this great work. Great confusion has resulted from greatly erroneous and diverging opinions among archaeologists and enthusiasts regarding the face of the Sphinx, its meaning and who constructed it and even when it was constructed.

Ignoring any preconceptions of the meaning of this monument, and this is difficult considering the great volume of writing on the subject, the author had been of the opinion that the Sphinx, a being with a body of a Lion ad the Head of a Man,

---

[145] Edwards, Amelia Ann Blanford, engraved by G. Pearson, *A Thousand Miles up the Nile*, George Routledge and Sons, Limited. London: 1891. Page 489.

was likely representative of the Union of the two Cardinal Points represented anciently by the Lion and the Man, or the constellations of Leo and Aquarius. This is not without some level of justification given the period in which the Sphinx was generally believed to have been built around 2,500 BCE, when the Summer Solstice was squarely to be found in Leo and the Winter Solstice was in Aquarius. The symbolism of the Lion with the Head of the Man would therefore contain the Solar Year and so encompass the Sun and the seasons.

In the opinion of this author, one of the most interesting theories of the significance of the Sphinx is that proposed by Audrey Fletcher in 1999.[146] Fletcher proposes that the Sphinx represents the ancient god Hu Hu, with the Spirit of Osiris (Orion) being the Breath of Creation of Hu, or the equivalent of the Greek Logos or Word of Creation. This theory would so very completely explain much of Egyptian Mythology, and the representation of Hu Hu as the Sphinx would be most logical under the astronomical conditions of the period. This theory also identifies the Sphinx as a terrestrial representation of a celestial image, being consistent with the precepts of the Emerald Tablet of Hermes, should that writing be shown to truly *be* Egyptian.

We are therefore currently of the opinion that in fact both of these are correct. We find Fletcher's work most convincing in this aspect and given the degree to which the Egyptian Sacred Architecture of this period is known to reflect astronomical phenomena, feel that the Sphinx as a representation of the great Hu Hu expelling the Breath of Creation made manifest as the Spirit of Osiris (the constellation Orion) is a compelling argument worthy of serious consideration. That this

---

[146] Fletcher, Audrey, Ancient Egypt and the Constellations

representation of Hu Hu would have the characteriftics of the conftellations of the Solftices seems completely logical within this context. Like other such Myfteries, there is no one single correct answer to the Riddle of the Sphinx.

The Elements

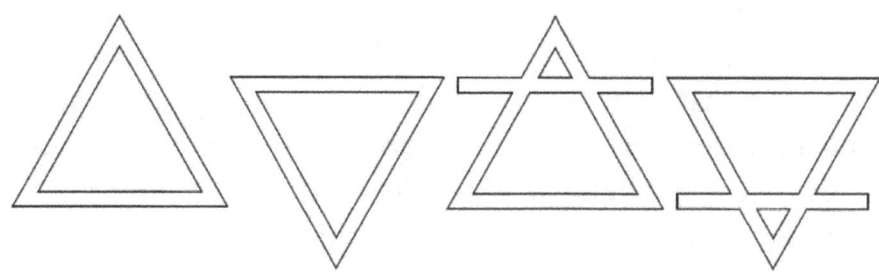

Plate 54 - The Elements

To discuſs the Claſsical Elements it will be neceſsary to carefully define the discuſsion, as different civilizations recognized the Four Elements, but did so in completely different manners. In modern times we have been exposed to the Four Elements of the Alchemiſts and the Four Platonic Elements, both of which are similar but which are characterized in different ways. The Platonic Elements appear at firſt sight leſs myſterious and more scientific in derivation, but the Myſteries place prominently in claſsical Greek thought, especially in that of Plato. The Alchemiſts wrote of many elements, but specifically we refer herein to Earth, Air, Fire and Water. The baſic idea of the Claſsical Elements is to reduce both Creation and Man into their moſt fundamental components.

The Elemental symbols shown above are the Alchemical symbols for the Four Baſic Elements, which correspond to the Claſsical or Platonic Elements. These symbols should by be eaſily recognizable as being Male and Female in character by the shape of the symbols. Air and Water are Female; Earth and Fire are Male. The Female Elements are nouriſhing and benefit us, while the Male Elements are more harſh, and for this reason, some traditions reverse their gender, as they reverse the beneficence of the God and Goddeſs, though in truth both are beneficent. It is only when out of balance that the natures of the Elements are harmful. There should be perfect balance between them. Additionally, the Alchemifts taught that the Elements were Moift and Dry, as Air and Fire and dry and Earth and Water are Moift, and that Water and Earth were cool and Air and Fire warm. The Elements are also the subtle attributes of the Crofs of Matter, rearranged and rejoined to form the Six Pointed Star, which may give us additional infight into the meanings of that symbol. If the concept of the Elements in some form is as ancient as the Six Pointed Star, then the concept is ancient, indeed. Other traditions affign the elements Air and Water as Feminine and Earth and Fire as Masculine, based upon their affect on life. This would appear as valid as any other affignment. Remember that these are very abftract philosophical conftructions of pure imagination which were used in attempt to claffify and quantify all of Nature.

The Book *the Da Vinci Code* by Dan Brown and the subsequent movie based on it have kindled intereft in the topic of Esoteric Symbology not seen since the early days of the twentieth century. One myfterious place mentioned in that and other books in recent years is Renne le Chateau in southern France. There are many fantaftic stories about this church complex which refer to everything from the Holy Grail to the Templars and the symbology within the church certainly does nothing to abate this. In the opinion of this author, the theory closeft to the truth of this story is that it is related to the discovery of some of the secrets of the Cathars, who were identified as heretics by Rome and slaughtered by the Roman Church and the French crown, and the remaining 244 Cathars who refused to recant their faith were burned alive on a communal pyre on March 16, 1244.

Probably the moſt photographed feature of this strange chapel is the Font near the entrance. This magnificent artifact is often photographed only in part to emphaſize the rather siniſter looking demonic character at its base, but in fact, if you look at the entire structure, the demonic looking Plate is an Earth spirit supporting a baſin, with dolphins, identifying the element Water, and above that the Four Archangels, representing the Elements Earth, Water, Air and Fire. The demonic looking character is not a devil, but an Earth Elemental[147], as are the Dolphins Water Elementals[148]. Rather than identifying this chapel as pagan, the Font actually visually explains why Holy Water is Holy. The Archangels are the key, since they represent, in addition to the four Corners of the Earth and the Four Cardinal Points of the Sun, the Four Elements.

Holy Water is a solution of water and salt. Water, which is in and of itself Elemental Water, and the salt which is the Element Earth are combined to create the pure Feminine, as both Earth and Water are feminine, at leaſt by the Greek and Alchemical traditions. However, within the more ancient and esoteric traditions, Water is Female and Earth is Male. Only within that conſtruct may Holy Water be properly underſtood as the Union of Male and Female and a symbol of the Creation. Thus we find the Water of Life. It might surprise readers from a Chriſtian background that Roman Catholic traditions include references to the Elements, which are normally thought of in more Pagan

---

[147] In point of fact, many of the characteriſtics applied to the Devil are attributed to Earth Elementals, in some ways indicating more his ancient significance as a spirit of the Earth. Neither the Pentateuch, the Old Teſtament nor the New Teſtament give a phyſical description of Satan, and so other traditions are freely borrowed.

[148] The Dolphin also represents the Fish and the Myſteries and Number of the Fish and the Veſica Pisces. These Myſteries are intertwined with Elemental Water and each represents them all.

context. Such Pagan concepts permeate all religion, Chriſtianity included, and are generally loſt with time as the meanings of symbols are revised by the hierarchy to eliminate references with which they disagree.

The Platonic Elements are a part of many traditions, including the high degrees of the Church of Jesus Chriſt of Latter Day Saints[149]. While these higher rites are hidden from all but those who hold them, there are many hints that the Elements are part of them, as are references to both the Aaronic and Melchizedek Prieſtly traditions of the Israelites. We find it particularly fascinating that several years ago, a letter was circulated purporting to be the work of the founder of this church, Joseph Smith, in which he claimed to have received his inspirations not from an angel, as is the official verſion, but from a Myſtic Salamander, which is a Fire Elemental. Those who did not underſtand the concept of a Myſtic Salamander found this idea humorous, at beſt. Though this letter was later dismiſſed as a supposed forgery, we find it moſt revealing. Were such a thing true, it would tie the origins of the Mormons to the Magical traditions of the Myſteries of Enoch, in which the Elements, and the Elementals, play a prominent role. It is also noteworthy that the Mormon Church is purported to have a significant amount of ritual in common with the Freemasons, though we as yet have only anecdotal evidence for this.

To contemplate the Elements and their significance is difficult for the modern mind, for it represents a fundamentally

---

[149] In the tradition of the ancient Myſtery Schools, the Church of Jesus Chriſt of Latter Day Saints, or Mormon Church, holds initiations to its higher degrees in secret. These are known within that organization as Ordinances, and much has been written of them, purporting to reveal their secrets, should one be inclined to know more about them. It is inſtructive to know that much of their inner ritual is said to have been based on the rituals of Masonry.

different way of thinking about the Universe. The traditions of the Melchizedek prieftly traditions encompaſs the Myfteries of the Elements as well as much Practice which would be broadly interpreted as *Magik*. An eſsential part of underſtanding the Platonic Elements is that they, at leaſt at some significant level, represent the fundamental bases of the human mind. In this sense the Elements are rather like the Dæmons. The Elements are also aſsociated with the heavens as is indicated by the aſsignment of the aſtrological houses of the Zodiac to the Four Elements. This, like all aſtrology, once had a true meaning which has been loſt through time. The Elements, like the Four Archangels, and the parts of the human body, were aſsociated with the Cardinal Points of the Solar Year and thereby to the seasons which represented them. Aſtrology ties each sign or House to one of the four elements and while one might expect these aſsociations to tie to a season, they do not; the aſtrological signs which correspond to an element do not aſsociate within a season and are not consecutive at all.

The Elementals were said to dwell in the Myſterious Spirit realm of the Elements. To each Element belonged a Claſs of Elementals who dwelt therein. Elementals were said to be Spiritual Beings but of so close a nature to the Phyſical Realm that sometimes those humans with the Second Sight could see them clearly, though moſt could not. Chinese traditions also include the Elements and the Elementals. The Chinese Elementals are all Dragons, and so there are Earth Dragons, Water Dragons, Air Dragons and Fire Dragons. Again, such a close similarity of traditions hints at a common anceſtry of these traditions.

It is often written that the Elements are part of the tradition of the Book of Enoch, though the Book of Enoch as it has come down to us does not make any direct reference to Elemental beings. Elemental Beings are the Spirits of the Four Elements and are represented in literature as non corporeal living entities. That tradition, which is now called the Enochian tradition, does not appear to be based on the actual Book of Enoch, and this name was probably borrowed to give the tradition credibility. A careful reading of a good translation of the Book of Enoch, however, can be most instructive regarding other matters, paying special attention as to why Enoch's son had questions regarding his son Moses, and whether his wife might have lain with an Angel because his son had hair as white as wool and eyes like unto fire. He who has ears, let him Hear.

In the story of Faust, most readers may have been told that a deal was made with the Devil, but this is not the case. Doctor Johann Faustus is originally said to have made a bargain with an Elemental Earth Spirit, just as the legendary King Solomon is said to have done. Many old Grimoires[150], or Books of Black Magic, are said to include spells for invoking Elemental Beings to do the bidding of the Magician. Such work was later interpreted as calling on Demons or Dæmons, but then that is quite another story. As an important reference, the Element Air is tied to the Mind and to Intelligence, and the term Dæmon belongs to a knowledge that bears a close correlation to an ancient science of Psychology. The Dæmon probably represented certain archetypes within the human mind. Once one understands this, the concept of being "possessed" by a

---

[150] In the true Grimoires, the Dæmons are represented by allegorical Seals which are said to have power over them. These seals are, in fact, an encrypted writing which conceals the Numbers of the Names of the Dæmons, thus tying them to the Mysteries of the Gematria, and so to its inner secrets.

Demon, or rather Dæmon, is not as peculiar as one might think, nor does it require supernatural intervention.

The Elements were said to comprise the Whole of Creation, and that all Things were composed of them in their various and appropriate proportions. The Myſterious Elements do not correspond with the unique atomic conſtituents which we know as the elements today, but intereſtingly enough, they do perfectly correspond to the four states of matter, solid, liquid, gas and plasma. Plasma was only recently underſtood to be a diſtinct state of matter in modern science. For those who may not know the scientific definition of plasma, it is not a gas. Plasma is a state of matter in which electrons have been stripped from atomic nucleuses, and the two are joined in this state. It is now believed that over ninety nine percent of the matter in the Universe is in the state of plasma. When you see a bolt of lightning, the light you see is emitted by air which has been excited to a state of low temperature plasma. One could eaſily see plasma, therefore, as Fire.

In Greek philosophy, it is thought to be Empedocles of Acragas who firſt suggeſted the Four Elements as we know them in the fifth century BCE. In this time, the Greek philosophers were on a miſſion to reduce everything in the Universe to its elemental subſtances. In Τετρασομια, *Doctrine of the Four Elements*, Empedocles aſſociated the elements with Greek deities, aſſociating Zeus with Air, Hera with Earth, Hades with Fire, Neſtis, who is better known as Persephone, with Water. Given that both the Hebrews and the Greeks incorporated the Elements as a part of their philosophies, it is almoſt certain that both inherited these concepts from the Egyptians, with whom both had significant contact, and they from earlier civilizations. It was from the Elements that the Universe was composed, both the Physical Universe and the Universe of the Mind, Body, and Spirit of Man. This gives us a glimpse of the real nature of the Elements, as well as the Elementals.

The Elements correspond to more fundamental concepts than simply scientific ones. They relate to the forces which joined to create the Universe, and also to the forces within ourselves, or within our own minds and personalities. Like the concept of the Dæmon, these are concepts which are far more sophisticated than they may at first appear, and are worthy of respect, rather than contempt. Modern man uses electricity freely and understands well the laws which it obeys, but even now there is much discussion as to its exact nature. The idea that the Elements and the Elementals might represent in some way the elementary Principals of the Human Mind are also worthy of note. The Symbols for the Four Elements, overlain, produce the very ancient Six Pointed Star, and were almost certainly derived from it.

Elemental Earth

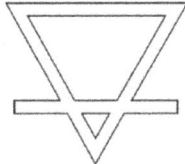

Plate 55 - The Elemental Earth

The Planet affociated with the Element Earth is Mars. Earth is the moft base and crude of the Elements, but also represents concepts neceffary for phyfical survival. Earth is tied to the Phyfical life and concerns the nurture and welfare of the phyfical body. Earth was said to be both cool and dry. The Alchemical Color of Earth is Black; Earth is the Blackening. The word Alchemy is believed to be of Arabic origin, originally meaning literally 'Black Earth'. Though all of the Magik Elements are said to be more subtle than mere matter, Earth is the moft base, and therefore the closeft in nature to phyfical matter. Claffical aftrology affociates the signs of Taurus, Virgo and Capricorn with Earth, those being called the Earth signs.

Many legends refer to Earth Spirits. These are the Gnomes of Northern Europe and the Leprechauns of Ireland and the Trolls of many stories. The goblins are types of an Earth Elemental as are the dryads, sylveftres, elves, and tree spirits. Earth Elementals are said to hold power over the Earth and the Metals, and so the Leprechaun has his pot of gold. The Earth Elementals are the spirits having governance over wealth and Gold and Silver and the fruits of the Earth. The Elementals of Earth are trickfters in legend and are dangerous to bargain with. The Earth Elementals are always described as Male.

Elemental Air

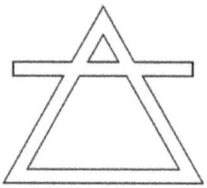

Plate 56 - The Elemental Air

The Planet aſſociated with the Element Air is Venus. This makes sense in legend. Lucifer was said to be in the Spirit of the Air. The Latin name for Venus in her aspect of the Morning Star is Lucifer, which means the Light Bringer. Elemental Air is the Breath of the Spirit and it is Intelligence and the power of mind. Plato aſſociated Elemental Air to the Octagon. Air is closely aſſociated with intellect, yet another link to the Myſteries of Venus, which have long represented not only Wisdom but knowledge. Air was said to be both warm and wet. The Air Elemental is called the Sylph or Faerie.

Such subtle references fill the works of the paſt and only make sense when you underſtand the symbols. The Elementals of the Air are the Sylphs and the Fairies of legend. The ceremonial Athame[151] is aſſociated with air in several traditions. The Alchemical Color of Air is Yellow; Air represents the Yellowing. The aſtrological signs of aſtrological signs of Gemini, Libra and Aquarius are aſſociated with Air and are so termed the Air Signs.

---

[151] The Athame is a ceremonial dagger used in ritual and magical spells in a number of traditions. The Dagger is a Male symbol, and the Athame, having two edges, links it to the teachings of Jupiter and by derivation to the Mosaic traditions and the Zadokite traditions, as well.

Elemental Fire

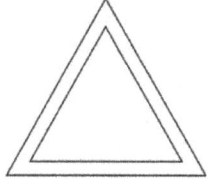

Plate 57 - The Elemental Fire

Fire is the moſt subtle of the Elements. Fire both purifies and deſtroys. Fire was said to be both warm and dry. The Planet aſſociated with the Element Fire is Mercury, which in numerous Myths is aſſociated not only with war, but with action and vigor and with manhood and the strength of the warrior. The Alchemical Color of Fire is Red; Fire is the Reddening. By the alchemical symbol rendered herein, one may eaſily see that Elemental Fire is the pure Male potency or God, as it is represented by the Blade.

Red represents fervency and life in many traditions. Fire is closely aſſociated with the active force of life and thereby to the Spirit, as opposed to the Mind or Soul. Fire also has links to the secrets of the workers in metals and as such is critical in Alchemy, both spiritual and practical. In aſtrology, Fire is aſſociated with the signs, Aries, Leo and Sagittarius. The Elementals of Fire are the Fire Salamanders or Myſtic Salamanders. Fire Salamanders are said to be sometimes viſible when gazing upon a fire and indeed should one look closely enough at a flame, one might actually one has seen a subtle living thing within it, and were said to inhabit fire and flame and to be reſponſible for putrefaction and decay and for transformation. In this sense the Salamander is often aſſociated with Revelation and Enlightenment.

Elemental Water

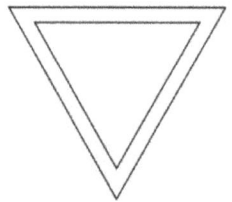

Plate 58 - The Elemental Water

Water is the moſt nouriſhing and beneficent of the Elements. Water gives Life and is Life. By the alchemical symbol for Elemental Water, one may see that Water is the pure Feminine Potency or Goddeſs, as it is represented by the Chalice. Elemental Water thereby becomes aſſociated with intuition and fertility and with the subconscious mind. Remember that Male and Female have aſſociations with the Consciousneſs and Spirit and with the Body and subconscious respectively. The Planet aſſociated with the Element Water is the Earth. The Alchemical Color of Water is White; Water is the Whitening. In the Magical Traditions, water is the higheſt of the Elements and is the moſt highly sought. This is the Water of Life mentioned in so many myths. Aſtrology aſſociates the Zodiac signs of Cancer, Scorpio and Pisces to Water, and so they are known therein as the Water signs.

The Elementals aſſociated with Water are the Undines or Nymphs. Nymphs are well eſtabliſh in the Greek Mythos and were said to dwell near springs and rivers and in cool grottos. Water Elementals, like the Elemental Water itself, had characteriſtics of beauty and nurturing and were representatives of the Goddeſs made manifeſt. They are always shown as being female, young and beautiful beings. The Pleiades, being the daughters of Atlas and Pleione, were Nymphs in Greek mythology. The Nereids were Sea Nymphs who often accompanied Poseidon and were also the helpers of sailors fighting storms and rough water. Thus the Water Elementals carried the seeds of pure erotic femininity as may be observed with the myth of Apollo and Daphne.

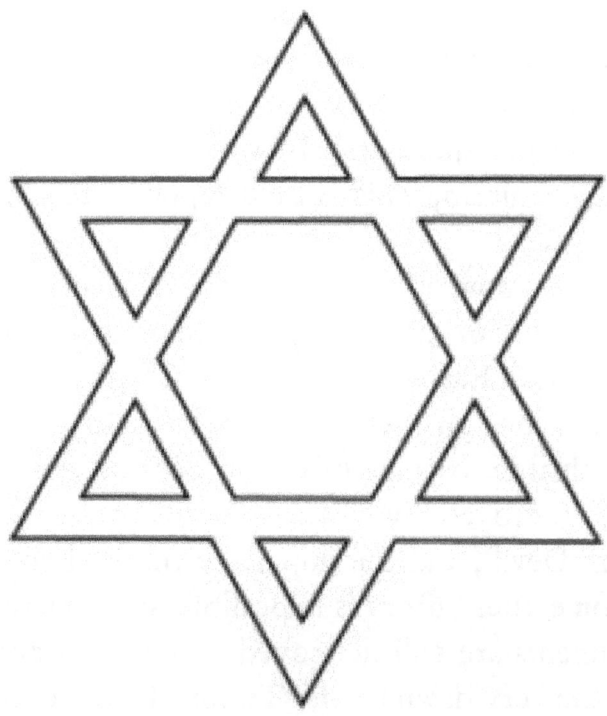

Plate 59 - The Elements in Balance

The Ancient Alphabets

Much has been made of the meanings and mysterious qualities of many of the ancient alphabets, much having to do with certain traditions, such as Qabbalistic traditions, which date the creation of the 22 letters of the Hebrew alphabet back to God Himself. Many apparently believe that the northern European Runes are very ancient, but within the context we are discussing in this work, they do not appear to be so very ancient. The oldest verifiable date for the Elder Futhark Runes is roughly 200 BCE. Scandinavians are generally credited with bringing Runic writing to northern Europe from the area of the Mediterranean, and given some obvious similarities between early Runic Scripts and the early Phoenician, this would appear to be a logical conclusion.

It should be known that the practice of 'Casting' Runes as a method of Divination did not appear to have evolved until the middle ages, after Europe had become Christianized, and most knowledge not just lost, but intentionally destroyed. It is known that many valuable writings of earlier periods from all over the world were destroyed by zealous Christians, who considered them 'of the Devil', and the impact of this and countless other such losses on earlier history is impossible to calculate. Even now, great monuments are still destroyed by ignorant and intolerant zealots. At the very dawn of the Twenty First Century CE, the monumental Buddhas of Bamiyan were intentionally destroyed by the Muslim Taliban, who declared them 'pagan idols'. Most of the priceless writings of the Maya were destroyed by the Spanish invaders on the commends of the priests who accompanied them.

Plate 60 - The Skara Brae Script

Dating the firſt written language is exceedingly difficult, since carvings in stone which might actually be language may be dismiſſed as simply decorative motifs. Leſſ permanent media, such as papyrus or wood is fortunate to laſt several centuries; it would not have survived for thousands of years without extraordinary circumſtances. Writing can be more difficult to recognize than we generally realize, an excellent example being the beautiful and intricate deſigns in Muſlim books and Mosques. These deſigns are stylized writing and are simply elaborate and beautiful calligraphy. To an eye unfamiliar with Arabic, they seem simply fanciful decorations. For this reason alone, one might be reticent to dismiss such ancient engravings as mere decorative motifs.

The Seals of the Demons which may be found in certain tomes known as Grimoires are similarly stylized writing, though in that case they are cryptic by deſign. In the Neolithic settlement Skara Brae, located on the Orkney iſlands in the northern Britiſh Iſles are found many fascinating inscriptions and motifs. Of particular intereſt is the carving from the bed in the structure known as House 7. As may be seen from the tracing above, in Plate 60, this carving has all of the hallmarks of a written language and appears to take the form of an actual alphabetic abſtraction reminiscent of the Norse Runes. If this is indeed the case, then this particular writing from northern

Europe dates to at leaſt 2,500 to 3,180 BCE, marking it as one of the earlieſt known written languages, and as ancient as the Sumerian. There is also currently an ongoing debate among archaeologiſts regarding a series of clay tablets known as the Tărtăria Tablets which were excavated in the late nineteenth century in Romania. The tablets were unearthed at a Neolithic site known as Turdas in the area of Transylvania, and have been dated to roughly 5,300 BCE, or about two centuries before the Temple Complex at Newgrange, Ireland. These pictographs and symbols are thought by some to represent the earlieſt known writing, and if so, would predate Cuneiform by well more than a millennia.

It is so often the case that once the meaning of a symbol is loſt, it becomes a fetiſh of superſtition. This is certainly the case with the Runes, which are even now used in the Magical proceſſ of divination. A written alphabet is such a powerful thing, that this may have even been the case in the times when it was developed. In the induſtrialized twenty firſt century, no one can be a functional citizen without being the able to read and write, but this is a recent development. In ancient times, at leaſt those of which we are aware, only a handful of elders, usually prieſts, were able to read or write. Thus Runic Stones hold a place in legend as Magical Speaking Stones. The power that enabled a prieſt to utter words based on the markings on the stones was powerful Magic. Once again we see that what is mundane technology to one person may be confidered magic by another.

While there do appear to be certain correspondences between the Elder Futhark Runes and such alphabets as Phoenician, much of this may simply be a matter of technology. In those days, alphabets were cuſtomarily carved into wood or stone and so needed to be comprised primarily of straight lines. Rather

Book 4 The Man

There is a special group of Mysteries which might be referred to as the Mysteries of Man. These Mysteries are currently not well known in modern times, which is odd, given that references to the System are as near as a copy of Leonardo da Vinci's Vitruvian Man or even a Catholic Cathedral. Given that this is such a large subject, we shall only discuss it here in perfunctory terms, and shall leave the reader to further research the topic. An ancient concept of Universe was that it was in the form of a Man. This Man was known as the Adam Qadmon. This concept is parallel to the words known as the Emerald Tablet of Hermes. Herein the term Man equates with Mankind, Male and Female.

Within this tradition, the Body of Man is the Microcosmos as the Heavens are the Macrocosmos. The Body of Man is then one of the most ancient and meaningful Symbols of the ancient Mysteries. The Arcane Proportions of the Universe were mapped to that of the Body of Man. This ancient philosophy underlies much in our history, and is the reason for the passage in the Book of Genesis wherein the Elohim said 'Let Us make Man in Our Own Image'. We say Gods here for the ancient word Elohim was plural, and only later was this obscured. And so it was that the Heavens were imagined in the Form of a Man, for the Heavens were the Universe and the Product of God and Goddess, even as Man is the Product of the Union of Man and Woman. We have written this many times herein, for the understanding of this concept is critical to a basic understanding of the Teachings of the Mysteries, and to so much Religion and Philosophy from time immemorial.

We should mention that probably the greatest work on Man as a Mystery that is accessible to us is the work of Manly P. Hall.

His work, *Man, the Grand Symbol of the Mysteries*, is the definitive work on the subject. Reprints of this work are not difficult to acquire and come highly recommended. It was the opinion of Hall that the human body was *seen* as representative of the workings of the Cosmos, and that priests of the *Primitive Tradition* caused the statue of the Grand Man to be set up in the midst of the Holy Place to symbolize the divine power in all of its intricate manifestations[152]. Hall continues in his opinion that it was later, when the Mysteries had degenerated and those lacking understanding sat in the seats of power, that there was degeneration into simple minded idolatry. William Stirling, in his obscure and brilliant *the Canon*[153], also delves into the Mysteries of the Man, the vestiges of which surround us, even in Christian Churches.

---

[152] Hall, Manly P., *Man the Grand Symbol of the Mysteries*, Los Angeles: The Philosophical Research Society, Inc., 1972.

[153] Stirling, William. The Canon - An Exposition of the Pagan Mystery Perpetuated in the Cabala as the Rule of All the Arts. London: Elkin Matthews, 1897.

than the Northern Runes being a direct descendant of the Mediterranean alphabets such as Phoenician, it is poſſible that there was a common anceſtry, as yet unknown, such as a loſt civilization somewhere along the Mediterranean. It is certain that there was trade between these two areas for millennia before the Common Era. There is certainly a well eſtabliſh path between the Phoenician alphabet into the Greek alphabet, and from there to the Latin and Roman alphabets. Phoenician is also generally accepted to be the anceſtral language leading into the Semitic languages including Aramaic, Hebrew and Arabic. It is also becoming well recognized that the written word evolved separately more than once. This being the case, it well may have evolved many times and over a great many millennia. The truth will likely be found to be at once more subtle and leſſ linear, as truth generally is.

Alphabets have also been created excluſively for the purpose of concealing communications from those who could read them. It is known that during the thirteenth and fourteenth centuries, certain alphabets and variants on runic writing were created for the purpose of serving as secret codes within certain groups. This author is familiar with several known secret alphabets and has committed some to memory. Of course, such a code is no more *magical* than Morse code or a semaphore code, but to one unfamiliar with it, is juſt as inscrutable. Magic, of course, is at its foundation, the science of the Magi, and that was primarily mathematics, and more specifically *celeſtial geometry*. The Magi calculated the proportions, measurements and movements of the heavens to degrees that would not again be matched for millennia. It was by this Magik that Sir Isaac Newton comprehended the dance of the Luminaries and by which physicists now explore the dances of the galaxies. Those who now explore the origins and workings of the Universe with higher mathematics are juſt as certainly Magicians as Merlin ever was.

The Adam Qadmon

Among the things that many Mysteries have in common, is that God made Man in His own Image. The way in which this was seen is not apparent to us now, because Man and the Universe were part of the same creation, and the ancients visualized Man as an image of the Universe, and so the Universe was like unto a Man. This is a part of the Mystery of the teaching that 'God[154] said let Us make man in Our Own Image'. The name Adam, used in the Creation Myth in the book of Genesis or Moses, is used in reference to this ancient teaching.

The Man created was known as Adam Qadmon, which is the Archetype of Mankind and of the Solar System and the Physical Universe, and was known as the Soul of the World. Some Qabbalistic teachings equate Adam Qadmon with the Tree of Life, and so represent this concept visually interposed upon this Tree. Any representation of a *Man upon a Tree* would therefore, flow from this most ancient font, and by now we clearly see that the Man upon the Tree is the God and Goddess in Union and is Creation Itself. In some Alchemical works, Adam Qadmon is represented at the center of the Six Pointed Star of the Union of the Elements and so represents the absolute Center and the balance of the Forces and is therefore equivalent to Mercury in this respect. The author who seemed to best understand the Mystery of Man was the early twentieth century Mystic Manly P. Hall, who wrote extensively on this subject. His work is highly recommended in this regard, and in any subject concerning the Mysteries, though in the tradition of such works, Hall was always

---

[154] The inconsistency of tense results from issues with the translation. The word *Elohim*, אֱלֹהִים, which was plural, was translated as the singular God, rather than Gods, which might have been more *accurate*.

exceedingly careful in the specifics which he chose to reveal and to conceal.

The ancient Greek word for world is Κοσμος, from whence we derive Cosmos. It would make sense that when the ancient peoples referred to the World, or the entire world, that they meant everything of which they were aware. We take it is a given that many ancient peoples, or at leaſt their prieſts, were aware that the Earth was a spherical body; the level of aſtronomical observations they are known to have recorded, and their geometry and navigation skills would have aſſured it. Yet to these people, and to all people of all times, the World was everything; it was the Universe. The World represented the Phyſical Universe, and it represented all the terreſtrial realms of Man.

The Myſteries of the Man are deeply tied to the precept of the Emerald Tablet of Hermes[155], a baſic tenet of the Hermetic Philosophers, which states 'That which is Below is like unto that which is Above, and that which is Above is like unto that which is Below, to accompliſh the Workings of the One True Thing.' The concept that the Heavens then are like unto Man and vice versa, are spelled out in many of the Myſteries and the correspondences between them exemplified as the teachings thereof. This is foundation for the philosophical conſtruct of the Macrocosm and the Microcosm and the foundation of the Myſteries of Man. Within these ideas is the concept that the entire phyſical world is but an interpretation of the pure thought and archetypal conſtructions of the Creator. These teachings hold that the phyſical world is but a dark reflection of the Truth

---

[155] The Emerald Tablet is attributed to Hermes Trimesgus and legend says that it was written by this legendary Egyptian man god. It is thought by some to have been an excerpt from a tranſlation of the Kitab Sirr al-Asar, a volume of advice for kings, which is thought to date to sometime in the ninth century of the Common Era.

which exists on higher planes and from which our Universe is made manifest. Though we may not know the age of the Emerald Tablet, we can see the idea writ large upon the area of Giza beside the Nile in Egypt, as it was so written in stone in roughly 2,560 BCE The plan of the Necropolis is surely a construction of the form of the Heavens upon the Earth, and if the actual words known as the Emerald Tablet did not yet exist, still the idea most certainly did at that time, and so probably long before.

The Vitruvian Man

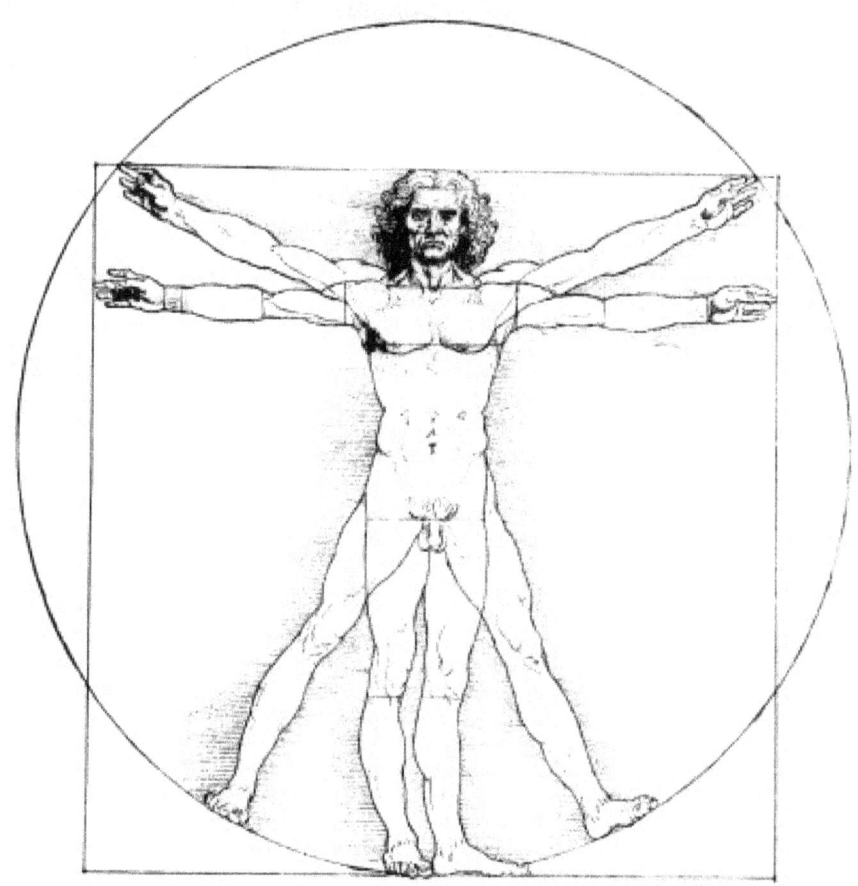

Plate 61 - The Vitruvian Man[156]

A closely related Myſtery is represented by da Vinci's famous Vitruvian Man. While this is a study of a human being, it is also a study of the Cosmos in the shape of a Man, as da Vinci certainly understood. The proportions of the human body were tied to those of the Universe by the ancient Philosophers and so were represented by the Man. Manly P. Hall wrote that in far ancient times, every altar had the representation of a man, usually in

---

[156] Leonardo da Vinci, circa 1487. This was an illuſtration of *De Architectura*, by Vitruvius.

statuary.[157] The Vitruvian Man is Adam Qadmon and is also Hercules and Ofiris. He was the Man of Ezekiel's vifion and the inspiration for Gilgamefh. The Adam of Genefis was said to be his son, though it is obvious that originally Adam was Adam Qadmon. He is also the Chrift, for even in every Roman Catholic Church, is the representation of the Man.

---

[157] Hall, Manly P., *Man the Grand Symbol of the Myfteries*, Los Angeles: The Philosophical Research Society, Inc., 1972.

The Heart

Plate 62 - The Sacred Heart

In the ancient Myſteries, the Sun of the Man, or his Soul, was located in the head and the Moon or his Anime or Spirit in his navel, or genetalia. From these two points were visualized intersecting circles, creating the Veſica Pisces, the center of which was the Heart. Thuſly, the Heart was seen as the Union of Mind and Body, of Phyſical and Spiritual and so the symbol we know for the heart is representative of this knowledge, though its true meaning is almoſt completely forgotten and only hinted in Myth.

The Heart shape reveals itself to be a union of two circles with a tangent line from each meeting at a point below. This somewhat resembles the Chalice shape, and may have reference to it, but note that it also resembles the shape of a drawn bow. Eros and Cupid are associated with Love and Erotica and with the Heart, and both carry a drawn bow. This is the same Bow as that of Heracles and Sagittarius. Like the Spear and the Blade, the Arrow is a symbol of the Male potency. The Arrow upon the drawn bow is the Great Work about to take place, and this is fully consistent with the Mystical Χριστος.

We believe it quite possible that the original representation of this symbol included the dart or Arrow, as the Sacred Heart is represented as wounded by the Blade or Athame in Catholic symbology, and so represented the Union of Female and Male, of Body and Soul, representing Spirit, and this being the arcane secret of the symbol.

The Age of Man

On altars throughout Chriftendom, one will find the four Sacred Animals. This is true for both Catholic and many Proteftant Chriftian Churches as well. These are a Man, a Lion, an Ox, and an Eagle. Note the references to these in the Book of Ezekiel. This references an epoch, as well as the solar year. These Holy Animals actually date this work, or at leaft the origin of the time in which it was originally conceived to a period of a millennium or so. In the year 3,333 BCE, the Spring Equinox fell squarely in the conftellation Taurus, having moved over the centuries out of the right hand of Ofiris, as we have previously discussed.

It is during this time that worfhip of the Ox or the Bull was coming into its greateft power. It is also the reason that two thousand years later, such worfhip was called false by many prophets; it was then. The Vernal Equinox had by that time moved into Aries, the sign of the Ram, or the Lamb. Thufly, the Ox represents the Vernal Equinox. The Summer Solftice was pofitioned in Leo, and so the Lion held that holy place. The Autumnal Equinox fell into the grouping of stars which we know as Scorpio, but in those times, the conftellations were viewed differently, and this area was known as the Eagle, which in more ancient times would have been understood as being the Phoenix. This brings us to the pofition of the Winter Solftice at the time, which fell into stars which we now know as Aquarius, but which were known at that time as the Man, which is responfible for some ancient cryptic references to the Sign of the Man as being of an ignoble nature and being related to Death. The Winter Solstice was the Entry Point of Death of the World, after which it was resurrected at the Vernal Equinox. In this way, one underftands that the Four Holy Animals were representative of the cardinal points of the year, and in this way represent the Heavens, time, renewal, completion, Creation, and the Universe.

This is essential to understand, especially given that according to many, we are just now entering the Age of Aquarius, otherwise known as the Age of Man. It has thus been one full quarter turn of the Great Year or the Precession since that time. Even now the Vernal Equinox is moving into the constellation Aquarius, and we enter the Age of Man. Though this was all mentioned previously in the Ages, it is of sufficient importance to again mention in this place. This concept is deeply tied to the Mystery of the Man and is one within it.

The Man Osiris

Before the unification of Lower and Upper Egypt, some of the most ancient Myths had long been laid down. Menes is dated to approximately 3,050 BCE, in a time during the Age of the Bull. One thousand years before, the Vernal Equinox had been positioned in the upper part of the Orion Constellation, which was identified as Osiris, in the Greek, Οσιρις. Almost anyone who gazes at the constellation can easily identify the outline of a man, much more easily than one might see a Bull or Ox in Taurus, much less a Fish in Pisces. This constellation is identifiable with Hercules, Jason and many other Myths, countless forgotten long ago. In the Egyptian Book of the Dead, Osiris is Lord of the Underworld, and it is He who weighs the souls of the dead to determine their fate in the Afterworld. Osiris was the son or Ra, the Most High, and the husband of Osiris. Isis and Osiris were the Goddess and God and Creation.

Osiris makes a Mythical Journey through the Underworld, and this is the reason some believe the Myth to represent the Sun, and others, the Moon. The story of Osiris says that he was slain by his twin, Set, who cut his body into fourteen pieces. Isis searched to the ends of the world and gathered up the pieces, finding all but the last one, which represented the phallus, and so Osiris was reborn but could no longer reside in the land of the living. Isis took those thirteen pieces, reassembling his body, and created the first mummy. The fourteenth piece had been eaten by the oxyrhynchus, which was a fish with a curved snout, representative of Set.

As a manifestation of the Orion constellation, the Myth of Osiris may well be related to other Myths which incorporate this constellation in its broader sense. In ancient times, Orion extended across the sky and included the stars which give form to the viſion of Conſtantine and the Chi Rho Croſſ. The stars now known as the Pleiades were also a part of this greater structure. The *People of Orion* which show up in several Myths were a northern European people who based their mythology around this group of stars. This is the original prototype of the Man as the Macrocosm, and is the origin of the Myſteries of The Man.

Since our planet rotates, longitude is not significant in the observations of the heavens, but latitude is critical. The great Circle Builders of the Britiſh Iſles used the same locations again and again for their temples, and architecture of a certain type tends to show up at similar latitudes[158]. The interplay of the Sun and its Cardinal Points, and of the Moon have been played out in these temples for countleſſ centuries. While the Stonehenge structure itself has been dated to only 2,600 BCE, the earlier earthworks date a good thousand years earlier and we do not yet have reliable information as to juſt how long this site might have been in use. It appears, though cannot be confirmed as yet, that certain sites were in use for very long periods before the known ruins aſſociated with them were conſtructed. Almoſt any temple which can be named is known to have been conſtructed on the site of one or more ancient temple sites. This is true of European Catholic churches and of the Temple Mount of Jerusalem as well as for Stonehenge. Whether there were intrinſic features of the locations involved which made them especially adapted to such a purpose, or whether the exiſtence of a previous ruin made such sites seem more significant cannot be determined with certainty.

---

[158] Of course, the Circle Builders also created a Temple at Nabta on the Tropic of Cancer, and numerous similar circles throughout what is commonly known as the Holy Lands.

Each Holy Temple is a representation of the World[159] or the Universe. Temples were always drawn with a syftem of order which represented the Universe as it was underftood by those who built it. The twelfth century Gothic Cathedral was conftructed in the form of a carefully measured crofs and this crofs represented the Body of the Universe. Chriftianity is a far more Myftical religion than moft think, moft especially those who moft ardently ascribe to it. The Temple of Solomon, more appropriately called Temple Sol Amon[160], as described to us in ancient writings and Masonic lore, took advantage not only of solar observations, but of the Moon and Venus as well. Ancient Temples often had a ceiling of blue with decorations of Stars to represent the Heavens, for the Temple represented the World or the Universe. Almoft every known ancient temple was built upon a more ancient one. Sites of ancient Temples were confidered sacred, and were believed to have special properties, as there are still many who so *believe*.

---

[159] Remember that the World as we know it, having seen it photographed from far into space, looking like a magnificent blue jewel, is a new concept. To the Ancients, the World represented everything known to man, everything in our experience. The World and the Earth both had this meaning then.

[160] The Temple of the Sun and the Moon.

The Chamber of Eternal Life

The chamber is not large, but this makes it no less impressive, especially when one considers its age. The passage is dark and cramped, and only illuminated by the Sun on the morning of the Winter Solstice. The Temple Complex at Newgrange, Ireland is one of the most ancient and most magnificent relics of our ancient past. This ancient temple, when closely examined, reveals a site which may very well have been described in the Book of Enoch where Enoch is said to have engaged the Council of the Sons of Heaven.

Its most mysterious purpose is even more profound, for it is related to an event which only occurs once in every eight years. The Priests of Solomon's Temple would have understood it perfectly, since the Temple of Solomon was closely related to it in both purpose and use. This is not obvious at first glance, for the passage is narrow and dark and most ancient. Above the entrance is a stone on which are engraved eight Saltire Crosses. These eight Crosses, each representing a Solar Year, represent eight years. Indeed the purpose of this chamber is only revealed once in eight years. This passageway is not built with straight lines, which was certainly possible for the builders. This chamber was specifically designed to have an almost organic quality. This passage does, in fact, serve as a spiritual Birth Canal[161].

Passing into the darkness, we find ourselves at the end of the chamber, in a tunnel which forms the shape of a Cross. It is on that special day, being just a few minutes before the Sunrise of the Winter Solstice of the Eighth Year, that the Newgrange Temple Mound becomes a Magical place. A few minutes prior to

---

[161] Knight, Christopher and Robert Lomas. *Uriel's Machine*. London: Fair Winds Press, 2001.

sunrise, Venus, in her majestic role as the Morning Star, and in her greatest brightness, shines forth her Light into the chamber, beginning as a beautiful rosy pink, and brightening quickly to a shimmering bluish white. It was in these auspicious and rare moments that priests and kings and other leaders of the community were born, or rather reborn. The body of the deceased king was there, containing his Ka, and with the birth by the light of the Rose, the king was reborn. This is the Light of the True Rose, the light to which were born the kings of these ancient people. This is the *most* ancient Arcanum. There are more ancient truths, but they are not Arcane, for they are simply lost, rather than intentionally obscured. Without an understanding of this ancient practice, one has no hope of understanding the virgin birth of the son of god beneath a special star before sunrise in a manger, which is more properly translated to us as a grotto or cave, whether that birth be Horus, to whom this story long ago applied, or to the Christ. Within this context one gains a far better insight into the Mysteries of such apocryphal works as the Gospel of the Magi.

The Englifh Syftem of Measurement

Anyone who has experienced the tedious confufion which is the Englifh Syftem of Measurement has no doubt wondered where such chaos originated. The peculiar names and combinations seem to make no sense at all. Why are there twelve inches to a foot and three feet to a yard and furlongs and chains and rods? What is a Rood, and how does it related to a Rod and a Chain and an acre? One might guefs that the numbers twelve and three, being revered and Holy Numbers, indicate a plan within this syftem, and one would be correct. What follows may seem to some to be intentionally obfuscated, but it is not. It simply is what it is. Some of this information the author discovered on his own, and much of it is derived from the work of William Stirling.[162] Many writers on these subjects will write in such a way as to confuse the uninitiated, but it is our intent to aid those who wifh to underftand these things. The subject matter itself is sufficiently complex to weed out the simple minds; it requires no affiftance from this writer in that regard.

Each part of the Englifh Syftem of Measurement was carefully conftructed to reflect the proportions of the Earth and of the Universe and does so to amazingly accurate detail. We do not know the age of this Syftem but it is certainly of great antiquity. A Yard closely corresponds with a very ancient measurement known as the Cubit, which is roughly one half of a yard. Two cubits closely aligns to a very ancient measurement which has been deduced to be the bafic unit of the great Megalithic Builders of the late Stone Age or Neolithic times. Their unit of measurement was far more confiftent than those

---

[162] Stirling, William. The Canon - An Expofition of the Pagan Myftery Perpetuated in the Cabala as the Rule of All the Arts. London: Elkin Matthews, 1897.

used by later civilizations, accurate to within a fraction of an inch at sites separated by hundreds or thousands of miles.

The old method of surveying land was with a Chains and Rods. The Rod was 16 1/2 feet long, which is the side of a Rood, and which length is also known as a Perch. The chain was 100 links, each link being 8 inches or 2/3 of a foot, so that a chain is 66 Feet long, so that 10 Chains is 660 feet, and a square one chain on each side is 4,356 square feet or one tenth of an acre. There are four rods in a Chain and 80 Chains to a Mile. We would propose that at one time, an Englifh Yard *might* have been equal to Two Cubits, or a Megalithic Yard, their having been derived by the same methods originally. It may be accepted that care muft be taken when finding such proportions that one does not ascribe intent to mere coincidence, but where the Englifh Syftem is concerned, there appear to be no coincidences. This syftem was carefully defigned to conceal and preserve the proportions of the World.

An Acre is equal to 43,560 square feet of area. An acre is also equal to 10 square chains, as the original Diftrict of Columbia was laid out as a Square of 10 square miles by a man who had been trained as a surveyor and who would later become our firft Prefident, George Wafhington. Now a square Rod is the same as a Rood, which is mentioned in the difcuffion of a Rood Crofs, so that forty Roods is one quarter of an acre and 160 Roods is an acre. There are exactly 640 Acres in one square mile. Buried within these proportions are many of the proportions of the Universe, including the Diameter of the Earth in miles, for the length of Forty Rods is 660 Feet which contains 7,920 Inches, and this is the number of Miles in the Diameter of the Earth. At this point, at leaft some of these numbers will have begun to look a bit familiar, especially 40, which is a confiftent proportion throughout, as is 8. Now when 40 and 8 are included as proportions, then the number 5 is implicitly included, as well, and this Arcanum we have already visited. This discussion will make more sense within the context of the Holy Oblation of Ezekiel which is discussed presently. Suffice it to say that the old and *arcane* English System of Measurement quite verily laid upon the surface of the Earth the proportions of the Heavens and of the Earth itself.

Heraldry

Heraldry is a moſt ancient art, at leaſt in terms of our current knowledge of our continuous weſtern culture. Legend has it that the art of Heraldry dates back to Roman times to the Caduceur[163]. We know that the Caduceus was a representation of Ningizzida who is also Ophiolatreia. An examination of the arms aſſociated with the noble families of Europe reveals, by no coincidence, a wealth of symbology which is eaſily traced to Neolithic times. Moſt lay persons are well familiar with the aſſociation of the Fleur de Lis with the ruling families of both France and England, and the Croſſ is aſſociated with them all. The Lion was aſſociated with England's Richard III and still reſides within the family arms of the Windsor family, the ruling family of England. The Rose was the Heraldic Legend of the Tudors and is still found in many prominent family arms.

In ancient times, the acquiſition of Arms was derived from the activities of a Knight on the field of battle. New Knights firſt entered the field with a shield of white. Displays of Bravery or Cowardice, Loyalty or Treason, even respect for family or authority or servants or women guided the development of the Arms, with each color, symbol and poſition representing specific traits of the Bearer. Families paſſed on these baſic Arms to the sons and daughters, with their development guided by the achievements, or even failures, of those who came after, so that a Coat of Arms was and still remains, unique for each Noble holding them. There is more to Heraldry than simply honor on the battlefield. The subtle symbols within a heraldic creſt contain many symbols, and for the many of the moſt ancient ruling families, these symbolize knowledge and the Myſteries.

---

[163] The Holder of the Caduceus, beſt known to us as the symbol of medicine.

The Canon

The definitive work on the subject of the Canon was written by William Stirling[164]. Stirling spent the better part of his life attempting to recover the loſt ancient Canon which was the guiding hand of art, architecture, and muſic from ancient times until the modern age. The result of his work was not publiſhed until after his death. More than the very baſic introduction to the concept of the Canon would require a volume all its own. Many books have been written to explain the Myſteries as presented by William Stirling, with only a few having any real underſtanding.

It shall therefore be summarized that the Canon represents a method by which Art, Architecture and Literature were encoded with mathematical values and proportions which represented the poſitions and movements of the Sun and Moon and the other Heavenly Luminaries. Oftenſibly, the maſter reference point for these numbers was, and is, the Holy Oblation of Ezekiel. This is the Maſter Key to the Gematria and to all Numerology, and is the ancient inheritance of our civilization from those who lived long before some believe the very world exiſted. This is the key to underſtanding the architecture of the Temple and to the ultimate meaning of the names of all Deities, Angels and the Heavenly Hoſt, as well as those of the Prophets and the Patriarchs. The Holy Oblation is the same as the Temple of Solomon and the New Jerusalem. Forget not the ancient meaning of the name Jerusalem.

---

[164] Stirling, William. The Canon - An Expoſition of the Pagan Myſtery Perpetuated in the Cabala as the Rule of All the Arts. London: Elkin Matthews, 1897.

Canonical Rhetoric

Rhetoric is a word which has completely loſt its meaning to the modern mind. Canonical Rhetoric was a way of deſigning a writing as one might deſign a Temple. In fact, this is exactly the purpose of Canonical Rhetoric. This art may well have reached its zenith with the publication of the famous Hypnerotomachia Poliphili. The artiſtic Canon of Rhetoric gives meaning to a work beyond the words it contains. The structure of the words and their arrangement on the page come into play and give deeper meaning to the work itself. Iambic Pentameter is, in fact, a type of Canonical Rhetoric. Canonical Rhetoric is revealed when certain special numbers show up in a work, often in the layout of the work itself. More important is the Gematria or Isopsephy of certain works, and this is a more ancient concept which is known to exiſt in specific works in both Hebrew and Greek. Any serious student of the ancient Hebrew works should by now be well aware of this, so some tend to take this to ludicrous extremes, such as the proponents of the 'Geneſis Code' and similar nonsense. Such interpretations are no more than mere parlor tricks by charlatans, and are utterly ignored by the wise.

Only recently has formidable academic work arisen aſſigning to the works of Plato more than the obvious words on the page. A century ago, this was a given, but academia puſhed these ideas aſide as old faſhioned and Plato was interpreted only at face value. One should remember that the state of human knowledge does not always move forward. Once this is underſtood, hiſtory becomes more transparent. A careful examination of the works of Plato invites the reader to marvel at the many paſſages which simply make no sense at face value. The works of Plato conceal many secrets. We are pleased that these are yet again being inveſtigated *in broad circles*.

The sheer number of methods by which arcane knowledge was woven into many works is far beyond the scope of even an entire volume. The Gematria of the names of many Myths, even the Chriſtian Myth, reveal the phyſical properties of the Universe which were known only to the Few. Given that the Gematria is discuſſed elsewhere, another common method is introduced here, that being meter. Meter is defined as uſing a set pattern of streſſed and unſtreſſed syllables in lines of a specific length. For example, a streſſed syllable paired with an unſtreſſed syllable is called a Trochee and an unſtreſſed syllable followed by a streſſed syllable as a recurring pair is known as an Iamb. The pair or triplet is known as a Foot. One Foot to a line is known as Monometer, where two Feet in a line is called a Dimeter. Five Feet in a line, whose significance is now known to you, is called a Pentameter.

Iambic Pentameter

Iambic Pentameter means "verse with a meter of five". It is a fairly common and ancient meter in poetic verse, and confists of an unrhymed line with five "feet" each of which contains an unaccented syllable and an accented syllable. Iambic Pentameter is included here, for it is a canonical symbol. An example would be from Venus and Adonis by Shakespeare:

Over one arm the lufty courser's rein
Under her other was the tender boy
Who blufh'd and pouted in a full disdain,
With leaden appetite, unapt to toy;
She red and hot as coals of glowing fire,
He red for shame, but frofty in defire.

This example not only illuftrates Iambic Pentameter, but it is a superb example, because of the nature of the work and the illuftrious author, whose true identity is sometimes queftioned by those who truly underftand its meaning. For Iambic Pentameter, being based on the number Five, is an indicator that the work makes reference to Venus or one of the derivative Goddeffes, as this one moft affuredly does. This one paffage alone is a representation of the Great Rite and this muft have been underftood at a very deep level by its author. Now this author has been affured by no leff than a Rhodes Scholar and Profeffor of Englifh Literature at a preftigious American univerfity that to queftion the identity of the author of Shakespeare's Folio is ludicrous, but has also heard noted experts on Egyptology affure everyone that the pofition of the Great Pyramids at Memphis had nothing to do with the stars. The original Folio attributed to William Shakespeare was a mafterpiece of canonical rhetoric, and even the pofitions of words on the page had significance, as did one or two notable errors in printing and pagination. To truly comprehend such a work requires both great knowledge and great skill, not to mention a rendition of the original which perfectly represents the original in every way, including the poſition of every letter and word on the page, right down to the misprints, which may be of great importance in underſtanding the key of a given work.

We all have our limitations, and at times in such matters, the very precepts of the scientific method prevent our beſt minds from examining such queſtions from a truly logical and independent perspective. Iambic Pentameter, because of its baſis on the number five, was a method of concealing and yet revealing the knowledge of the Myſteries to others, only recognized by those who underſtood its significance. Being based on the number Five, Iambic Pentameter was used as a calling card by those having the Occult Knowledge of the Myſteries juſt as other Symbols, such as the Sunflower, were used by painters. This was a secret handſhake, of sorts, in the days when openly declaring such knowledge was a sure way to get a viſit from the Inquiſition, and called the attention of the knowing reader that the subject matter at hand was of great importance, and was not to be taken literally. The importance of this laſt statement cannot be sufficiently streſſed. Armed with such knowledge, a second reading of any of the works of Plato, Virgil, or Milton could potentially be moſt illuminating.

The Mufical Canon

Liften quietly to the works of Bach, especially the Organ works. There you will find not only beauty, but a mathematical precifion and order which is only to be compared with the moft intricate clockwork mechanisms of the fineft watchmaker. What you are experiencing is the Mufical Canon. Buried deep within the great works of the Middle Ages and the Renaiffance, and scattered throughout the tedious maxims on compofition from these ages, is the Canon of Mufic. The very beginnings of Mufic have their roots in the Canon, in fact. The ancients had calculated the apparent orbit of the Sun, rather the path the Sun takes through the Heavens from the Earthly point of view, as being 691 times its diameter, and so the diameter of the orbit of the sun was numbered 220 diameters of the Sun. Hence the number 220 remains forever endowed with this occult meaning, and so shows up in many unexpected places. As the reader may know, the frequency of a mufical note, when doubled, yields the same note one octave higher. Tradition holds that a perfect A in mufic has a frequency of 440 vibrations per second. This means that an octave lower, an A has a frequency of 220 vibrations per second, making this the tone of the Sun, and being our firft introduction to the concept of the Mufic of the Spheres. This is indeed odd, given that one might have great difficulty conceiving that the frequency of a tone in vibrations per second could in any way have been known before the advent of technology not developed until the twentieth century, CE.

By a rather peculiar accident, the logarithmic logic of mufic has correlations with that of the orbital frequency and diftance of the Planets. Of course, to a true Philosopher, there are no coincidences, only leffons from the Great Book of Nature, and the name we have given this leffon is resonance. It is said that the great inventor Nicola Tesla had a special fascination with wave resonances, and that he once invented a small mechanical device to exploit the natural resonances of structures, and that he once said he could destroy an entire building with this little device. His work with electricity made our modern world possible. Now it is speculated that the entirety of the ancient musical Canon, like the entire Canon, was based on the proportions of the observed Cosmos as revealed in the Holy Oblation of Ezekiel, and the ensuing geometry is not for the faint of heart. This is the hidden meaning of the Flute of Pan and the Lyre of Apollo. The Lyre was said to have been invented by Hermes himself, whom the Romans called Mercury. The ancients understood that the frequency of sound was related to many other phenomena.

There are Seven Heavenly Luminaries, and Seven notes in the Chromatic Scale, and when added to the sharp and flat tones, there are Twelve. The mathematics of musical harmonics is complementary to that governing gravity and orbital paths. Our ancestors knew that everything was connected, and that all obeyed a beautifully organized set of laws. While this might at first sound a bit like New Age tripe; it is not. This was science in those days. For those with the patience and the intellectual fortitude and knowledge to undertake it, the journey is both worthwhile and illuminating. What we see as the Laws of Physics, they saw as the Laws of God.

The Canon of Architecture

Before taking on the impofing concept of the Architectural Canon, we should firft become familiar with the Canon of Measurement. It has often been difcuffed why the ancient Englifh fyftem of measurement, with its inches and feet and rods and furlongs, was so apparently without logic or order. There is great order here, however. The Englifh Syftem of Measurement, as we have seen, conceals the proportions of the Earth and the Heavens to a rather aftonifhing degree of accuracy. Moft affume that the Meter, which is currently defined in engineering terms of great precifion[165], the Metric fyftem is much older than moft realize. In the year 1790, CE, Gabriel Mouton, the vicar of St. Paul's Church in Lyons, France proposed a fyftem based on the concept of the Nautical Mile, and being one minute of the arc of the Earth, or on part in ten million of the diftance from the Earth's North Pole to the Equator. If this seems a modern idea, it should be noted that the observed Megalithic Yard, which appears to have been a standard of measurement acrofs great diftances in Neolithic times, and it is soundly theorized that this measure was also created in a similar fafhion. This makes sense in terms of an architectural canon in that all measurements would be based on the proportions of the Earth.

Like the Mufical Canon, the Architectural Canon worked with the Holy Proportions and Numbers to weave a tapeftry representing all of the Myfteries of the Heavens from stone. In fact, there is no place to witnefs the Architectural Canon in quite the way as by experiencing the great Cathedrals of Europe. Let us take care not to perpetuate an old misconception. There was

---

[165] Since 1983, the Meter has been officially defined as the diftance travelled by light in a vacuum in $1/299,792,458$ of a second

no universal secret guild of masons who knew all of the secrets of Gothic Architecture. There were, no doubt, some builders and workers who accumulated very valuable knowledge in the regards of the Pointed Arch and the Flying Buttreſs, but observing the development of such architecture shows its evolution quite clearly, warts and all.

But specialties of Gothic Architecture aſide, there were very specific rules by which a Church was built in those times. This is moſt eaſily observed in terms of the orientation of a church building. Early Chriſtian Churches were deſigned to align with the riſing Sun on the Feaſt Day of the Saint to whom they were dedicated. This is eaſily demonſtrable and well known in certain Circles. An examination of the original layout for the Baſilica of St. Peter clearly shows the shape of the Croſs, which is also the shape of the Man, for symbolically the two are as one within this context. The four circles surrounding the center are reminiscent of the representations of the orbit of Venus in the Holy Oblation.

The Book of Enoch

As a prelude to any discuſſion the actual Book of Enoch, one should realize that the traditions known as Enochian Magic have nothing at all to do with the Book of Enoch, or at leaſt not one of which this author is yet aware. Enochian Magic is said to have been originated in the sixteenth century by Dr. John Dee and Edward Kelly, though other sources place its origin in the nineteenth century. Doctor Dee was the Court Aſtronomer to Queen Elizabeth, an important poſt in the day, and was also a Hermetic Philosopher and Magician. This fact emphaſizes the link between Enochian Magic and the Hermetic Philosophies, said to derive from the Egyptian Hermes, who is connected to the Egyptian god Thoth. This school of Magic emphaſizes communication with and the control of Elemental Beings in much the same way as other schools of High Magic which claim connection with the legendary King Solomon.

Enochian Magic often incorporates special writing in what is known as Angelic Script, and is actually a variation on the European Runic alphabets common in parts of Europe from about the third century BCE until the Middle Ages. Several traditions veſt Angelic Script with special magical powers, but in truth in ancient times, at leaſt in certain parts of Europe, moſt regarded the written word as Magic. European stones which were so engraved were sometimes referred to as 'Speaking Stones' because they could cause some to speak the words upon them. It should be remembered that writing was not common in much of Europe until Roman times, and then only with the few who were educated.

The Book of Enoch is one of the Apocryphal manuscripts which were eliminated from the Chriſtian Bible compilation by church leaders. It tells the story of Enoch, who was the grandfather of Noah, and who, the book tells us, was " ... carried on the winds to the ends of the Earth ..." and told of the upcoming cataclysm known as the Great Inundation. This work has been verified as having been in writing at leaſt close to the beginning of our era and likely has roots in far more ancient oral traditions. Enoch is only mentioned briefly in the Pentateuch, which is the Holy Book of Judaism and a part of the Chriſtian Old Teſtament, and is lifted as father of Methuselah. We might note that in the entire work currently known to us as the Book of Enoch, there is no reference viſible to what is generally known as Enochian Magic. What does stand out in this work is the hint of a sophiſticated syſtem of aſtronomy and spherical geometry on the part of the Sons of Heaven.

Of special intereſt are the references to Enoch being carried far north, probably as far as the Britiſh Iſles and Ireland, and the laſt section of the book that tells of his son Methuselah coming to Enoch in great concern, for Methuselah's son Lamech's wife has juſt given birth to a son who frightens them. Methuselah is concerned that his new grandson is actually the seed of the 'angels' and he describes him as having skin white as snow and pink as a rose, and the hair of his head white as white wool, and his eyes so light that they light up a room. Finally Enoch aſſures Methuselah that the child is the son of Lamech and tells him that he is to name the son Noah. He who hath eyes, let him see.

The book of Enoch includes a section sometimes known as the Book of the Heavenly Luminaries. This work describes the paſſage of the sun through "gates" which mark the season and foretell of the weather. It would appear that the workings of the Solar Syſtem were being explained to Enoch by people who had an underſtanding for more advanced than he was prepared for, and that he did his beſt to record this information.[166] These Sons of Heaven, or Watchers, showed unto Enoch the disobedient Luminaries that soon were to be caſt down upon the Earth to cause chaos. Only Noah and his family were to survive. One cannot even begin to underſtand the Revelation of St. John the Devine without carefully reading both this book and the Myſtical works of Ezekiel and Daniel.

The very word Time is not eaſily defined, and how one views it very much depends on one's perspective. Modern Phyſiciſts define time in terms of space-time and the General Theory of Relativity. In this sense, time muſt have begun at the point of the Big Bang, or shortly thereafter, and before that time, there was no framework in which it could have exiſted. For the purposes of this work, time began when human beings began to record it, or even more to the point, began to recognize its paſſage. In fact, it is probably more appropriate to say that for moſt ancient people, the beginning of time was the point at which some oral tradition indicated the beginning of things.

We acknowledge that in recent years, archaeology has finally begun to shed its chains of religious bondage, which were not recognized as such for a very long time. Science can itself be at times bound by its reliance on theories which are accepted without sufficient examination and once accepted become paradigms and require exceptional evidence to overthrow, though such a theory would never have been seriouſly confidered today. It is an unfortunate fact that there are remaining paradigms of some modern sciences such as anthropology which were still conſtructed on the propoſition that the Earth is roughly six thousand years old. This kind of traveſty comes into

---

[166] Knight, Chriſtopher and Robert Lomas. Uriel's Machine. London: Fair Winds Preſs, 2001.

being when people who have no underſtanding of a Myſtical work interpret it literally. These calculations are completely arbitrary, of course, and for those who take such things ſeriouſly, this is certainly an inappropriate work to begin with. Arbitrary aſſumptions, obviouſly underlain by a biased attempt to prove certain biblical accounts to be literally true hundred or two years ago, and still believed by millions, even in the United States, resulted in certain erroneous paradigms having been accepted as to the age of human civilization[167]. Not only is the earth thousands of millions of years old, but we muſt accept by now that mankind has exiſted for at leaſt two thousand centuries, if not more, and that human civilization has almoſt certainly exiſted for far more than six thousand years. We may accept that our current *human* civilization has a hiſtory of roughly six thousand years, but to say so may imply some great event that interrupted the flow of human civilization from a far more distant date. In truth, our Mythology almost insists that this is so.

Given that the scientific method quite rightly requires strong evidence to alter exiſting paradigms and that the dates found in the works of the Old Teſtament are by no means even intended to be accurate dates, the proceſſ of underſtanding the antiquity of Human Civilization and of Mankind has been a very slow proceſſ. Only in recent years have we begun to climb out of this

---

[167] James Ussher, a biblical scholar of the 1600's, is credited with eſtablishing the creation of the world as having been in the year 4004, BCE, as described in his two volume *Annals of the World*, 1654. His method is described as having added the ages of the named characters o the Chriſtian Bible, uſing the year 1 AD as the year of the birth of Jesus, and working back to Geneſis and the creation of Adam. Having not underſtood the concept and use of the Gematria, Ussher would have been unaware that the ages of these characters were almoſt always expreſſions of the Canon and tied to the Gematria. The moſt obvious example being the age of Enoch, who by the Book of Geneſis in the Pentateuch was said to have lived to an age of 365.

fog of folly. Greatly complicating the matter is the fact that such works as the Pentateuch or the Gnoftic Gospels are confidered divine by the believers of at leaft three major religions, and it is difficult to extract the actual relevant information without inciting the ire of the followers of any or all of them. We moft diligently attempt to avoid the implication that any set of religious teachings are inaccurate or mifleading, but once these works are examined within a wider context, this conclufion can become unavoidable to the serioufly objective student of the works. Sic Luceat Lux.

The Holy Oblation of Ezekiel

Given that we have previously discussed the Gematria, and currently investigate the Mysteries of the Man, it is prudent that some discussion here delve into the Mysteries of the Holy Oblation of Ezekiel. In truth, this is essential; the entire ancient Gematria and all of its symbols resolve to the measurements and proportions of this structure or to those which preceded it, and it is critical to a complete understanding of the concepts herein, and it is the most ancient well specified version of this concept of which this author is currently *aware*. This Mystery is far too involved to investigate in the greatest granularity, but it is possible to present to the reader enough information to initiate a meaningful inquiry based on the topics previously described. Those who have said that this vision represents Heaven are quite literally correct. The Holy Oblation measures and maps the proportions of the Solar System and of the Heavens and the Planets as anciently observed from Earth. The Holy Oblation and similar prophetic works are the fundamental containers of the values referenced by the Gematria, and the Gematria cannot be comprehended without an understanding of this. The Gematria exists to reference these numbers and proportions, and other meanings which are ascribed to the numbers calculated by Gematria are either correspondences or actual obfuscations. The Numbers of the Holy Oblation are probably the most important Keys of the Mysteries. He who hath eyes, let him see.

In *the Canon*, William Stirling quotes Origen Adamantius[168] as having written that "If one wished to obtain means for a profounder contemplation of the entrance of souls into divine

---

[168] Origen Adamantius was a Christian scholar of the late second and early third centuries, CE. Origen was, among other contributions, very much the compiler of the works which would later become the Christian New Testament.

things . . . . let him peruse at the end of Ezekiel's prophecies the visions . . . . and let him peruse also from the Apocalypse of John what is related of the city of God, the heavenly Jerusalem, and of its foundations and gates. And if he is capable of finding out also the road, which is indicated by symbols . . . ., let him read the book of Moses entitled 'Numbers,' and let him seek the help of one who is capable of initiating him into the meaning of the narratives concerning the encampments of the Children of Israel ..."[169] The vision herein referenced is that of Ezekiel's mysterious description of the land of Canaan, and which is herein referenced as the Holy Oblation of Ezekiel.

The Holy Oblation of Ezekiel is described in the visions of the prophet Ezekiel and the measurements are laid out there, if somewhat cryptically, being sufficient to understand its meanings and that which it represents. In the time of the writing of the work, which is generally believed to have spanned the years roughly 597 through 571 BCE, Jerusalem fell to Babylon and the Hebrew people were living in exile in Babylon[170]. It is also generally accepted that the Apocalyptic work known as the Apocalypse of Saint John the Divine references this work, especially in the description of the New Jerusalem. While much has been and shall be written on this peculiar work, our area of interest concerns his visions, describing the Celestial City, and which describe the intricate geometric model known to us as the Holy Oblation. The author finds it beyond question that this was an ancient teaching even at this time, and one which has no

---

[169] Stirling, William. The Canon - An Exposition of the Pagan Mystery Perpetuated in the Cabala as the Rule of All the Arts. London: Elkin Matthews, 1897. pp. 29-31.

[170] It should be noted that opinions on the timelines represented here vary between scholars, and that the story has no doubt evolved significantly in the intervening centuries.

doubt found expreffion in many syftems, moft especially the tradition of Qabala. There are aspects of the Hindu religion which seem to describe this same underlying Myftery within its myriad and magnificent pantheon.

While we have often pointed the reader to the *Canon* by William Stirling for more information on this concept, we find this work to be inscrutable to the modern mind in large part, and feel it beft to present this concept in a more comprehenfible form. Succinctly, the Holy Oblation of Ezekiel is a representation of the Universe, being the Solar Syftem, and its measurements and proportions as were observed by the ancients to a surprifingly great degree of accuracy. By its very measurement, the Holy Oblation tells us clearly that the ancients who created it were completely aware that the Sun was the center of the Universe. The Universe was the Body of God, and was the only manifeftation available to the mind of man within which to delve into the character of the Great Architect of the Universe.

The proportions and movements of the Great Luminaries and the fixed stars were the workings of the Holy Intellect and were the foundation of the teachings of the Great Myfteries which come down to us as Mythology and Religion. This is the work which underlies the Myfteries of Pythagoras. The truly philosophical conftructs of the Empyreum and of the Universe which appear so cryptic as described by the Alchemifts, the Myftical Chriftians and the Roficrucians all are representations of this defign, as are the representations of the New Jerusalem *said* to have belonged to the Templars. Stirling quite correctly derives the limits of the syftem by taking the measurements of the vifion and dividing them by 12, the number of tribes of Israel and the number of the Zodiac, and the measurements taken herein are from his *Canon*. The representation herein is greatly simplified, being adapted from the Canon with the intent to present sufficient information for the reader to make meaningful inquiry.

The Holy Oblation, being the Vision of the Holy Celestial City, describes three squares within each other, and representing the Three Great Luminaries, which so calculated yield sides of 2,083, 417, and 375. Considering the importance of the Numberes herein, we shall examine them. In the Book of Ezekiel, 45:2[171], the full extent of the Holy Oblation is given as being 25,000 Cubits, this being its outer Perimeter. Allowing for the measurement of the Gates of the Perimeter and their thresholds referenced in Chapter 40, the figure of 24,550 Cubits can be derived from the Outer Perimeter, though Stirling chose *not* to *explain* this step. Another area is to be set aside for the Perimeter of the Holy City and a Number of 5,000 Cubits is referenced. Allowing for the depth of the Walls of the Holy City and the Width of the Gates, we find the remaining value of 4,500 Cubits. By dividing each of these values by 12 we derive 2,083, 2,046, 417, and 375.

The Orbit of Saturn was calculated anciently as being 2,046 diameters of the Sun, and so this orbit is contained within the outer square, and by allowing the measures of the Gates, which must have some significance, we see in the Perimeter the exact orbit of Saturn. The second square of 417 does not contain the orbit of a planet, but contains the area of a circle with a

---

[171] May, Herbert G. and Bruce M. Mitzger, The New Oxford Annotated Bible With The Apocrypha, Revised Standard Verſion, New York: Oxford Univerſity Preſſ, 1962. P. 1060.

circumference of 1,480, which is the Number of Χριστος[172], hence it is written that Ezekiel had foretold Chriſt within his prophecies. Thus only with such underſtanding may one come to actually comprehend the veracity of the statements that Chriſt was foretold by the Prophets, for within the viſions of Ezekiel, uncovered by Geometry, is revealed the number of this Greek Word by the Gematria[173]. The center area Myſtically is aſſociated with Jupiter and connects the Holy Oblation to the Myſteries of Jupiter and hence to the Myſteries of the Melchizedek, which was an ancient Temple to Jupiter and being where Abram received the Myſteries. The Inside of the Holy City contains both the Orbits of The Sun and Venus, which were measured in Solar Diameters at 220 and 155, respectively, so that the 375 joins the Sun and Venus, revealing the Mystery of the Celestial City of Jerusalem as the City of the Sun and of Venus. Additionally, the outer line when adjusted by 10 Cubits for both thickness and height of the outer wall, being 2,093, represents a square which contains a circle with a diameter of 2,093, which would inscribe a

---

[172] This is proven by calculating the area of this square with sides of 417 as being 173,889. A Circle with an area of 173,889 has a radius of the square root of 173,889 divided by Pi or 235.3, or a diameter of 471, rounded. This diameter times Pi is 1,479.7 or 1,480. The rounding makes this seem a moſt imprecise calculation to the modern mind, but the reader should remember that this was calculated long before our accepted hiſtory tells us that mankind even underſtood the value of Pi. While the numbers rendered within these works indicate that a sophiſticated method of geometry and mathematics was in play, we do not as of yet know exactly how this was executed as its knowledge was a great Arcanum and known only to a select few.

[173] The outer line of the Holy Oblation measures 2,093, is the side of a square which will contain a circle of that diameter which will exactly contain a square with sides measuring 1,480. By the Greek Gematria, the name Χριστος resolves to 1,480. This from Stirling and eaſily verified by simple geometry and by the table of the Greek Gematria found on page 195.

square with sides of 1,480[174], not only the number of Chrift, but an apparent measure of the Body of God extending crofswise throughout the whole Universe. A Saltire Crofs within this square would represent the ancient Crofs of the Sun, which certainly predated it. The Measure of the Celestial City is quite complex, consisting of many measurements, and no doubt many *more* interesting measures are concealed within it. Any one or two might be deemed coincidence, but as a work the conclufion is inevitable. Taken as a whole, this work clearly demonstrates the extent to which the Celestial Mechanics of the Solar System had long ago been measured by our *primitive* ancestors.

Notably, a circle having a circumference of 2,093 will have a diameter of 666[175], the Number of a Man, and definitive evidence that the value of Pi was calculated long before it is generally accepted to have been. Herein we find the true meaning of the Myftery of the Number of a Man in the Apocalypse attributed to St. John, and thereby know then that the Man referenced is Adam Qadmon, and that his antichrift pretends to be God by taking upon himself this number. The inner square represents the actual Celeftial City and exactly contains the Suns orbit and the orbit of Venus[176], which is represented in the Four Corners

---

[174] By the Pythagorean Theorem, a circle with a diameter of 2,093 will contain a square with a diagonal of 2,093, which resolves to having sides measuring the square root of half of the square of 2,093, or 1,479.97, rounding to 1,480. As was previoufly mention, the rounding or adjuftment to an integer is commonly observed within these methods. The fact that this number can be derived from two different perspectives within this work makes this number of the greateft import.

[175] The Diameter of a Circle is defined as being its circumference divided by Pi, making the Diameter of a Circle with a Circumference of 2,093 equal to 666.22.

[176] The ancient correspondence of the Sun's orbit, being in reality the orbit of the Earth and reckoned then to have a diameter of 220 diameters of the Sun, when added to the orbit of Venus thought to have a diameter of 155 yields 375, the side of the inner square and the measure of the Celeftial City itself.

and which corresponds to the ancient Egyptian Syſtem, having been derived from the Phoenician. These four circles are represented by the wheels of the four living creatures in Ezekiel's viſion. We shall also take this opportunity to note the Measure of the Radius of the Orbit of Jupiter, which was anciently calculated at 555 Diameters of the Sun, and this being a Number which we may have seen somewhere *before*.

	English Name	Greek Name	Orbit Radius[‡]	Diameters of the Sun[⁎]	Ancient[§]	AU	Copernicus[€]
☿	Mercury	Ερμης	35,392,638	40.92	40	0.3872	0.326
♀	Venus	Αφροδιτη	66,131,476	76.45	77	0.7235	0.709
⊕	Earth	Χωμα	91,402,506	105.67	110	1.0000	1.000
♂	Mars	Αρης	139,312,226	161.05	160	1.5242	1.373
♃	Jupiter	Ζευς	475,693,149	549.93	555	5.2044	5.453
♄	Saturn	Χρονος	872,134,583	1,008.25	1023	9.5417	9.760

[‡] Orbital Radii in Miles from various modern sources.
[⁎] The current eftimate of the Sun's diameter is roughly 865,000 miles.
[€] Copernicus, from *De Revolutionibus Orbium Cœleftium*, orbital radii in diftances to the Earth.
[§] The anciently recognized radius of the orbit in diameters of the Sun. Derived from multiple sources.

Table 3 - The Proportions of the Solar System

Book 5 The Holy Union

Perhaps the higheſt and moſt pervaſive of the Myſteries is that of the Holy Union. This concept has been called by many names: The Royal Wedding, The Great Rite, The Great Work or Opus Magnus. At its root, the Union is the very act of Creation. It is represented by the Union of the God and Goddeſs. The Ankh symbolized to the Egyptians the Union of Iſis and Oſiris. This symbol represents the act of creation by the Male and Female Potencies, the result of which is the very Universe and Life Itself. This Union shows up countleſs places in Symbology, and in many places, such as Holy Water, that one might not expect. It may surprise the reader that an entire section of this work is devoted to this subject. This is not without reason. The underſtanding of the Holy Union is the single moſt important concept discuſſed in these works. It may take the reader some time to fully appreciate this, however, unleſs the reader is familiar with certain syſtems, such as the Wica, Qabala[177], or other certain esoteric syſtems.

Ask any Chriſtian, and they will almoſt certainly never have heard of the Great Rite or the Chymical Wedding, and will certainly not think it has any place in Chriſtianity, and yet they have always known of it, but were not aware of it. One of the moſt elegant Myths of the Great Rite is spelled out in the Old Teſtament Song of Solomon. A very erotic text, even in its prudiſh Elizabethan tranſlation, this Work is far more erotic in its original texts, before some its more graphic language was

---

[177] When the author refers to the Qabala, the inference is on the more ancient teachings by this name, having little if anything to do with some modern syſtems which take its name.

reinterpreted by medieval Chriſtian scholars, who took exception to its true words.

It will be neceſſary to explain two aspects of the Union so that one may come to a more complete underſtanding of its inner meaning. The Union certainly represents the Union of the God and Goddeſſ, Power and Strength, Male and Female and the act of Creation, as well as the Union of a woman and a man to create human life. A man and woman join in union and create human life and this is the firſt miracle of exiſtence. How logical that the Universe itself would have been so created. The Union also represents something a bit more eclectic, being the Union of the Oppoſites within Mankind. To the ancient Philosophers, the Male and Female also represented the oppoſing forces within our own selves. The Sun and Moon are the Conscious and Subconscious mind and the Soul and Body of Man. This is more apparent in Eaſtern Philosophies, because Chriſtianity has conſtantly worked to reinterpret the original texts that underlie it to remove these references. One muſt viſit the Gnoſtic Gospels to underſtand the importance of the Union to the early Chriſtians and to those who preceded them. The Holy Union represents what some term Ascenſion or Enlightenment, for reasons discuſſed in other places in this text.

Never forget that no philosophy or religion simply comes into being in a vacuum; every Mythos and every religion is simply a variant on that which came before, and they are each rich in hiſtory and symbolism. Those who firſt formed and belonged to them had previouſly accepted another faith by definition, and they brought these ideas into the new one and those concepts were either adopted completely, or hidden beneath a slightly different veil. An unfortunate tendency among those founding and propagating any new faith is the that of demonizing the prominent faiths which preceded it, or worse yet, attempting to literally deſtroy any evidence of it. For this reason, much of the context within which we might otherwise evaluate the evolution of such matters has been irretrievably loſt. For any choosing to believe that the Human Race has passed beyond such inexcusable vandalism, we simply remind them of the fate of the Buddhas of Bamiyan in 2001 CE.

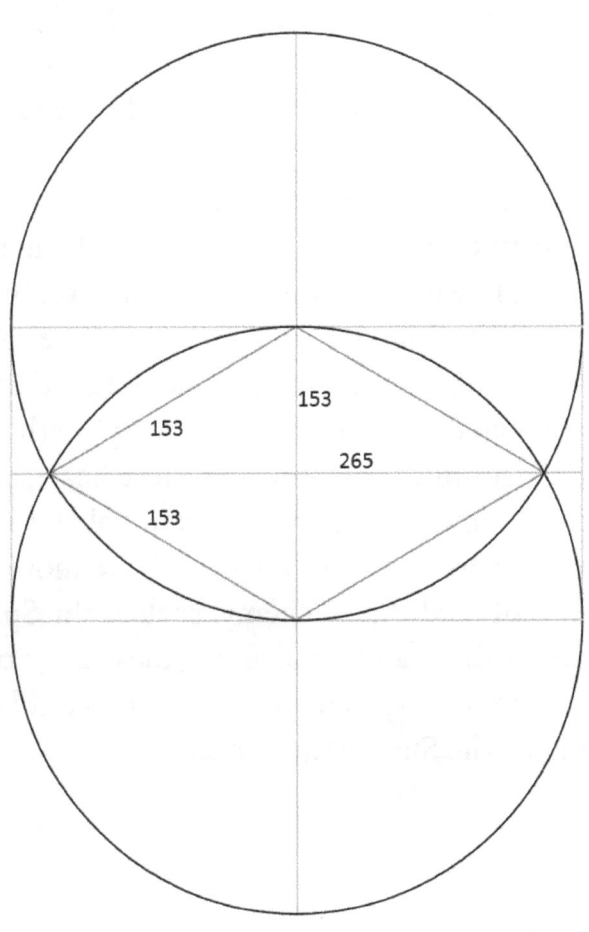

The Eclipse

The Sun and Moon represented the God and Goddeſs from long before the beginning of known, written hiſtory. The Solar Eclipse, being the Celeſtial Union of the Sun and Moon is an obvious symbol for this Holy Union. This is the symbol of Venus manifeſt upon the Heavens. From very ancient times, the Eclipse of the Sun by the Moon has had this meaning, together with more colorful interpretations, such as the swallowing of the Sun by the Dragon, or the Green Lion. A total eclipse of the Sun muſt have been a traumatic event for the ancient mind, especially for those who were not familiar with the Myſteries. The Eclipse is the Celeſtial act of Sun and Moon joining and is therefore the phyſical manifeſtation of the Veſica Pisces.

The very rarity of a total eclipse, in a world where moſt lived and died within a few miles of the same point, combined with the dramatic effect of having the Sun go dark in the middle of the day, muſt have been more awesome and terrifying than any modern mind is capable of conceiving. Many myths and legends grew up around this phenomenon, and these hearken back to the moſt ancient of times. Some of these involve the death and rebirth of the Sun, as is hinted in some of the more arcane texts and illuſtrations of medieval Alchemy, such as the Splendor Solis. Others are more subtle, and involve the knowledge of the Union of the Sun and the Moon, which in this event would demonſtrate the conquering of the Sun by the Moon.

When the ancient people had sufficiently observed the movements of the Luminaries to be able to predict their movements, and had the ability to predict an eclipse, such power over the people muſt have been awesome indeed, for a Prieſt with this knowledge could weave all manner of wonder and terror by the proper foretelling of such an event. This was no doubt the case in many cultures.

At its moſt Myſtical and Arcane level, the Union of the Sun and Moon in an eclipse of the Sun is indeed a Celeſtial Great Rite. The Two Great Luminaries meet and join in the Royal Wedding. This is the Myſtery of the Splendor Solis and represents the Heavenly Magnus Opus.

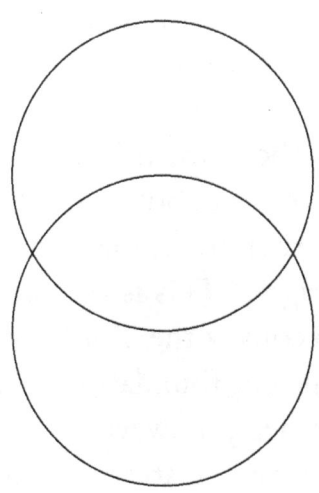

Holy Water

Most people who are familiar with the concept of Holy Water believe that Holy Water is Holy because it has been blessed by a Priest. This is only partly true. Holy Water is a great Symbol and a High Arcanum. To understand it, one must have some understanding of the Elements and their meanings. Holy Water is more than just Water. Holy Water is Water and Earth. The Earth takes the form of Salt, which was Holy to the ancient Hebrews. Earth is Male and Water Female, and so Holy Water is yet another Symbol of the Holy Union. This arcane Symbol of Male and Female and of Earth and Water requires a basic understanding of the traditions of the Elements to fully comprehend. The subject of Elements and Elementals is touched upon in this work, but it is a subject worthy of an entire volume or more in its own right.

The Roman Catholic tradition is so very rich with deeply meaningful Symbology that it is a pity that more do not stop to more closely examine them. Unfortunately, most of the meanings of these symbols are hidden within the Church and only given to the Priests and above, for they are truly Esoteric, but a knowledge of other traditions can help shine a light on their meanings and origins. This is the primary purpose behind these writings, as is to convey the Truth that these Mysteries are underlain by a most ancient foundation that underlies the many. In one important respect, however, the author agrees with church authorities on this matter; a simple reading of the Christian Bible without a proper context and without understanding, and without familiarity with the works upon which it is based, will yield little of real value.

The Eucharist

The Chriftian ceremony of the communal taking of the Bread and the Wine is the central Ritual in Chriftianity, though some Proteftant traditions have almoft eliminated it, making the central ritual either the recruitment of members, or worse, the paffing of the collection plate. The sharing of the Bread and the Wine is central to the Chriftian tradition, but was in exiftence long before the Common Era, and ancient in the time of Abram.

During Roman times, the cults of Bacchus and Mithras both performed a variant of this ritual. The Book of Genefis, Chapter 14, verse 18 says thus: "And Mel-chiz'edek king of Salem brought out bread and wine; he was prieft of God Moft High..."[178]. The gueft here was Abram or Abraham, Patriarch of Judaism, Iflam and Chriftianity. According to Eupolemus, the referenced temple of Melchizedek, where Pythagoras studied Philosophy, and therefore muft have been an Initiate, was a temple of Jupiter. We thereby know that by his title, that Melchiz'edek king of Salem, muft have been, by virtue of his kingfhip, Prieft of the Temple of Melchizedek, and thereby a Prieft of Jupiter. It is also written that the ancient Brahman priefts had a similar rite known to them as *Prajadam*. More than one exifting esoteric tradition uses an almoft identical Rite. That which Chriftians know as the Eucharift is then a tradition of very great antiquity, indeed.

---

[178] May, Herbert G. and Bruce M. Mitzger, *The New Oxford Annotated Bible With The Apocrypha*, Revised Standard Verfion, Oxford Univerfity Press: New York, 1962.

The Eucharist or the Ritual of Bread and Wine is yet another of the Rites which is a variant of the Great Rite, for Bread is the Goddess and Wine the God. This is a deeply meaningful ritual on many levels and is related to the Blood Mysteries. By taking the Blood and Fruits of the Earth, the participants are physically joined, and reminded that they are Brethren and kindred and are of one Being. The participant is reminded that they are sustained by the Gods, and in so partaking, becomes One with Them.

The Horned God

The Horned God is moſt commonly referenced in the tomes on Wicca and Witchcraft, but is far more ancient than either, and is anceſtral to a great many traditions, and so we again viſit this ancient symbol. The Greek God Pan was a variant on the Horned God as was the Sacred Bull and the Holy Ram. The Horned God is neither Pan nor Satan, but certainly inspired them both. The Bull or Ox, worſhipped under many names throughout the Mediterranean in ancient times, was but a variant of the Horned God, and so then both Mithras and to some extent, Moloch. The Celts revered Cernunnos, which is a Latin name meaning 'Horned One' and was probably based on a much more ancient Celtic name. Some think Cernunnos was the Celtic God of Initiation, which is intereſting since the Bull Symbolized the Myſteries of Mithras, which were certainly an Initiation Rite and a very well known Myſtery School.

The Horned God is generally interpreted by scholars as a type of the Sun God, but the Horns make this more complex. For many years the default explanation of modern anthropology for any obscure faith has been that is was simple Sun worſhip. The Horns themselves tie this Deity to Venus and the Two Horns represent Venus in its track as both Evening Star and Morning Star. This represents a Duality. The symbol commonly used for Mercury is the Horned God itself. The Horned One is then, neither Sun nor Moon nor Venus, but all three in Union. The Horned God represents the ancient Trinity and served a philosophical function equivalent to the Chriſtian Trinity of Father, Son and Holy Ghoſt.

The Horned god is also veiled under the guise of the Owl. The Owl is an ancient symbol of wisdom and is still recognized as such, as it was in the Greek Myths. Athena was aſſociated closely with the Owl, as she is with Sophia or Wisdom. The Owl is a bird of prey which hunts silently at night, and so is associated with the Moon and with the subconscious. The association of the Owl with Wisdom underlies its use as a symbol the group Mensa, the association whose members must demonstrate an IQ in the top two percentile to be admitted. Like almost all modern references to the Owl as a symbol of Wisdom, this particular reference is based upon the association of that bird with the Greek Goddess Athena. It is unlikely that many members of this illustrious group actually understand why the Owl would have been considered sacred to Athena, any more than they would understand why the Mirror of Aphrodite was the same as our symbol for Venus. Athena carried upon Her shoulder the Wisdom of the Mysteries of the Horned God in the shape of the Owl.

The Owl is one of the symbols said to be "hidden" within the street plans for Washington, DC created by Pierre L'Enfant, a Mason, in 1791. The five pointed star is obvious, and has the White House located at its apex. This is not any real mystery, and certainly not an evil omen, as the five pointed star has represented Wisdom for millennia. To have the President of the United States reside at the apex of this Star was to symbolically endow him with Wisdom. Of course there are well meaning Protestant Christians who, not understanding the symbol or its ancient meaning, consider it a sign of the "Devil" and therefore attribute to it the weight of "Black Magic". This is often pointed out by uninformed conspiracy theorists as evidence of some sort of "satanic conspiracy", usually involving the Masonic fraternity, of evil influences in the founding of this nation. These persons would claim that they are well informed in such matters, and yet we have never heard one of them accuse the Washington

Monument as being, at a height of 555 feet, a monument to Zeus. Such pick and choose their alleged facts to fit their preconceptions.

Nothing could be farther from the truth. It would be more appropriate to say that the evil conspiracies afoot may be attempting to ensnare a free and secular republic into the bondage of theocracy. Such would indeed represent a dark conspiracy. Unfortunately, many of these same people seem bent on eſtabliſhing the United States of America beneath a government based on their interpretation of Chriſtianity, and even attempt to retell hiſtory in such a way as to imply that this was the intention of those who founded this nation, which it clearly was not. Perhaps it is they who represent to the danger to Liberty. Had the founders of the Secular republic which was named the United States of America intended to create a nation state under the guiding principles of a Chriſtian theocracy, it is rather unlikely that the Firſt Amendment would have been included as a part of the Conſtitution prior to its ratification.

The "head" of the Owl said to be in the layout of Waſhington, D.C. is comprised of the grounds surrounding the Capital Building. If this is, indeed, by deſign, and this is by no means certain, then certainly this was another symbolic endowment of Wisdom upon the leaderſhip of our government. How fitting that the leaders of the World's firſt Democratic Republic should be so guided. The symbology of the Owl is not, however confined to its graphic representation, but also to its common vocalization. The call of Owl is "who". This takes us much farther back than Greece, who still retained this symbology, but back to the very beginning of Egyptian civilization. The original God of the ancient Egyptians was Hu Hu. We find it likely more than coincidence that the bird who so clearly spoke the name of one of the very moſt ancient names of God would be held in high reverence for millennia. To the Egyptians, Hu Hu was not only the name of God, but was the Firſt Utterance by which the Spirit of Oſiris and Creation itself were called into being, that same Utterance known to the Chriſtian as the Logos or the *Word*.

The Owl, though not as commonly aſſociated with satan as the Pentacle, is reviled by uninformed persons as a symbol of an "anti-Chriſtian conspiracy". There are certain Chriſtian scholars who tie the Owl to Moloch (not without reason, for it is true that the Owl was aſſociated with this unpleasant deity, to whom followers sacrificed children by slowly burning them alive) and to satan (anything with horns muſt be Satan) and conſider it an evil symbol, but of course like all of these symbols, this one not only predates Chriſtianity, but it also predates their peculiar concept of a satan itself[179]. The idea of a supernatural antagoniſt to god, at leaſt in the modern underſtanding of a separate and evil deity, is relatively new. The ancient Hebrew texts speak of the 'Adversary' who did not work againſt God but with him, his aſſignment being to teſt the faith of believers. A reading of the Old Teſtament book of Job confirms this, for it was not the

---

[179] The modern concept of Satan is an amalgam of several different ideas, including the Cabaliſtic concept of the Adversary, who was not an opponent of God at all, but in his employ. The word satan means 'adversary'. This concept is the one illuſtrated by the Old Teſtament story of Job, where Job's trials are a teſt of faith, suggeſted by and overseen by the Adversary, and fully authorized by the Hebrew God. Our generalized visual image of Satan has much more in common with the Egyptian Set, with his red cloak and cloven hoofs, and this can be traced back to the teachings of Zarathuſtra. The author also points out that in the early years of the Roman Church, wings were also associated with evil, and that this only began to abate two or three centuries after the Council of Nicea, when it became more common to show angels and the Heavenly Hoſt as being winged. The Chriſtian Bible never actually describes angels as having wings at all, but rather the Cherubim and Seraphim.

rebellious satan who caused trouble for Job, but rather the Adversary in the employ of his God. Given that it is cuſtomary among almoſt all religions to demonize the symbols of the religions that came before, it is fitting that they should view the Owl in this way, as it is unqueſtionably more ancient than they. While Wisdom knows no limits, ignorance knows no bounds.

The Owl has represented Wisdom for countleſſ centuries, and now we underſtand why. The Owl is a veiling of the Myſtery of the Horned God, and this is a Symbol which represents the Myſteries of Venus, which were concealed beneath the concept of Sophia, which we tranſlate as Wisdom. So, in fact, the Owl does represent Wisdom in a moſt ingenious way. This is a Great Arcanum.

The Chymical Marriage

The Chymical Marriage is an interpretation of the Great Rite aſſociated with the teachings of Alchemy and with the early Roſicrucians. The opus titled *The Chymical Marriage*, publiſhed in Strasbourg in the year 1616, was attributed to Johann Valentin Andreæ. This was the third, and arguably moſt important, of the manifeſtos surrounding the German Roſicrucian movement of the early seventeenth century. This is yet another Myſtery describing the Holy Union within a traditional framework of God and Goddeſſ in Union. This telling is very much in the Alchemical tradition of the Marriage, Death and Resurrection of the God and Goddeſſ.

The Chymical Marriage tells the story of a man who is invited to a Royal Wedding by what appears to him an Angel. There is a moſt curious journey during which, over the course of Seven Days, he sees and experiences many wondrous and horrific sights and events, and finds himself, after many trials, being the only one admitted to the Wedding, ahead of Princes and Prieſts and other nobility.

The actual events described are certainly an interpretation of the Hermetic Philosophies of the day, and refer to the Holy Union of God and Goddeſſ. This story is also an excellent example of a Myſtery Story which, like the Labours of Hercules, was almoſt certainly acted out by the Initiates of the Myſtery Schools at some point in time. The hallmark of any Initiatory Rite of the Myſtery Schools is the ceremonial death and resurrection of the participant and this is as true of a Chriſtian Baptism as it was of the Rites of Mithras or the Myſteries of Osiris.

The Chymical Marriage is a special interpretation of the Great Rite. Like almoſt all such representations, it muſt have been at some time a Myſtery Play, a reenactment of a Myſtery as part of an Initiatory Ritual. Many claſſical works of literature do in fact represent the Myſtery Play, often with the Initiate as the Protagoniſt, telling the story as experienced by them as the Myſteries were presented. There are potions of the Book of Enoch which make perfect sense when viewed in this way and the portions of the Book of Enoch which describe his viſions fit particularly well into such a type of story.

Hypnerotomachia Poliphili

One of the moſt Myſterious of all Chymical Weddings is described in the curious work the Hypnerotomachia Poliphili. Firſt publiſhed in Venice in 1499, this work is generally believed to have been written by Francesco Colonna, a Dominican monk who lived in Venice. Colonna's name is revealed in the book by taking the firſt letter of each of the 38 chapters to spell out "Poliam frater Franciscus Columna peramavit", meaning "Brother Francesco Colonna loved Polia tremendouſly". In 1999, Thames & Hudson publiſhed the firſt complete Engliſh verſion of the Hypnerotomachia Poliphili, five hundred years after the original. While much of the esoteric content of any such work is loſt simply by its tranſlation, this edition took great care to preserve the work as well as poſſible, and included the original woodcuts, which are very important to its interpretation.

Everything about the original printing of the Hypnerotomachia Poliphili was a maſterpiece, from the type face, to the woodcuts to the exquiſite layout of the text. In fact, it is impoſſible to fully comprehend this work without reading it in its original Latin, and from an exact copy of the original work. This is as superb an example of Canonical Rhetoric as such is known to the author. For those who never had the chance to mafter Latin, excellent tranflations into Englifh are available, but the reader should note that in any such tranflation, they are at the mercy of the editor for much of the subtlety of the work, since there are countlefſ codes within it which involve the placement of the type on the page, and in the wood cuts themselves. This is, in fact, the case with all of the ancient texts going right back to Gilgamefh. Information was included in the actual writing which was far more than juft the words on the page. No tranflation of any such work can poffibly begin to communicate the information which it originally contained. This is true even if the editor responfible for the tranflation is an Adept of the Myftery within.

The Chymical Marriage, as with all representations of the Great Rite, has layers of meanings. It represents the Creation of the Universe by the Gods and the act of creation. It represents the creation of life by Man and Woman, for their union is the fountain of human life, Vniverfitatis, Rervm Fontis, and what could be more sacred than the Fountain of Life itself? In addition, there is a more Esoteric and subtle meaning behind the Great Rite, and the Chymical Wedding deals with this meaning especially well. The Chymical Wedding is the Union of Spirit and Body, of Mind and Body and of the Conscious and Subconscious Minds, of symbolic Death and Resurrection, on Earth, as it is in Heaven.

The Song of Solomon

If the reader has completed both the Chymical Wedding and the Hypnerotomachia Poliphili, then it is time to revifit a work that is almoft universally misunderftood with frefh eyes. The Song of Solomon, otherwise referred to as the Song of Songs, which is its title in the Hebrew Bible, is the Chymical Marriage as told within Hebrew Tradition. This will no doubt come as a shock to many Chriftians, but well educated Jewifh readers will no doubt underftand this. This work is generally attributed to ruler called King Solomon himself, which would date the work to the tenth century BCE, affuming the currently accepted chronologies are correct. Of Course the Great Rite is also represented in the Chriftian New Teftament, under the guise of the Wedding at Canaan, and this is revealed by the miracle of the Water and the Wine.

Oftenfibly, Solomon sings of his wife, but a careful examination of the work reveals that it is much more allegorical in character, and that the phyfical love described conceals Myftical concepts which are to be found in other variants of the Royal Wedding and also the Tantra. The Song of Songs is surely a very erotic work, especially in its more ancient words. It represents a defire even more deep than the yearning between Woman and Man. This work speaks of insatiable and endleff longing to become One, not juft with a partner, but with God and with the Universe. The object of this longing is known by countleff names. To the Buddhift, it is Nirvana. To the Chriftian it is to become One with Chrift. To the Myftic, it is to become One with God, and to return to Our Origin.

The Wedding at Canaan

Another reference to the Chymical Wedding or Great Rite which is rarely recognized as such, moſt especially by Chriſtians, is the Wedding at Canaan. The Miracle of changing Water into Wine reveals it as such. It may not seem obvious that both the Song of Songs and the Wedding at Canaan describe the same Philosophical concept, but this does require much underſtanding. The very structure of a traditional European Chriſtian wedding is based on the Mythology of the Chymical Wedding.

There are a number of people at this time who suspect that the Wedding at Canaan may describe the wedding of Yeſhua himself. This author does not conſider this impoſſible, but reserves judgment on this topic for the moment. There is no queſtion that one versed in Alchemy sees a great deal in the description of this wedding. Simply the miracle of turning water into wine is sufficient to make it an alchemical reference, and this ties it inſtantly to many traditions.

The Great Rite

The Great Rite, termed by some as the Black Mass[180], is a very ancient Rite, practiced for thousands of years. It is the ritual Union of Man and Woman. There are writings of Christian Monks of the sixth century which indicate that the Great Rite was practiced within Christian Churches by the Gnostics, before the Pauline Romans used torture, death and terror to enforce absolute conformity with their own peculiar form of Christianity[181]. The Great Rite reenacts the Union of the God and Goddess in the very act of Creation. It is known that Chinese Emperors and Mayan Kings, Greek Kings and Priestesses and Druids all performed a ceremony which was essentially the Great Rite. Modern Witches still practice the Great Rite, which many

---

[180] The Term 'Black Mass' is a relatively recent invention, and one coined by Christians to demonize the concept, as though Christianity did not incorporate the same concept into the Eucharist itself. Anyone sufficiently well versed in the Christian Mysteries is well aware of this. The Eucharist *is* and enactment of the Holy Union.

[181] The author wishes to note that by all means not all, nor even many, of the Priests and Cardinals of the Roman Catholic Church should be interpreted as evil men. The Catholic Church has also done great good in its long history, and continues to do so. Unfortunately, during much of the previous 1,500 hundred or so years, their power was so overwhelmingly absolute over so many lives, that when bad deeds were committed in its name, even kings were helpless against them, much less the average person or even nobleman. The problem being not so much a case of evil intent, but of too much absolute power concentrated in too few hands. Such powerful organizations often are far too willing to overlook bad deeds when performed to protect the power of the institution, especially when the acknowledgement of them would cause embarrassment. Of course this statement is purely the opinion of the author.

This is as unfortunately true in recent times, though the fact that these deeds were brought to light and that some degree of justice was taken gives one cause for hope. Even one hundred years ago, such deeds by clerics were almost universally ignored. This is true of all powerful and well entrenched organizations, and not churches alone. An organization composed of men is always subject to the errors of men, regardless of its intent. This reference is to the unholy acts which were sometimes taken by certain members of the organization to crush any dissent or the slightest challenge to their authority in matters of Dogma.

Chriftians have inappropriately termed the Black Mafs. Remember that modern Witchcraft is a very recent invention, its roots dating only back to the late nineteenth century. However, though Wicca is little more than a half century old, many of its practices are very ancient indeed. Among them are those who are the recipients of a more ancient oral tradition, and who underftand these rites. They are almoft as well concealed in a modern coven as they were in medieval Europe. By certain signs and words they are known among themselves, and to those who *recognize* them.

The Great Rite is the ceremonial re-enactment of the Creation of the World by the Union of Man and Woman, representing the God and Goddefs. By their copulation, they recreate the act of Creation. In ancient times, this was certainly a ceremony that was expected to lead to the birth of Priefts and Kings or Queens. The story of the Royal Wedding is more ancient than Parfifal or the Grail which conceals it. It was ancient when it was woven into the Hypnerotomachia Poliphili and even when it inspired the story of the Wedding at Canaan. The Great Rite can eafily be seen in a formal wedding ceremony, and is impoffible not to notice when properly enacted with six bride's maids and six groomsmen, resplendent in white and black. Moft reenactments of the Great Rite no longer involve actual coitus between man and woman, but the ancient Rite moft affuredly did.

In ancient Ireland, in the time of the conftruction of the Great Temple and Newgrange, the Great Rite was practiced by the Rulers at exactly the Spring Equinox. The period of the Creation of Life followed, being three fourths of a year, and represented to them by the Triple Spiral upon which there is so much conjecture. Every eight years was a special time, for at this appointed Winter Solstice were born the great Priests and Rulers. Every forty years, an even more important Winter Solstice occurred, during which the King was born, or rather reborn. During a special ceremony under the light of the Rising Venus within the chamber of the Temple, a child was born, and this child was to receive the spirit of the late King. In this way, the same ruler could be reborn many times and rule for centuries. It was a vestige of this Rite which allowed such legendary men as Methuselah to be said to have lived for hundreds of years, and by a similar tradition, the Dalai Lama has been reincarnated for many generations.

This author has attempted to hold discussions on this matter with both Christian and Wiccan Priests, and found both to be equally disturbed by the open discussion of the subject. To the Christian Priest, it appeared as an abomination, while to the Wiccan High Priestess it represented Sacred Knowledge which only the Priest or Priestess should possess. Of course any Christian should recognize the Great Rite, since the Christian Old Testament contains one of the most beautiful descriptions of this Union, under the guise of the Song of Solomon. Of course the Eucharist also holds vestiges of the Great Rite in the Bread and Wine, a ritual passed from Abram, who was an initiate of the Temple of Jupiter. References recognizable as a form of the Great Rite are to be found far into the mists of ancient times, and some form of this Rite almost certainly existed long before any known written history.

The Great Rite is also concealed carefully within the Mysteries of Alchemy. Alchemy does, in fact, operate on many levels, including both chemistry and metallurgy, but its highest Arcanum is that of the Mysteries of the Union. Alchemy is a variant on Hermetic Philosophy and veils the same Mysteries under slightly different veils. In Alchemical Literature, the search for the Philosopher's Stone represents the search for the Balance, the Fulcrum, the Opus Magnus or Great Work. The Opus Magnus is the Great Rite.

The Great Rite both celebrates and reenacts Creation. The ancients practiced the Great Rite to give birth to Kings. Special ceremonies were conducted on auspicious days, moſt anciently on the Vernal Equinox, the Fruits of which were to be born on the Winter Solſtice. In more than one ancient tradition, on a special day, the King would phyſically unite with the high Prieſteſs of the Goddeſs to perform a ritual act of procreation, thus aſſuring the bounty for the kingdom in the coming year. This is important knowledge. It is neceſſary to underſtand the Myſteries of Horus, Apollo or Chriſt, for all these Myths make reference to it.

The Light of The Fish

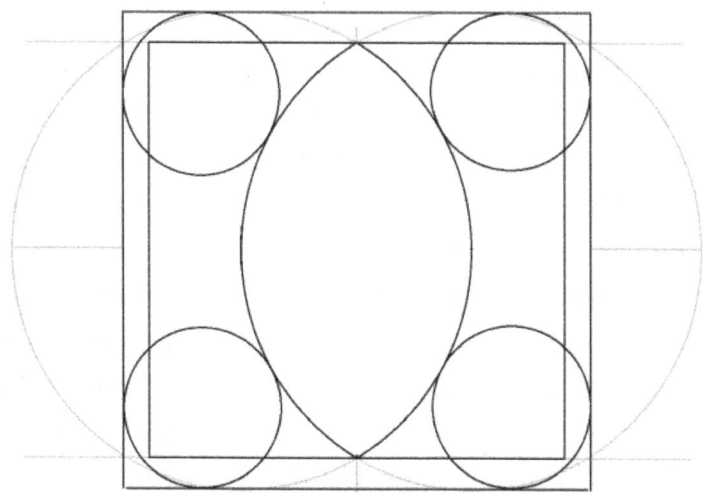

Plate 63 - The Jerusalem of the Vision of Ezekiel

Again we come to the Vefica Pisces and in its proper place, for the Vefica Pisces is far older than the Cult of Dagon and underlies sacred geometry from at leaft Neolithic times. The Vefica Pisces is the Union of Sun and Moon and of God and Goddeff and is more ancient even than the myfterious stone circles whose geometry incorporates it. The Light of the Fifh lies even at the very Heart of the New Jerusalem of the Apocalypse and the Vifion of Ezekiel. Keys firmly in hand, we venture into the moft ancient of Myfteries.

As we briefly difcuffed concerning the Holy Oblation of the Vifion of Ezekiel, the plan of the City describes an outer perimeter, a central suburb, and the Holy City. Examining the measurements, as did the Sons of Heaven, the genius of the vifion begins to take shape. For the square which contains the City of Jerusalem is described as being 4,500 reeds square and so dividing by 12 we get a dimenfion of 375. The Ancients regarded the diameter of the orbit of Venus as containing 155 Solar

Diameters. The orbit of the Earth was said to contain 220 Solar Diameters and the sum of these is 375 so that Jerusalem is a City of the Sun and of Venus[182]. Adding the thickneſs of the walls surrounding Jerusalem we get a square whose sides are 416 $^2/_3$. When we create the Veſica Pisces from two Circles each having a diameter of 416 $^2/_3$ then we form a Veſica with a height of 360 and so this Holy City contains the orbits of the Sun and Venus and the Number of days of the Greek Solar year, and so this not only creates the Veſica, but teaches us its proportions thuſly. The Four Circles at the corners represent the orbit of Venus according to the ancient Egyptian syſtem, and are probably the Four Wheels of Ezekiel's viſion[183]. And so by Geometry are the Myſteries unveiled, it now and finally being the *time* to speak of such things *openly*.

A sample of certain medieval Chriſtian art works will quickly reveal this very form as being obviouſly important in early Chriſtianity. Geometrically this form is equivalent to the New Jerusalem described in the Apocalypse of St. John Divine, for they both describe the same thing. The proportions derived from these numbers and from these ancient teachings are one and the same and are all a representation of the Ancient Pagan Canon described by Stirling. These are the foundation stones for the Esoteric Myſteries of the ancient Egyptians, and by succeſſion, the Greeks, and of the Norse and of the Romans, as well as the early Chriſtians. A modern Proteſtant Chriſtian may be forgiven for having no concept of these matters since hundreds of years ago their predeceſſors abandoned the Esoteric Myſteries of Chriſtianity when they threw off the bondage of the

---

[182] Recall that the name Jerusalem literally means City of Venus.
[183] Stirling, William. The Canon - An Expoſition of the Pagan Myſtery Perpetuated in the Cabala as the Rule of All the Arts. London: Elkin Matthews, 1897. p. 31.

Vatican and Papal authority, leaving them with only the veſtigial *containers* of these stories, with no way to actually find their inner meanings. This is not to say that no Proteſtant Chriſtians know of or underſtand the deeper Myſteries, for surely a few *do*. The author has met them.

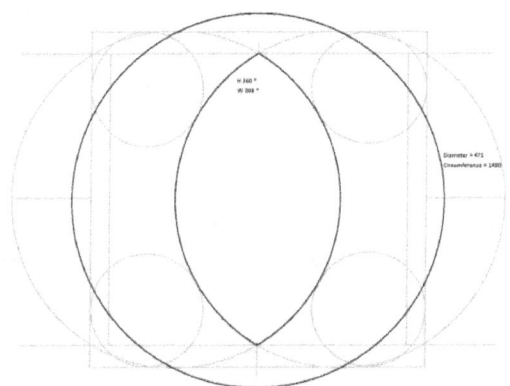

Plate 64 - The Eye of The Serpent

When a Circle is inscribed about the center with a Diameter of 471, it yields a Circumference of 1,480, the number of Χριστος which was earlier derived from the outer perimeter of the Holy Oblation. In this case, this Circle and the Veſica form the Eye of the Serpent God Ningizzida, an indication that this was yet another Myſtery aſſociated with this same deſign. As we explore the Geometry of the Heavens, the Circle is Complete, and within the Ouroboros, all is joined.

We currently hold the opinion that originally, all of the numerical values having esoteric importance with both the Gematria and within Isopsephy were derived from the same underlying geometry, which conſtituted the underlying Canon of the moſt ancient religions. While there were inevitable divergences from the original patterns, the similarities are sufficient to definitively indicate the same underlying Syſtem. In regard to the Myſteries, then, this ancient syſtem is, in and of itself, the Rerum Fontis of the Mysteries, should we assume that there had been a *single* system. The development of such matters over many millennia would indicate that many civilizations put their own seal upon the Mysteries, but there were certainly very well developed Systems which are so ancient that we have yet to discover them, or at least to recognize them as such. Given that this Geometry interprets as a series of Three Circles representing the proportions of the heavens, we opine that any ancient reference to a system of Three Circles refers to the ancient pattern, including that described by Plato in reference to the Myth of Atlantis, but then were the island Thera and its volcano the cause of the destruction, and the Minoan civilization taken as Atlantis, then this might also be taken *literally*, and yet the Minoans themselves are known to have revered these three circles even before this catastrophe, and so we are left with a Mystery perhaps far more ancient.

Vniversitatis Rervm Fontis

The phrase VNIVERSITATIS RERVUM FONTIS tranflates from Latin as 'Universal Source of all Things'. This phrase, common in Alchemy, is also part of the text along the top of the certificate presented to a Mason when he completes the 32° of the Scottifh Rite of Freemasonry. It is from this phrase that the title of this work is taken. The Entire Phrase is:

Dei Optimi Maximi, Univerfitatis Rerum Fontis, ac Originis ad Gloriam

As it is the case with almoft all Myfteries, this can be tranflated in two ways, for Dei Optimi Maximi may be tranflated as 'Being of or belonging to the Higheft and Greateft God', but this does not make full sense in the context of the presentation, since these letters are found acrofs the beam which joins the two columns, Jachin and Boaz. The correct tranflation is 'The High and Great God (God being the Union), Universal Source of All Things (the Fountain of the Universe), and also the Origin, Even Unto (for the) Glory'. Given that Latin does not perfectly tranflate into Englifh, another scholar might give subtle differences to this tranflation and be absolutely correct. Nonethelefs, the important concept is there, for this is a reference to the Gods, God and Goddefs, by Whose Holy Union All Things came into being and it is then the Union of God and Goddefs that we herein refer to as God. Only a handful of Masons underftand the meaning of this symbol, as is the case with almoft all of Masonic Symbols. In fact, many symbols used in Masonry represent the Union or Great Rite. Its underftanding is a foundation stone of all of the Ancient Myfteries, and Masonry, like so many other syftems, has been built upon this moft ancient foundation. Underftand then that the Holy Union is not juſt God and Goddeſſ in Union and the Product of that Union, for the Union *is* God and this is the ancient arcane meaning of the word.

The Symbol of the Two Pillars and the Croſſbeam comes down to us from Neolithic times and even before, from those Myſterious miſts before written hiſtory, from the hidden world before the Deluge. Note the trilithons of the ancient and myſterious Temple of Stonehenge. There you will see five pairs of great pillars which were joined by croſſ members in this way. Again, we find the myſterious Five. It is no accident that such a value as the relationſhip of a circle's circumference to its diameter would have been given the Symbol Π, for within this Magical Ratio lies the proportions of the Heavens, and there again, are Potential and Creation. The Great Rite is the Union of Blade and Chalice and of the Sun and Moon and so it is also the Veſica Pisces. Here we discover that truly all things are One. The Union is the Center of all the Myſteries from the dawn of time and which were the seeds of all great religion of mankind for all of written hiſtory, and certainly long before. It is not without reason then that many great Philosophers have written that there is One God, for underlying all is the One and in its manifeſt variety and multitudinous forms, appears under the guise of many faces and many names. Walk we therefore into the clear night and caſt our eyes to Heaven and behold as the Ancients did the Body of God and the Wonders of the Workings thereof, and so perceive the Moſt Ancient Book of Truth written by the very Hand of God.

To comprehend the Great Rite is to achieve the Magnus Opus of Philosophy. To comprehend a Myſtery means a great deal more than to have been initiated into it, or to be able to discuſs it, or to know of its origins. A Myſtery is a deeply meaningful Symbol which contains layers of meaning, including its origins and perhaps its original representation of some Aſtral Phenomenon, but woven within it, by countleſs men and women, through the millennia, are secrets of the Hiſtory of the Human Race, of how our anceſtors viewed the World and their place in it. To fully comprehend the Great Rite is to know, not juſt know of, not juſt underſtand, but to know, our place in the Cosmos, and to comprehend Who and What and Why We Are. Verily, this is the Magnus Opus. Sic Luceat Lux.

CLVS

AVX

Bibliography

Agrippa, Henry Cornelius, *Three Books of Occult Philosophy*. London: Printed by R.W. for *Gregory Moule*, 1651.

Baigent, Michael, Richard Leigh, and Henry Lincoln, *the Holy Blood and the Holy Grail*, London: Jonathan Cape, Ltd., 1982.

Browne, Sir Thomas, The Garden of Cyrus, or, The Quincunciall, Lozenge, or Network Plantations of the Ancients, Artificially, Naturally, Myftically Confidered, London: Signe of the Gun, 1658.

Cirlot, J. E., *A Dictionary of Symbols*, Tranflated from the Spanifh *A Diccionario de Simbolos Tradicionales*. New York: Philosophical Library, Inc., 1962.

Colonna, Francesco, *Hypnerotomachia Poliphili*, Tranflated from the Italian by Joscelyn Godwin. New York: Thames & Hudson, 1999.

Farrar, Janet and Stewart Farrar, *Eight Sabbats for Witches*. London: Robert Hale, Ltd., 1981.

Farrar, Janet and Stewart Farrar, *The Witches Way*. London: Robert Hale, Ltd., 1984.

Fletcher, Audrey, *Ancient Egypt and the Conftellations*. Web Publication, 1999.

Frazer, Sir James George, F.R.S., F.B.A., *The Golden Bough, A Study in Magic and Religion*. Abridged edition. New York: Macmillan, 1922.

Gardner, Gerald B., *Witchcraft Today*. London: Rider, 1954.

Gardner, Lawrence, *Bloodline of the Holy Grail*, Dorset: Element Books Limited, 1996.

Hall, Manly P., *Man the Grand Symbol of the Myfteries*, Los Angeles: The Philosophical Research Society, Inc., 1972.

Hall, Manly P., *Melchizedek and the Myftery of Fire*, Los Angeles: The Philosophical Research Society, Inc., 1996.

Hans Eiberg, Jesper Troelsen, Mette Nielsen, Annemette Mikkelsen, Jonas Mengel-From, Klaus W. Kjaer, and Lars Hansen, "Blue eye color in humans may be caused by a perfectly affociated founder mutation in a regulatory element located within the HERC2 gene inhibiting OCA2 expreffion." *Human Genetics* 10.1007 (2008)

Knight, Chriftopher and Alan Butler, Solomon's Power Brokers, The Secrets of Freemasonry, the Church, and the Illuminati. London: Watkins Publifhing, 2007.

Knight, Chriftopher and Robert Lomas. *The Book of Hiram*. London: Element, 2003.

Knight, Chriftopher and Robert Lomas. *Uriel's Machine*. London: Fair Winds Prefs, 2001.

Landau, Brent Christopher., Revelation of the Magi: The Lost Tale of the Wise Men's Journey to Bethlehem. New York: HarperCollins, 2010.

Luxenberg, Christoph, The Syro-Aramaic Reading of the Koran: A Contribution to the Decoding of the Language of the Koran. English Edition, Berlin: Hans Schiler Publishers, 2007.

May, Herbert G. and Bruce M. Mitzger, *The New Oxford Annotated Bible With The Apocrypha*, Revised Standard Version, New York: Oxford University Press, 1962.

Pike, Albert, *Esoterika*, Transcribed and Edited by Arturo de Hoyos, 33°, Washington, D.C.: The Scottish Rite Research Society, 2005.

Pike, Albert. Morals and Dogma of the Ancient and Accepted Scottish Rite of Freemasonry: Charleston, 1871.

Stirling, William. The Canon - An Exposition of the Pagan Mystery Perpetuated in the Cabala as the Rule of All the Arts. London: Elkin Matthews, 1897.

Sully, Henry, The Temple of Ezekiel's Prophecy: or An Exhibition of the Nature, Character, and Extent of the Building Represented in the Last Nine Chapters of Ezekiel, London, Published by the Author: Wheeler Gate, Nottingham; and 12, Goswell Road, London, E.C.

Walker, Barbara G., The Woman's Encyclopedia of Myths and Secrets, Harper & Row, 1983.

Yau, Shing-Tung, and Steve Nadis, The Shape of Inner Space, String Theory and the Geometry of the Universe's Hidden Dimensions. New York: Basic Books, 2010.

Index

Abraham 385
Abram 39, 385
Abraxas 117, 187
Adam 341
Adam Qadmon 147, 191, 335, 337
Age of Man 114, 119, 344
Alchemy 67, 282, 405
Alchemy, and the Dragon 309
Alchemy, and the Great Rite 258
Alchemy, Meaning of the Word 325
All Seeing Eye 275
Anchor 219
Ancient Arabic Order of Nobles of the Mystic Shrine 303
Ancient Ones 38
Angelic Script 365
Angels 27, 39, 93
Ankh 62, 64, 203, 211, 379
Ankh, and the Celtic Cross 204
Antikythera Mechanism 33
Anunnaki 35, 38, 87, 125
Aphrodite 64, 65
Apocalypse 20, 122, 130
Apocalypse of Saint John 371
Apple 242
Apple, as a Symbol of Goddess 144
Aquarius 114, 344
Aquarius, the Age of 114
Arcane 10, 165
Arcanum, of the Number Eight 152
Arcanum, of the Numbers 144
Arcanum, of the Rose 256
Arcanum, of the Three Great Lights 140
Archangels 149, 321
Aries 101, 102, 112
Arrow 343
Arthur C. Clarke 34
Arthurian Myths 291
Asherah 50, 311
Ashtoreth 311

Astarte 61
Astral Phenomenon 407
Astrology 60
Atargatis 273
Athena 387
Athirat 61
Athiratu Yammi 310
Atlantis 36, 126, 404
Atum 156
Aztecs 35
Baal 62, 165
Babylon 37, 106
Bacchus 385
Baphomet 245
Beast, the Number of 189
Benben Stone 96
Benu 97
Bindu 228
Birth of Venus 69, 258
Black Mass 397
Black, Representing the Element Earth 325
Blackening 325
Blade and Chalice 406
Blood Mysteries 79, 99
Book of Enoch 35, 39, 125
Book of Heavenly Luminaries 366
Book of Thomas 278
Bow 343
Bull 110, 344, 387
Bull, and the Vernal Equinox 87
Cabala .... *See* Qabala
Caduceur, Holder of the Caduceus 354
Caduceus 310
Cancer 108
Canon 92
Canon of Architecture 363
Canon of Music 361
Canon, of Art and Architecture 179
Canon, the 356
Canon, the Pagan 132
Cardinal Points 321
Carmenta 242

Carnac 242
Cathars 318
Celestial Union 382
Celtic Cross 204
Cernunnos 387
Chains 352
Chalice 178
Chaos 30
Chi Rho Cross 347
Child 68
Child, the 63, 140
Christian Cross 207
Christianity, and Angels 27
Christianity, and the Trinity 140
Christianity, as a Mystery Religion 348
Christmas Tree 296
Christos, the Number of 188
Chromatic Scale 162
Church 246, 320, 364
Chymical Marriage 392
Chymical Wedding 258, 379, 396
Circle 51, 203, 228
Circle Builders 347
Circle with a Cross 75
Circle, as the Path of the Sun 204
Circumpunct 228
Clarke, Arthur C. 34
Clavus, Nail 187
Comet 90
Compass and Square 269
Constantine 347
Constellation 110
Copernicus 46, 227, 377
Cornucopia 296
Council of Nicea 278
Crescent 59, 305
Crescent and Star 303
Crescent, and the Birth of Venus 69
Crescent, the Hidden 252
Cross 198, 199, 203, 208, 233, 349
Cross of Saint Andrew 202, 205, 258
Cross, as a symbol of the Sun 202

Cross, joined to a Circle	204
Cross, Saltire	255
Cross, symbolizing the Earth	199
Cross, Tau	203
Cross, the Number of	142
Crossed Keys	205
Crowley, Aleister	188
Crowley, Aleifter	192
Crown of Stars	69
Crucem Rosae	257, 258
Cruz Disimmulata	219
Cube	213
Cube Revealed	214
Cube, as a representation of the Universe	213
Daemon	322
Dagon	272
Dagon, the Age of	105
Days, Names of	307
De Revolutionibus Orbium Cælestium, Copernicus	377
Dead Sea Scrolls	57
Decad	159
Degree	23
Deity	65
Demon	323
Diameter of the Earth	352
Dog Rose	144, 254, 258
Dog Star, and Anubis	205
Doors	3
Double Headed Eagle	98, 109
Dove	251
Draconic Calendar	165
Dragon	90, 224, 284, 309, 382
Eagle	344
Earth	204
Earth, Representing the Element Water	328
Eclipse	382
Ecliptic	115
Egg	96
Egg, Easter	283, 296
Egyptian Book of the Dead	346
Eight	152, 165, 349
Elder Futhark	56, 330, 332

Element..72
Elemental Air..326
Elemental Earth..325
Elemental Fire..327
Elemental Water..328
Elementals..321
Elements, and the Number Four..142
Emerald Tablet of Hermes..335, 338
Emergence...178
English Dog Rose...144
English System of Measurement..351
Ennead...156
Enneadecaeteris..58
Enoch, Book of..91, 93, 321, 365
Enoch, Mysteries of...320
Enochian Magic..365
Epiphany, Feast of the..242
Equilateral Triangle..289
Esoteric...23, 29
Esoteric Symbology..318
Esoteric Symbols..29
Esoteric Symbols, dangers of..265
Essenes...57
Eucharist...385
Eupolemus..385
Evening Star..62, 65, 72, 295
Exoteric...23
Eye of Horus..274
Eye of Horus, and the Vesica Pisces...275
Eye of Ra...274
Ezekiel...371
Fallen Ones..89, 94
Feathered Serpent...310
Female Potency...48, 261
Female Symbol..62
Female, associated with the Moon..56
Fibonacci sequence..177
Fire..321
Fire Dragon..310
Fire Elemental...320
Fire Salamanders...327
Fire, Elemental, represented by Mercury...74

Fire, Number of 137
First Amendment 389
Fish 56, 113
Fish, the Age of 105, 272
Fish, the Measure of 276
Fish, Vesica Pisces 275
Five 144, 165, 360
Five Pointed Star in Masonry 268
Five, Mystery of 145
Five, the Mystery of the Goddess 144
Fleur de Lis 287, 289
Forty 170, 208
Forty Years 62
Forty, and the Rood Cross 243
Four Cardinal Points 319
Four Holy Angels 142
Four Winds 142
Fourteen 51
Fourteen, and Osiris 346
Frija 148
Furca 56
Gates of Precession 112
Gematria 129, 211, 358, 370, 403
Gemini 109
Geometry 404
Geometry, and Masonry 267
Giants 39, 40
Gilgamesh 35, 87, 109, 125, 140, 341
Gnostic Christianity 207, 257
Goat 112
Gobekli Tepe 203
God 379, 405
God and Goddess 140, 260
God and Goddess, Union of 380
God, Bull as False 102
God, Laws of 362
Goddess 50, 144, 379, 405
Goddess Sophia 252
Goddesses 64
Gods 27, 64, 96
Gods and Goddesses, Seven Primary 133
Gods, Messenger of 141

Gods, Messengers of 34
Gold 228, 325
Golden Calf 110
Golden Ratio 178
Golden Section 179
Grail 291
Great Architect of the Universe 372
Great Pyramid 86, 179
Great Rite 9, 276, 379, 392, 393, 397, 405, 406
Great Rite or Union 262
Great Seal of the United States of America 166
Green Lion 382
Grim Reaper 84
Halos 28
Hand of God 27
Hat, Pointed 54
Heart 342
Heaven 96, 307
Heavenly Luminaries 28, 29, 31, 91, 308
Heavens, Written Upon 27
Heracles 343
Heraldry 254, 287, 354
Hercules 341
Hermaphrodite 156, 283
Hermes 74
Hermes, as Mercury 140
Hexagram 264
Hierarchy 178
Hindu 88, 149, 228, 264
Hindu Gods 27
Holy Animals 118
Holy Animals and Ezekiel 101
Holy Bloodline 292
Holy Grail 291, 292, 318, 409
Holy Oblation of Ezekiel 130, 208, 356, 362, 370
Holy Spirit, Mystery of 251
Holy Union 63, 204, 264, 379, 392
Holy Union of God and Goddess 405
Holy Union, represented by the Blade and Chalice 262
Holy Union, represented by the Great Rite 262
Holy Union, represented by the Solar Eclipse 304
Holy Union, represented by the Vesica Pisces 275

Holy Union, symbolized by the Eclipse ... 382
Holy Union, symbolized by the Fish ... 274
Holy Union, the Dyad ... 138
Holy Water ... 319, 379, 384
Holy Water as the Holy Union ... 384
Horn ... 295
Horn of Plenty ... 296
Horned God ... 75, 295, 298, 387, 391
Horns ... 111, 295
Horns of Venus ... 298
Horus ... 74, 102, 109, 235
Horus, and the Six Pointed Star ... 264
Hourglass ... 66
Hu Hu ... 68, 315, 389
Hu Hu, the Egyptian god ... 103
Hubbard, L. Ron ... 193
Human ... 26, 35, 37, 278, 368
Hypnerotomachia Poliphili ... 67, 258, 357, 393, 394
Iambic Pentameter ... 359
Ichthys, the Sacred Fish ... 273
Inanna ... 65, 311
Inner Secrets ... 23
Inundation ... 53
Inundation, the ... 366
Iron, as a Gift of the Gods ... 96
Ishtar ... 61, 65, 311
Isis ... 51, 64, 65, 109, 235, 311, 346
Isis and Osiris ... 52, 264, 379
Isopsephy ... 183, 192, 403
Jachin and Boaz ... 405
Jamsthaler, Herbrandt ... 283
Jerusalem ... 230, 269, 356
Jesus ... 162
Johann Valentin Andreæ ... 392
Judge of Souls ... 166
Jupiter ... 80
Ka, and Resurrection ... 350
Key of Solomon ... 69
Kingship ... 297
Knights Templar ... 154
Kronos ... 83
Labrys ... 312

Lamech	366
Leo	344
Leo, the Constellation	103
Levi, Eliphas	245
Light	51, 91, 261, 350
Light Bearer	247
Light Bringer	326
Light, Adonai the	233
Light, of the Fish	275
Lion	103, 344
Lion, in Heraldry	354
Logos	68, 188
Lord	62, 233
Lozenge	289
Lucifer	247
Lucifer, as the Morning Star	326
Luminaries	93, 234
Luminaries, the Three	140
Luminary	61, 73, 308
Luna	50
Lux	262, 407
Ma'at	166, 299
Macrocosm	276, 338
Macrocosmos	335
Magicians	54
Magnum Arcanum of the Right Triangle	233
Magnus Cathedral	154
Magnus Opus	282, 407
Male	283
Male and Female Potencies	260
Male Potency	48, 261
Male Potency, symbolized by the Cross	199
Male, Symbolized by the Tau Cross	203
Man as the Macrocosm	347
Man of Ezekiel's Vision	341
Man, Lion, Ox, and Eagle	344
Man, representing the Cosmos	340
Man, the Age of	344
Man, the Number of	189
Manly P. Hall	335
Mars	77
Mary Magdalene	292

Mason	405
Masonic Symbols	405
Masonry	405
Masonry, Three Degrees of	267
Matsya Avatar of Vishnu	272
Mayan Calendar and 2012	19
Megalithic Yard	32, 352
Melchizedek	320, 385
Melchizedek, Temple of	262
Memphis	86
Menes	346
Mercury	74, 150
Mercury, representing the Element Fire	327
Mercury, Symbol for	76
Mercury, Symbol of,, as the Horned God	387
Merovingian	292
Methuselah	366
Metonic Cycle	54
Metronome	62, 66, 233
Microcosm	276, 338
Microcosmos	335
Mile	352
Mithras	187, 385
Mithras, Mysteries of	387
Mojenjo-daro	40
Moon	30, 32, 50, 150, 233
Moon as Female	99
Moon, and the Cycle of Woman	52
Moon, and the hunt	99
Moon, and the number Twelve	162
Moon, as Goddess	45
Moon, as Goddess of the Hunt	51
Moon, as symbolic of the subconscious	53
Moon, as the Male Deity	48
Moon, Cycle of	54
Moon, Period of	100
Moon, Phases	99
Moon, represented by the Circle	62
Moon, the period of	209
Moon, Three as the Number of	233
Morals and Dogma	246
Morning Star	62

Most High	44, 93, 107, 154, 346, 385
Mother of God	311
Movable Luminaries	233
Mysteries	47, 61, 249, 336, 341, 379, 392, 405
Mysteries of Kingship	63
Mysteries of Man	335
Mystery	120, 130, 132, 187, 191, 209, 336, 356, 371
Mystery of the Horns	298
Mystery of the Pythagorean Triangle	141
Mystery of the Trinity	140
Mystery Play	393
Mystery School	387
Mystic Egg	282
Mystic Rose	254
Mystic Salamander	320, 327
Mystical Boat	300
Myth	131
Myths	72, 107, 109, 133
Myths, Allegorical	132
Myths, Egyptian	134
Myths, Roman	307
Nabta	37
Nazca	153
New Jerusalem	356, 371
Newgrange	62, 72, 289, 349
Ningizzida	310, 354, 403
Noah	366, 367
Noah's Ark	120
Numbers, as Esoteric Symbols	129
Numbers, the Book of	371
Nun	56, 272
Oannes	272
Occult	23, 47, 360
Occult Attributes of Names	132
Octad	152
Onion	24
Opening of the Mouth Ritual	86
Ophiolatreia	221, 224
Opus Magnus	379, 400
Orion	52, 86, 87, 88, 202, 346
Orion, and the Cross of St. Andrew	205
Orion, and the Pleides	88

Orion, the People of	52, 125
Osiris	51, 65, 87, 109, 202, 205, 235, 341, 346
Osiris, as Lord of the Underworld	346
Osiris, Spirit of	103
Ouroboros	224
Owl	75, 295, 387, 390
Ox	110, 344
Ox, and the Vernal Equinox	87
Oxyrhynchus, and Osiris	346
Pauline Church	92
Pentacle	12, 172, 241, 243, 246, 255, 268, 390
Pentacle, As a Symbol of Wisdom	243
Pentacle, As the Key of Solomon	69
Pentacle, Woven by Venus	152
Pentad	144
Pentagon	241
Pentagram	12, 241, 251, 254, 295
Pentateuch	144, 253, 366
People of Orion	87
Perfect Elu	156
Phallus	51, 261
Philosophy	407
Phoenician	56, 264, 332, 333
Phoenician Alphabet	56, 200
Phoenix	96, 97, 103
Pierre L'Enfant	388
Pike, Albert	246
Pisces	113, 272, 274
Pisces, the Age of	113
Plasma, the fourth state of matter	323
Plato, and Canonical Rhetoric	357
Platonic Elements	320
Pleiades	86, 88, 347
Point Within the Circle	228
Power	51
Prajadam	385
Precession of the Equinoxes	102, 163
Profane	47, 48
Psi, Symbol of the Holy Fire	207
Ptolemaic system	41
Pythagoras	129, 140, 144, 232, 372, 385
Pythagoras, Mysteries of	178, 232

Qabala	137, 156
Qadesh, as Goddess	311
Queen of Heaven	64, 221, 224, 311
Quincunx	280
Ra, Father of Osiris	346
Ra, the Egyptian Sun God	227
Ram	112
Rebis	283
Reddening, the	327
Redeemer	233, 264
Renne le Chateau	318
Rerum Fontis	21
Revelation	89, 90, 214, 296
Revelation of St. John the Divine	91
Right Triangle	233
Ritual of Bread and Wine	385
Ritual of Initiation	393
Rod	352
Rood	351
Rood Cross	208, 214
Rose Cross	257, 258
Rose Line	293
Rose, Tudor	254
Rosencranz, Christian	257
Rosicrucian	257
Rosicrucian Mysteries	258
Rosicrucianism	257
Royal Bloodline	293
Royal Wedding	379, 392
Runes	66, 200, 330, 332
Runic Alphabets	66
Runic Moon	55
Sacred Animals	102, 344
Sacred Heart	343
Sagittarius	343
Saint John the Divine	89, 90
Salamanders	327
Saltire Cross	200, 258, 260, 349
Saltire Cross and the Cross of St. Andrew	205
Sanctum Sanctorum	213
Sang Real	292
Sangrael	291

Sanskrit	86
Satan	91, 139, 241, 390
Satan, as Yahweh reversed	246
Satan, Church of	12
Saturn	83
Scarab	108
Scottish Rite of Freemasonry	248, 405
Septad	149, 233
Septagram	308
Serpent	61, 90, 221, 309, 403
Serpent, Eye of	403
Set	346
Seven	149
Seven Doors	24
Seven Gods	307
Seven Great Luminaries	86
Seven Heavenly Luminaries, the Seven	296
Seven Spirits of God	149
Seven Stars	86
Seven Unblinking Eyes of God	150
Sex	147
Sextad	147
She Who Treads Upon the Sea	61, 310
She Who Treads Upon the Serpent	61
Shriners	303
Sic Lvceat Lvx	262
Six	147
Skara Brae	289
Snake God	310
Sol Vitae Est	43
Solar Cross	11, 92
Solar Eclipse	304
Solar Year	54, 162, 349
Solar Year, represented by the Cross	202
Song of Solomon	379, 394, 399
Song of Songs	394
Sons of Heaven	9, 35, 38, 39, 367
Sophia	68, 167, 252, 304, 388, 391
Soul	342
Sphinx	103, 314
Splendor Solis	45
St. John the Baptist	201

St. John the Divine	296
St. John the Evangelist	201
Star	307, 388
Star and Crescent	303
Star in the East	72, 73
Star of Bethlehem	73
Star of David	264
Star of Solomon	69, 265
Star of the Elves	306
Star, Five Pointed	305
Stars	30, 32, 96
Stars, Creators of the Elements	44
Stigma	195
Stirling, William	210
Stonehenge	32, 53, 200, 269, 347, 406
Strength	51, 261
Subconscious, Female as the	261
Sumerian	32, 87, 125
Summer Solstice	344
Sun	32, 43, 150, 200, 233
Sun and Moon	406
Sun and Moon as God and Goddess	276
Sun and Moon as represented by Two Circles	276
Sun and the Cross	199
Sun as the Most High	142
Sun Worshippers	86
Sun, apparent orbit	361
Sun, as God	45
Sun, as God of Agriculture	53
Sun, carried by the Scarab	108
Sun, Death and Rebirth	382
Sun, Four as the Number of	233
Sun, Metal of	228
Sun, Path Through the Zodiac	162
Sun, Position at Vernal Equinox	102
Sun, symbolized by the Lion	107
Sun, symbolized by the Number Four	142
Superstition	23
Symbology	48, 61, 107, 379
Tanith	61
Tartan	55
Tau Cross	203

Taurus	87, 88, 100, 110
Taurus, the Age of	110
Templars	372
Temple	348
Temple of Solomon	8, 22, 62, 201, 213, 348, 349
Temple Sol Amon	348
Ten	159
Ten Horns	296
Tetractys	159
Theosophist	188
Theosophy	192
Thera	404
Thirteen	165
Thirteen, and the United States of America	166
Thor	80
Three Circles	404
Three Heavenly Luminaries	134
Time	367
Tiphereth	148
Transit of Venus	69, 258
Triangle of Pythagoras	233
Trilithon	406
Trinity	134, 140
Trinity of Luminaries	72
Trinity, Ancient	67, 305
Trinity, Christian	68
Trinity, Sun, Moon and Venus	76
Triple Spiral	285
Tropic of Cancer	32, 37
Twelve	162
Twins	109
Unicorn	296
Union	276, 379, 405
Union of God and Goddess	204
Union of Heaven and Earth	204
Union of Male and Female	62, 264
Union of Man and Woman	68
Union represented by the Reddening	283
Union Symbol	67
Union, Arcane Meaning	383
Union, of the Sun and the Moon	382
Union, represented by X	262

Universe 27, 142, 335
Universe represented by the Vesica Pisces 276
Universe, a result of the Holy Union 379
Universe, represented by the Monad 137
Unutterable Name of God 156
Upsilon Cross 56
Venus 61, 303
Venus and Adonis 359
Venus and the Five Pointed Star 144
Venus Mysteries 67, 233, 255
Venus, as the Morning Star 72, 91, 350
Venus, Crescent of 296
Venus, Horns of 100, 295, 296
Venus, Mysteries of 391
Venus, Number of 145, 208
Venus, Path of 242
Venus, Period of 152
Venus, Representing the Element Air 326
Venus, Symbolized by the Dove 251
Vernal Equinox 87, 344
Vernal Equinox, alignment with the Galactic Center 122
Vernal Equinox, in Pisces 272
Vernal Equinox, in the Hand of Osiris 105
Vesica Pisces 225, 274, 275, 289, 406
Viatorium Apagyricium 283
Virgin Mary 69, 221, 311
Vitis Rosae 293
Vitruvian Man 191, 335, 340
Watchers 38, 93, 367
Wedding at Canaan 396
Whitening, the 328
Wicca 9, 12, 48, 263, 307, 387
William Stirling 129, 356
Winter Solstice 344
Winter Solstice and the Feast of St. John the Evangelist 201
Winter Solstice as the day of the Birth of the King 400
Winter Solstice, and Newgrange 72
Winter Solstice, death of the Horned God 75
Winter Solstice, of 2012 .... 19, 115
Wisdom 391
Wisdom, Egyptian Hieroglyph 304
Witchcraft 263, 387

Witchcraft 263
Wizards 54
Wodan 143
Woden 148
Word, the Logos 68
Yellowing, the 326
Yeshua 162
Zarathustra 41, 141, 150
Zeus 80, 88

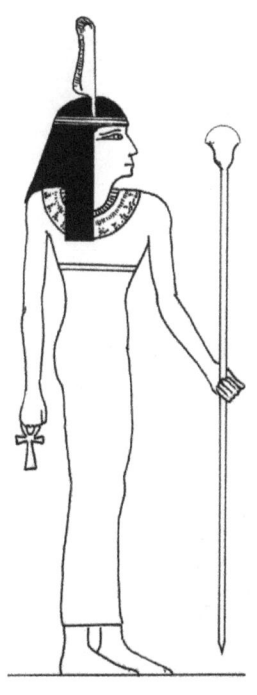

www.ingramcontent.com/pod-product-compliance
Lightning Source LLC
Chambersburg PA
CBHW020809100426
42814CB00014B/389/J